THESE GOOD MEN

MICHAEL NORMAN

POCKET BOOKS

New York   London   Toronto   Sydney   Tokyo   Singapore

Grateful acknowledgment is made to the following for permission to reprint previously published material:

Harcourt Brace Jovanovich, Inc. and Faber and Faber Limited: an excerpt from ''East Coker'' in *Four Quartets* by T. S. Eliot. Copyright 1943 by T. S. Eliot and renewed 1971 by Esme Valerie Eliot.

Naval Institute Press: an excerpt from *The Marine Officer's Guide*, 5th edition by LCOL Kenneth W. Estes, USMC. Copyright © 1985, U.S. Naval Institute, Annapolis, Maryland.

Opryland Music Group and Warner/Chappell Music, Inc.: an excerpt from ''I'm so Lonesome I Could Cry,'' written by Hank Williams. Copyright 1949, renewed 1977, by Acuff-Rose Music, Inc. & Hiriam Music. All rights on behalf of Hiriam Music administered by Rightsong Music Inc. International Copyright Secured. All rights reserved. Used by permission.

POCKET BOOKS, a division of Simon & Schuster
1230 Avenue of the Americas, New York, NY 10020

ISBN: 0-671-73173-4

First Pocket Books printing May 1991

10 9 8 7 6 5 4 3 2 1

For
Beth

I am grateful for the generous support of the Florence and John Schumann Foundation and its director, William B. Mullins. Without them, there would have been no book.

M. N.

Contents

There is only the fight to recover
    what has been lost
And found and lost again and again. . . .

T. S. Eliot

THESE
GOOD
MEN

PROLOGUE

THE WAY BACK

Sometimes I still hear his call. It does not come in a dream—I do not dream anymore. The guns are silent, the fields covered in green. Instead, it must be memory I hear, an old cry for help, echoing unanswered across all these years.

Bridge 28 was a scratch on a map, a small, open span of a ribbon of road that ran east and west through the dark green hills along the Quang Tri River. On the morning of Friday, April 19, 1968, the men of Golf Company, Second Battalion, 9th Marines, formed a rescue column and moved cautiously up that road. A few hours before, a squad from the company had been ambushed at the bridge; now the main force had arrived to retrieve the bloody survivors and gather up the dead.

The column wound slowly west. This was the hot time, just after the season of the rains. The morning sun beat down incessantly. The road, Route 9, was hard packed, but the rumble of convoys from Khe Sanh had left upon it a thick topcoat of powder, and now seven score pair of boots

1

moving west stirred the powder into the air. Soon a cloud of bitter yellow dust enveloped the column as if to mark its coming for the eyes ahead, hiding in the hills.

Leading the line that day was Charlie Squad of the First Platoon, ten men, among them: Belknap and Gonzales, two Texans, one of the country-club set in Waco, the other off Beeville's tortilla flats; "Squeaky" Williamson from Oklahoma, tall and barbed-wire thin; Pier Luigi Tartaro, or just plain "Louie," a pizza maker out of Queens, New York; Eric Karl Hefright, Navy corpsman, "Doc Hefright," to the men, a steady boy from a small town in south-central Pennsylvania; and Andrew James Payne Jr.,"Jim," a Californian, red hair, freckles, a mouth full of gleaming white teeth.

The men were hot, sweating from fear, wary as they moved up the road. At their right were steep slopes and razorbacks, at their left across the river on the opposite bank, an impenetrable wall of brush. Out in the open on the road like that, the men were defenseless—either flank could hold danger—so they looked hard for any sign at all that would give them a second to save themselves.

The enemy, cool in his trenches in the hills, watched and waited. He could see the long line of camouflaged helmets moving slowly below. He could hear the orders of the officers, the chatter on the radios, the hacking coughs from the bitter yellow dust.

All at once, the point man in Charlie Squad, spotting bodies on the bridge, brought the column to a halt and asked for orders.

Bridge 28 was flat and open, a simple concrete slab spanning a culvert that ran to the river. The topography was like that of a deep bowl. The enemy trenches were along the rim; the bridge was at the bottom. It was a knacker's yard, a perfect place for slaughter.

Gonzales was the first to go. Whatever hit him—shrapnel from a mine or grenade—tore him nearly in half; Doc Hefright reached for his belt to drag him from the field and came up with a handful of viscera. Then Belknap reeled backward into the dirt; his hip was shattered, one of his fingers blown off. Now came another volley; a corporal from Ohio grabbed his arm; a lieutenant from Missouri had a bullet hole in the front of his head (he was dead, one of the men reckoned, before his knees touched the dirt). As Doc Hefright lugged Belknap to safety, a piece of shrapnel sliced into his foot; the hot metal cleaved the Doc's skin; blood oozed through the seams of his boot onto the road. Finally, Jim Payne was shot in the stomach. Squeaky came upon him by the side of the road, sitting in the sun against a big rock, bleeding to death.

Payne was among the first to set foot on Bridge 28. A radioman, he had sent back word that he was crawling out to check the bodies on the bridge. As soon as he moved to the bottom of the bowl, fire from the rim ripped into him.

He grabbed for his transmitter, squeezed the handset to talk. His voice rang with shock at first, then turned weak with fear.

"NO! . . . NO! . . . NO! . . . Norman . . . help me . . . I'm hit. . . ."

He may have died for his country or for his god or for nothing at all. For a long time, I thought he died for me.

The battle for Bridge 28 lasted three days and two nights. In the end, only half of the 110 men of Golf who came up the road walked back again. The others were carried out, a score of them dead. It was an unrelenting fight, such as none of us had seen—or would see again.

I was a hundred yards back in the column when Jim Payne cried out for help. By the time I reached the foot of the bridge, they had lifted him to a truck and were driving him away. The truck bounced back down Route 9 east to the Battalion aid station at Ca Lu, but by then it was too late. He died on a gurney, still covered with yellow dust.

Like many men who meet at war, we were cronies of the

moment, companions of the road. He was more green than most, nineteen years old, still adolescent and unready. One night, on patrol, not long after we met, he got careless and opened fire on our rear guard; one of his shots sent splinters of shrapnel into my head. I was furious. Yet it was hard to stay angry with Jim. His insouciance had another side. Maybe it was the red hair and freckles; in that moribund place, he still carried the bloom of youth.

He was a rifleman, but wanted to tote a radio, like me, and asked for help. I was twenty, well-traveled, a college man. He played the eager junior, I the patient savant. I taught him the codes and procedures. The more we drilled, the closer we grew, and, in time, became confidants and friends.

That winter and early spring, I was the radioman for Charlie Squad. The day before the battle, our platoon commander, a lieutenant, decided to pull me into the command group to work the radio for him. When he asked me to recommend a replacement for the squad, I suggested Jim. He took my place in the line of march on the morning of April 19, two hours before Golf Company rushed to its bitter work at Bridge 28.

I felt the deep sorrow of that moment for ten years, might feel it still if Jim Payne's father had not turned me away. In the fall of 1979, I called him in California and asked to visit. I wanted to tell him what had happened, unburden the load.

He was polite, but demurred. He finally had learned how to live with his son's death. "I'll tell you, Mike," he said, "I really don't want to go back through it again. It's just too damn hard."

Five years later, in the spring of 1984, I again threw a line into the past, this time in search of something more significant than absolution.

At that point, my family was secure, my career well-established. But I was restless, filled with an inexplicable choler. Unsettled and irritable, I behaved badly. I sought solitude, then slandered friends for keeping away. At work I agitated for a change of assignment, then did nothing but complain when it came through. I barked at a son who revered me and bickered with my best ally, my wife.

She and I had been together since college. Over the years, of course, we had quarreled—about money, mostly; it took years to get used to the writer's life—but it had never been like this. She wanted another child; I wanted to leave.

I was not, as some men say of themselves, born at war. The roots of my restlessness went deeper than that. I had known the loop of anger and ennui as a child. I had struggled with the self long before I set foot on Bridge 28.

But I was sure that I had walked off the battlefield a more knowing man. Those who survive such a long and lethal assault emerge with at least a small piece of truth, some little lesson, a sliver of light. Maybe, across the years, chasing bylines and a bigger house, I had simply lost it.

I did not expect to clear the smoke or quell the disquiet. Not all of it, at any rate; nothing is that neat. But I could not even begin to get my balance without at least trying to recover what had been lost. And the fact that I had never been able to say exactly what that was did not make it any less important.

So, in the spring of 1984, in search of the ineffable, I set out to find the men I once held close, intimates side by side under a flame-white sun and at night belly to back in a fighting hole.

Those men had been a mirror of me; likely they, too, carried home some small verity. Perhaps my comrades had been more provident and not let a thing so dearly won slip so easily away.

The search began in my attic, in a battered plaid satchel, a repository for old letters and photographs. I had not looked at this musty litter in years—not, at least, with any purpose. The letters were bundled together with rubber bands and stuffed into a cheap leather pouch. They were useless really, just maudlin ramblings. Not so the photographs spread across the bottom of the bag.

Discolored and curling at the edges, they were a rich vein of remembrance. Some of the faces are smiling or mugging for the camera. Others are hollow-eyed, mechanical. There are men with cigarettes dangling from their lips, bare-chested, mud-stained men perched on a pile of sand bags, hungry men squatting in a circle picking through a box of green cans that held their dinner. It was hard to date some of the pictures, but the ones with men laughing came before Bridge 28—that much was certain.

A few days later, I had a list of eleven names. After a month of inquiries, I had numbers and addresses.

WILLIAM CRAIG BELKNAP went down in the first burst of fire at Bridge 28. When I saw him last, litter bearers were lugging him down the road in a bloody poncho. I found him in Mesquite, Texas, near Dallas, badly hobbled by his wounds, a recovering alcoholic who had become the executive director of a treatment center for drug-addicted and alcoholic women. He turned out to be steady and true. No man now is closer to me.

MICHAEL "SQUEAKY" WILLLAMSON has only lately come to rest, carving out a comfortable home in the green hills of eastern Oklahoma. He survived the battle at the bridge unscathed, but lost an eye during a firefight that fall. After the war, he wandered; might be on the move still if love had not found him.

DAVID JOSEPH TROY JR. was on leave during the fight at Bridge 28. After the war, he became an insurance executive, living in Mahopac, New York. The son of an Irishman (a rebel who fought the Black and Tans), Dave inherited two familial traits: a tendency toward fierce loyalties and the habit of reducing his experience to stories. The war gave him more material than anyone wanted to hear.

FRANK CIAPPIO, the lieutenant who led the rescue column at the bridge, was a wild man. "Demo Dan," we called him, because he liked to blow things up. Frank had risen through the ranks and was close to his men, maybe too close. "My kids," he called us, "my family." He went on to become a stockbroker in New Jersey. He never forgot his kids or recovered from the feeling that he had abandoned them.

ERIC KARL "DOC" HEFRIGHT of Huntingdon, Pennsylvania, was one of the company's two Navy medical corpsmen. Doc was wounded as he pulled Belknap to safety. He went home to become a policeman, then supervisor of an infirmary at a maximum-security prison. When I found him, he was holed up in his house high on a wooded ridge, trying to heal himself after a breakdown.

LT. COL. DAVID NELSON BUCKNER took command of Golf Company as a young captain a few days after Bridge 28. I became his radioman and bodyguard. When we met, he was hard and disciplined, a young commander with promise, positioned perfectly in time and place. When I saw him years later, in London, he was still in the Corps, his rise checked, however, his career near its end. The war was supposed to have been his golden opportunity. Instead it became his undoing. But fate had not left him bankrupt. He was among the most decent of men.

EUGENE "DOC" DEWEESE was the company's senior medical corpsman. I owed the Doc. After the bridge, I was in trouble, sick with mysterious pain, full of shock and dangerously adrift. Every night for two weeks, Doc sat at my side pulling me back. In January 1985 I went to Seattle, in a trip long overdue, to express my gratitude. I returned with an account of an unexpected metamorphosis.

MIKE CARON, quite simply, was the bravest man I'd ever met. He risked his life repeatedly at the bridge, dragging the dead and wounded from the field of fire. For a while he stayed in the Corps; a drill instructor at first, then a maintenance chief with a helicopter squadron. Later, in West Haven, Connecticut, he bounced from job to job, waiting for success, still undaunted.

CHARLES WHITFIELD of Savannah, Georgia, the platoon

sergeant, was shot in the head near the sea at Cua Viet a month after Bridge 28. The wound left him with a plastic plate in his skull and a blind spot in his field of vision. "The Marine Corps," he said, "was the best thing that ever happened to me."

PIER LUIGI TARTARO was the platoon clown. At Bridge 28 he was cited for extraordinary gallantry. After the war, he settled on Long Island, New York, and became a union shop steward at a bus terminal, still a comic character no one could forget.

Finally, there was JOHN ROBERT HAGAN, also of Savannah, after Ciappio, the commander of the First Platoon. No one really knew the lieutenant and no one, save Whitfield, was close to him. He was a hard case, out to make a career and win the Congressional Medal of Honor—or so we thought. We were wrong about Bob Hagan. All of us were wrong, especially me, his radioman at the bridge, the comrade who left him frozen on a hillside with the enemy a stone's throw away.

Some men had changed little. Belknap still howled at his own jokes and Frank Ciappio still liked to play with guns. Most settled remarkably close to where they had lived seventeen years before. Seven had children. None had achieved celebrity and only one, Louie, sought it. ("I want to be a big shot," he said, then laughed.) No one confessed to murder or to any of the crimes that society considers serious. Three of the eleven smoked cigarettes. There were no vegetarians in the group. They were about equally divided between Democrats and Republicans, liberals and conservatives. A few said they would carry a gun again if the call came. Others said this time they would shoot the caller. I am part of the latter group.

Five were receiving some form of government compensation for wounds suffered in combat. Squeaky was classified 100 percent disabled. Belknap was 90 percent disabled. No one complained of pain, but Jean Belknap, her eyes beginning to water, took me aside and told me that Craig was sometimes in agony. And there have been several moments during the last few years when a few of us have worried that Squeaky—with one eye gone and damage to the other— was about to go blind.

My comrades ranged in age from thirty-six to forty-three, "war babies" from our fathers' war. Four of the men were starting to gray. A few had filled out. Squeaky was still bean-pole thin. And Mike Caron, the former drill instructor, was just as fit and chiseled as he had been seventeen years before. Frank Ciappio, the stockbroker, lived in a modest house in a wooded section of suburban New Jersey. His backyard was home to brown rabbits and gray squirrels. Squeaky, living on government disability, had just moved with his wife into a small mobile home on a ten-acre tract of land in rural Oklahoma not far from the Arkansas border. His property was covered with thick brush and swarming with chiggers.

For the record, none of the eleven showed any signs of acute mental illness. A few, clearly, were troubled. Only the most insensate of men emerge from such a violent sojourn unmarked. But none of my comrades used their trouble to excuse the shortcomings they brought to war or the failures they suffered after it.

They asked for nothing from the society they had served—demanded no debt, claimed no arrears, wished for no reward.

A few of the men have drawn close to one another again, just as they did when danger was at hand. Most simply have stayed in touch. Nevertheless, we are linked forever and there are moments with some when this attachment can be as fierce as a blood bond, as enduring as a kinship.

We do not pretend to understand the forces that held us together or why, across all these years, they awaken us still, make us stir. We have spent long hours sifting the events that began in the spring of 1984, when I first set out to find the others, and culminated, more than a year and a half later, in a reunion at my home in Montclair, New Jersey.

I'm not sure even now that it is possible to relay the whole story of what happened between us—what is happening still—or explain the longing we felt, the desire, at least one more time, to huddle close.

Here, however, is how it began.

ONE

WHIPPOORWILL

The sight of him stunned me. Four stretcher bearers were lugging him down Route 9 in a bloody poncho. He was limp, the color of chalk. His hair was soaked in sweat. His eyes were watering. He looked afraid.

"Write my father," he said when he spotted me. "Tell 'im I'm all right. . . . Thanks, Norman." He stuck his thumb in the air, smiled weakly as they bore him down the road.

Until that moment, his last at war, Craig Belknap had seemed unassailable. He never flagged or lost his head. I used to think that men like that—men with more than the common measure—were somehow immune to harm. Now, watching them carry him off chopped up and helpless, I knew no one was safe.

Craig went home to Texas, into one hospital after another. We exchanged letters for a while, then lost touch until August 1969.

I had just finished a tour at the Naval base at Guantánamo Bay, Cuba, and had come back to Camp Lejeune, North Carolina, to await a discharge. It had been a miserable wait.

11

The racial strife that had ravaged Watts and Newark several years before had finally found its way into the military. Angry packs of whites and blacks roamed the base at night looking for stragglers to pummel. The hate and the sweltering heat from the Carolina coast only made those last days longer. I kept to the shadows and quiet corners and thought of other days. One night, listening for the sound of old footfalls, I decided to call Belknap.

He had been the center of our small cosmos—a loud, affable Texan, the backwoods wit, the would-be balladeer.

> Hear that lonesome Whippoorwill,
> He sounds too blue to fly.
> The midnight train is whinin' low,
> I'm so lonesome I could cry.

We laughed at this, of course. It was an act. Belknap was a college dropout from the suburbs, a country-club kid. Still, we encouraged him. His viscous twang made the pretense work. And the lonely strains of Hank Williams seemed to capture the mood of those melancholy days.

Once a month or so, Craig would get a package from home, and each time it drew a crowd. Carefully tucked inside a loaf of bread or a cookie tin were bottles of whiskey or bourbon. Often, his father sent along a six-pack of Pearl beer wrapped in newspaper. Belknap was generous with the liquor but hoarded that beer.

Pearl was his prize and he made a great ceremony of drinking it. "Boys, this here is Pearl beer," he would say, holding a can aloft. "This is 'Beer from the Land of Eleven Hundred Springs,' Texas beer." Then he'd close his eyes, lift the can to his lips, and take a long, deliberate swig.

He was just under six feel tall, about 170 pounds, with brown hair and a barrel chest, dark-framed glasses and an arrogant ribbon of a mustache. He was more self-important than anyone my age I'd ever met. (We figured everyone from Texas was like Belknap.) But he never cheated at cards, never overslept his watch, and never failed a comrade in trouble.

The thing that marked him most, his signature, was his laugh—a howl, really, unabashed, mouth wide open, head thrown to the sky. Oh, how he could laugh.

I needed him that hot summer at Camp Lejeune. The night I called, a rumor was going around camp that one of the gangs of white thugs had caught a black Marine, doused him with lighter fluid, and set him ablaze.

At a quiet telephone on the second floor of the NCO club, I got Craig's number from information. I cannot remember the details of our conversation, only that it did not last long. Belknap was wildly drunk and it was hard to make sense of anything he said. I let him go, quickly, had a Coke at the club, and went back to the barracks and the rack. A week later I was out of the Corps, headed north, away from the equatorial heat and the bitterness. Fifteen years passed before I called Waco, Texas, again.

"Man," he said this time, "have I got a story to tell you."

He was next to Tommy when he rushed the bridge. Gonzales went first; he slipped out behind him.

Suddenly, he was reeling . . . spinning . . . splayed out in the dirt. When he finally raised himself a little and looked around, he thought he had lost a leg.

He yelled for a corpsman. He yelled for his helmet. He yelled and yelled and yelled.

The corpsman went to Tommy first—Gonzales was on his back a few yards away, perfectly still—then scooted across the road to him.

He cut off his trousers, laced battle dressings over a deep wound in his hip.

His back felt wet—had he fallen in water? Beneath him, on the road, his blood began to puddle.

He hurt, he told the corpsman. "Goddamn it, shut up!" the Doc said, and kept working.

Another man had hold of his head now.

13

All at once, the man pulled away, shot in the arm. Then the corpsman rocked backward, bleeding as well. They'd been caught in a killing zone.

A sharp pain seized his right hand. He'd been hit. Again!

He turned his head to look at the wound. The bullet had laid him open—bones, tendons, raw flesh. He looked away, across the river to the dark green hills.

"I'm home," he thought. "It's almost summer, I'm home."

He went back to the red-brick house on Braemar Street, back to his old room and his parents' plans for him.

For as long as he could remember, the family had pushed him to study law. His mother and stepfather had a vision of him: an important man moving in important circles, perhaps, someday, even to Austin and the Statehouse.

All of this started innocently enough, a kind of joke on a young boy: "W. C. Belknap—Governor." It was funny. But along the way, the joke took on the aura of a prophecy, one he thought the family expected him to fulfill.

His stepfather, the purchasing agent at the local glass works, had given them—his mother, brother, sister, and him—a good life. He took golf lessons at the Ridgewood Country Club, went water skiing on Lake Waco.

At Richfield High, he became a cheerleader and sat on the student council. He went dove hunting and danced with debutantes. By his senior year, he had a regular girlfriend, Jean Allen, petite and ebullient, a banker's daughter who had gone to charm school. In 1964, at Christmas, he wrapped his class ring neatly in a box and gave it to her. They were inseparable that spring. At graduation she wrote in his yearbook:

> *Although the end of May means wonderful summer, it also means an empty one without you. . . . Needless to say, you have made my senior year the most memorable year of my life. I don't know what I would have done without your help, understanding, and sweet*

14

*smile. . . . As I look back on this year, I will treasure
all the wonderful memories of you and remember all of
the beautiful plans we have for the future. I only pray
that we will meet some day, never to part. Sweetheart,
may God bless and always keep you safe.*

I love you,
Jeanie

In the fall, Jean went south to a small college to study
English and drama and earn a teaching certificate. He headed
west to Lubbock and Texas Tech to major in economics
and English and prepare for a career in law or politics.

But he hated Lubbock, a place of sandstorms and bleeding red skies. He was homesick as well. He missed mornings at Braemer Street, evenings at Kim's hamburger stand,
Sundays at St. Alban's Church.

His grades that first year were B's and C's, undistin-
guished by the family's standards, but good enough to move
him ahead. When the summer arrived, he eagerly returned
to Waco, a job in the glass factory, and Jean.

They tried to rekindle the romance, but a year apart had
left them different, a bad fit. To him, she seemed too
small-town and studious. To her, he was all drinking and
discontent.

They had long talks about his future. He no longer wanted
to be an attorney, he said. He was satisfied simply to drift.
This premeditated aimlessness troubled her and that fall
they returned to college uncertain of each other.

Then came the break. In the spring, Jean told him that
she had fallen in love with someone else. And within weeks
Belknap had joined the Marines.

From the timing of these two events, Jean concluded that
she had driven him into the service, but, in truth, he had
been headed toward war since the fall, stumbling along with
bad grades and an academic warning.

Along the way, he said nothing to his parents. They had
paid his tuition, room, and board. They had been generous.
What would he say? That he felt restless? That he had
something to prove?

He had a vision of himself—a man at the end of a long trial, lean and fit, standing ramrod straight and wearing the most conspicuous uniform in the world: the fitted dress-blue tunic of a United States Marine. He meant to make that vision real.

In April 1967 he snuck off to Houston and signed the papers to enlist. By the fall, he was slogging through the monsoon, eating a bolus of C-rations, hiding and praying in the bottom of a deep hole.

October 15 [1967]

Dearest Brother,
By the time you get this I'll have over a month of my tour gone and already I'm starting to become an animal. Sometimes I just don't give a damn for anything. Don't let Mom and Dad know this as it would only hurt them. I just want to get home as soon as possible in the best shape possible.

His brother, Barry, or "the Bear," as he was sometimes called, was two years younger, a student at Baylor University in Waco. During the fall and into the spring, Craig regularly sent the Bear dispatches from the field.

November 15 [1967]

Dearest Bear,
My rotation date will be around the 10th of October [1968] so within 15 days or less of that time I should be home. Now if I can only get stationed in Texas all will be well.
Give everyone my love and keep plugging away at those books. I don't want you to do the same stupid thing I did.

When the Bear decided to transfer to Texas Tech in Lubbock, Belknap, sure that his brother would repeat his failures, made a melodramatic appeal.

You've got the drive to study and work in college I didn't have. Mom and Dad gave me all the money, credit cards etc. . . . and I used them wastefully. . . . I knew what was happening and didn't give a damn. Not only that but I wasted a year and a half of my life. Barry, I'll never be able to tell you how sorry I am now. I'll carry the scars of that mistake the rest of my life.

In January 1968 Golf Company was assigned to guard a bridge along the Cam Lo River. Belknap sent the Bear some jungle boots. "Christmas presents are impossible to find," he joked. The duty at Cam Lo was soft and relatively safe.

We're all getting fat and lazy here at Cam Lo. So how do the new cars look? Pretty sharp, I'd imagine.

In February he was promoted to corporal.

When I buy dress blues, I can have the red stripe on the blue trousers [the mark of an NCO]. Sounds nice.

In March when the Bear wrote that he wanted to quit college, Belknap erupted.

I'm violently opposed to this idea and for once I know what I'm talking about. This is no time to be thinking about the service. One fool in the family is enough.

Golf Company was on Hill 37 then, a small, bald, shell-pocked knoll on the edge of a wide plain not far from the Demilitarized Zone. From its position in the mountains, the enemy had the hill zeroed in and every day, usually three times a day, they fired their huge mortars. We could hear the tubes popping in the distance—*pah . . . pah . . . pah*—then *woosh,* as the rounds cut the air overhead, then *CRACK!* when they hit and ripped the earth apart.

Gouged and battered, the hill took on the look of a wasteland.

> *So far we've lost 10 men in 4 days. But so far I've kept my butt down. Knock on wood. . . . If I can just keep my butt low enough for the next 220 days I'll be on my way home.*

That spring the Bear changed his mind and decided to stay in school.

April 5 [1968]

Dear Bear,

I got your letter today telling me you'd . . . decided to study harder. You have no idea how much that relieved me. . . .

. . . I've been writing Jeanie since Christmas. It's no big deal as I made it plain to her that we were just friends and that was all. . . .

. . . We're supposed to return to [the battalion rear at] Camp Carroll the 9th of this month. Maybe we'll skate awhile. Be careful and take care of yourself.

Your loving brother,
Craig

P.S.—188 more days

Fourteen days later, on April 19, Belknap was headed down Route 9 toward Bridge 28.

APR 25 68
WASHINGTON D.C.
 THIS IS TO CONFIRM THAT YOUR SON CORPORAL WIL-LIAM C BELKNAP USMC . . . SUSTAINED MULTIPLE FRAG-MENTATION WOUNDS TO THE RIGHT HAND, RIGHT HIP AND RIGHT LEG FROM HOSTILE MORTAR FIRE WHILE IN A DE-FENSIVE POSITION. HIS CONDITION WAS FAIR WITH HIS PROGNOSIS GOOD. HE IS PRESENTLY RECEIVING TREAT-

MENT AT THE STATION HOSPITAL DANANG. YOUR ANXI-
ETY IS REALIZED AND YOU ARE ASSURED THAT HE IS
RECEIVING THE BEST OF CARE. YOU WILL BE KEPT IN-
FORMED OF ALL SIGNIFICANT CHANGES IN HIS CONDITION.
  LEONARD F CHAPMAN JR GENERAL USMC COMMANDANT
OF THE MARINE CORPS

I had come home whole. Twenty-eight combat operations, a year on the battlefield, and all I had picked up were
splinters of shrapnel, two concussions, and a bout with
malaria. Those of us who escaped harm measured our good
fortune against those who did not. Their long scars were the
yardsticks of our luck.

I had not seen Craig since the day he was carried
from the bridge, but in the spring of 1984 I was in contact with one of the men who had—Dave Troy. In 1969,
while Craig was recuperating at home, Dave went to see
him in Texas.

"What did he look like?" I asked.

"Well, he was still on crutches back then," Dave said.

"What about his hand?"

"Oh, you mean old Captain Hook."

I should have pushed for details, but the remark caught
me so flat-footed, all I wanted to do was hang up.

Belknap arrived at the airport an hour early and began to
pace the terminal. He had thought about putting up a
banner—something like "Welcome, Mike" or "Let's Go,
Marines"—but such a show seemed wrong and, as the day
approached, he became too anxious to do anything but sit
and wait. By the time my flight landed, a crowd had formed
at the gate. Belknap hung back, behind it.

He was easy to spot—same gray eyes, same smile. His
face was rounder than I remembered, more mature and
covered with a dark beard, neatly trimmed.

He wore a blue sport coat with brass buttons, gray trousers that carried a sharp crease, and a custom-tailored shirt.
He seemed so prosperous, so secure, I almost forgot . . .
and then he began to move.

His right leg and foot were canted outward at an odd angle, perhaps 45 degrees, and he limped, heavily, sinking toward the ground, then rising again with each step.

What used to be his right hand was now a kind of claw. Only two fingers were left—the forefinger and middle finger—and they curved in toward his palm like the talons of an eagle or the bent end of a crowbar. The thumb was stiff and disfigured; it appeared as if the joints had been fused so that the thumb jutted out from the hand and was frozen in the shape of . . . a hook.

I winced.

He tried to move easily through the crowd on this scorched Texas morning, but he was hobbled. There was no way to get past it or shut it out.

He stopped in front of me. His head was tilted slightly downward. He looked at me askance. His mouth was in a tight smile.

He had extended his bad hand now. I grabbed it, quickly, and pulled him into a long embrace.

"Goddamn," he said softly, his eyes beginning to water, "Goddamn, Mike, it's good to see you."

"We made it, boy," I said. "We made it."

A page from his medical record:

This 20-year-old CPL, USMC sustained a through and through gunshot wound through his right femoral neck, and shrapnel fragments through the right hand on 19 April 1968. He was found to have extensive bony loss of the carpal bones in his right hand, including the fourth and fifth metacarpals, and the fifth digit of his right hand was missing. He also had an open wound through and through his right hip joint with a fracture of the right femoral neck.

There was bone and soft tissue loss. . . The right hand and wrist [essentially] were completely blasted away. . . . The patient cannot flex or extend the right wrist, and it is fixed in the neutral position. The patient is right handed.

The patient was kept in traction for his right femoral fracture for approximately two months, and during this time he had daily

dressing changes to his right hand until the skin healed. . . .
He was placed in a walking spica cast for his fracture of the
right femur. . . . He was returned to the operating room and
a bone graft was done from the iliac crest to the proximal right
third metacarpal. The ring finger was amputated because there
was no tendon or nerve supply to this finger and it was essentially
functionless.

He has approximately one inch shortening to the right lower
extremity due to the femoral fracture, and he had only 20 degrees
abduction to the right hip. He is walking with crutches because of
some continued traumatic arthritis and pain.

A note from his mother's hand:

1968:	May 11	Arrive Lackland Air Force Base [Texas].
	May 12	Move to Corpus [Naval hospital].
	May 13	Operation [on hip].
	May 16	Traction began.
	June 19	New cast on hand, took first step in new body cast.
	June 20	New bottom on cast.
	June 25	1st leave home to July 8.
	August 1	Taken out of cast, crutches, hand back in cast.
	August 21	Hand operation: bone transplant, straighten hand and nerve surgery put hand back in cast, all surgery fell through, not successful.
	September 13	Removed another finger.
1969:	June 9	Admitted to Houston VA Medical Center.
	June 21	1st [skin] flap surgery for hand.
	June 26	Hip surgery 10-and-a-half hours.
	July 17	2nd flap surgery.
	August 21	Sewed hand to stomach for skin graft, 9-and-a-half hours.
	September 11	Removed hand from stomach.

A story from his local newspaper:

Waco News-Tribune
June 26, 1968

Marine Cpl. Craig Belknap arrived home Tuesday for the first time in 10 months, and friends and neighbors turned out to greet him.

The family's front lawn was draped with U.S. flags and signs reading "Welcome Home Cpl Belknap, U.S.M.C." and "Home of Leatherneck W. C. Belknap."

Belknap said he was quickly moved to [a transfer point in] Da Nang and flown to a Navy hospital in Guam where he spent about three weeks. He was then taken to Corpus Christi Naval hospital and allowed to take an 11-day convalescent leave to come home.

A picture accompanying the article shows Belknap standing on the lawn of the red-brick house on Braemar Street, his father on one side, his mother on the other. He is wearing casts on his right arm and his right leg. He is supported by a crutch, but seems to be trying to stand at attention.

We ate lunch in Dallas, in a cool place with palm leaves and white-tile walls. Then we stopped by his office at the halfway house he ran downtown before heading out the Thornton Freeway and east on Route 20 toward his home in the suburb of Mesquite.

The land was flat and brown, burned by the Texas sun. Along the road were stands of yellow sunflowers and large billboards that announced JESUS and, in only slightly smaller letters, the name of the preacher who had paid for the space.

We stopped for gas on a side road by a small field that long ago had been left to seed. The air barely moved the weeds and bushes. Sometimes a cicada would stir and screech at the afternoon.

"Goddamn, Mike," he said, standing by the pump, "being together, this is really something."

Belknap had come back a hero. Belknap had come back a drunk.

Released from the hospital in the fall of 1969, he arrived home just in time for the debutante season, with its whirl of parties and country-club dances. At these affairs, he could usually be found by the bar; everyone wanted to buy a drink for the man with the Purple Heart.

Jean, back in town, began to drop by Braemar Street:

"When he first came home, I was over there almost every day. I would get over there fairly early in the morning and he would still be in bed, but he began his day with a glass of scotch. People were waiting on him hand and foot. He didn't have to do anything for himself. I wanted him to get on with his life. I wanted to say, 'You're alive. You may not be in one piece, but you got to get on with it.' He was drinking at home all day long; I mean a big tumbler full of scotch. When he was drunk, he was not physically stable, especially in the beginning when, because of his fingers, he could not hold on to a regular crutch. He was just pitiful, a stumbling obnoxious mess who reeked of alcohol."

One night he was just too much.

As Belknap remembers it, "I was supposed to pick her up about eight o'clock for a party. That afternoon I was with a bunch of the guys and I got so drunk, I got home and passed out. So she broke it off. She didn't want anything to do with a drunk."

A year later, after a brief courtship, he married Patti Lachele, two years his junior, a girl around the corner he had dated in high school. Patti was a teacher in elementary school. With her salary and his disability pension, they moved into an apartment.

He decided to try college again, this time at Baylor University in Waco. As before, he embarked on a course toward the law. As before, he did not finish.

What he wanted, needed really, was a lesson in ontology. "I could not rationalize in my mind how God let good men die. I had gone to several Episcopal priests. I was sitting there with this one priest and said, 'Father, I don't understand this: How does God allow small children to be killed? What is this thing, this war, this bullshit? I got all these friends who are dead, and the government is getting ready to pull the plug on that place.' That priest, he looked me in the eye and said, 'I don't know, son, I've never been in war.' I said, 'I didn't ask you about war, I asked you about God.'

"I don't even know if I was asking the right questions. I had gone to my dad and to other vets. I wanted to understand it. I wasn't getting any answers and the pain I was having. . . . So I retired to our little one-bedroom apartment, drinking and trying to sort some of this stuff out."

He tried trade school next, training to be a cowboy, a "ranch and livestock manager," as the school called it. He bought himself a new gray Stetson, a pair of hand-tooled leather boots, and ambled off to class. But he was just marking time. "Hell, I knew there would be no jobs for a ninety percent disabled veteran with no farming or ranch background."

When the course was over, he started to drift. He spent his days in "some beer joint" shooting pool, drinking scotch, and growing despondent. Twice, as he remembers it, he went to the closet, took down his .38 caliber Smith & Wesson revolver, and put the barrel in his mouth.

One day the proprietor of his regular gin mill slipped onto the stool next to him. "You know what your problem is? You don't got any fire in your belly," the man said. "You got that Goddamn government check coming in and that wife working and no reason to do anything. So you don't."

"I said, 'Fuck you,' " Belknap remembered. "But he was right."

By 1977 he was drunk more often than not. He drank at home, he drank on the road, he had charge accounts at more than a dozen liquor stores. His drinking day began early. He and Patti had a daughter now, Amy, and he would get up in the morning to see her off to nursery school. By 9 A.M. he was loaded. Sometimes he would stay home and drink, sometimes drive to a beer joint. In the afternoon, he would take a nap until his family returned. Shortly before dinner, he'd start the happy hour. After the meal, he would drink until bed.

He began to have blackouts; turned ugly. Once, when someone offended him at a party at home, he retrieved his .38 from the closet and put the gun to the man's head.

In April he was attacked by their cat, a Siamese named Abercrombe. The cat had been in a fight and Belknap had intervened, driving the assailant off. When he went to check his animal for wounds, he bit him and badly clawed his arm.

At the hospital emergency room, he was given painkillers and warned not to drink. For three days, he stayed off the booze. On the evening of the fourth, watching television, he began to float. Something was wrong, he told Patti. He rose from the couch and climbed the stairs to the den. As he entered the room, he noticed a bolus of fishing line on the floor. He reached down to pick it up. All at once, the line began to wrap itself around one of his arms, then attack the other.

At first, the hallucinations fascinated him: the flowers on the bedspread turned themselves into crabs; Willie Nelson and Waylon Jennings were playing country music in the closet. Then the room filled with rats. Then the snakes on his arms began to bite.

Veterans Administration Hospital, Waco, Texas
Belknap, William C.
Alcohol addiction with delirium tremens

This patient has been drinking severely for quite some time, approximately a quart of scotch daily. The evening before he was admitted he began to see things which were not there. . . . The patient was detoxified on the infirmary service and was much improved by 5-1-77 when he was transferred to the Alcoholic Rehabilitation Unit where he made an excellent adjustment, took part in all the meetings, was cooperative, and began to gain self respect and an improved self image. His wife was extremely faithful. She had at least 10 interviews with the social worker. The patient's attitude improved sufficiently for him to return to old goals which he had deserted some years ago when he left college. He was discharged 7-15-77. He is competent.

He tried to turn his sobriety into a career and used the family's savings to set up an alcohol counseling service. At that point, he had more ambition than expertise and it was not long before he went broke.

Patti, meanwhile, had become pregnant again and in June 1978 gave birth to a son, Barrett. She was out of work now and the mortgage and car payments and weekly expenses quickly consumed Craig's monthly disability pension. They were in debt, falling further behind each week.

To keep going, he took a job at a friend's grocery store. "I wanted to be a big shot with my own business," he said. "I ended up stocking shelves. That was as low as it got."

But he stayed sober and it was not long before someone offered him a job managing a local alcoholic rehabilitation program that was in disarray. By June 1980 he had turned the program, and himself, around.

That year the class of 1965 at Richfield High held a fifteen-year reunion. He decided to go. So did Jean.

She remembered seeing him at a party five years before, a stumbling loud-mouthed drunk who reeked of alcohol and needed a bath. Now he was sober and handsome and headed her way.

"I was really nervous," she said. "I don't think I would have ever gone up to him, but he came over to me. He was so kind. He said he wanted to apologize for any—I can't remember the word—wrongdoings that he had caused me from his drinking. It was maybe a ten-minute conversation, but he was so, so gentle. And then he reached down and kissed me on the cheek."

She was working as a high-school guidance counselor and, at that point, had been married for almost ten years to a local businessman. By mutual choice, it was a childless union. During the week, they were absorbed by their jobs. On weekends, he went hunting and fishing while she shopped and had lunch with her friends.

A few days after the reunion, Belknap gave her a call.

"He told me he couldn't count the number of times he

started to dial and couldn't get through all seven numbers,"
she said. "I had butterflies in my stomach. My heart was in
my throat."

He was coming to Dallas on business, he went on. Would
she meet him for lunch?

They ate at a small Chinese place, then went for a walk.
"We had a lovely day," Jean remembered. "We went to
a lake. We kissed a lot. I was so nervous. Finally I said,
'Hey, you're married; I'm married; this is dumb. I still love
you, but don't call me again.' "

Two days later the phone rang.

"By this time," she said, "we were just gone over each
other."

They met often over the next few months. Craig and Patti
separated; she stayed in Waco with the children. For a
while, Craig and Jean shared an apartment. Then on October 1, 1981, sixteen years after they had first become sweethearts, they married.

"It was Camelot," Jean said. "It was high school all over
again."

The house was new, a one-story ranch of brown brick
with a small backyard of thick St. Augustine grass enclosed
by a stockade fence. A huge hackberry tree hung over the
back property. Nearby, a row of honeysuckle made the
summer mornings sweet.

When we arrived after lunch, Jean, flanked by Craig's
children, was standing in the center of the living room. The
kids had come down from Waco for the weekend. It was a
spacious room with a four-sided cathedral ceiling, a skylight
facing north, a stone fireplace, and polished dark-wood
walls.

Amy stood by Jean's side. Barrett, opposite, was sitting
on a coffee table. Jean nudged Amy forward to shake hands
and made Barrett rise from his perch. The girl had dark hair
and a round face, like her father. The boy was small and
shy.

Jean addressed herself to Barrett. "This is Mike Norman,

Daddy's friend. Mike was in the war with Daddy. Do you know what that makes him?"

I was sure she meant for the child to say, "a Marine." But Barrett assumed another connection.

"Shot?" he said.

Belknap did not complain of pain, but clearly he was suffering. That night, with the children asleep, he showed me his scars.

Here, standing naked on the living-room rug, was the part of war I had escaped. Swales of old skin and bright pink cicatrices marked his arms, legs, front, and back. The bullet that had shattered his hip tore off a part of his buttocks and, at the exit wound, left an enormous scar that ran from left of his buttocks to the outside of his right hip. He had scars from bone grafts, from skin grafts, from jewett nails and traction.

". . . And then they would cut under the skin. . . . They did that three times to get the blood flowing. . . . And they took bone out of this hip again. . . . The bullet hit me right here and they laid me open. . . ."

He said he felt arthritic; his shattered hip was turning stiff. If he tried to adjust by altering his walk, his knees would become sore and hobble him. More and more he went to his cane. And more and more he worried. He guessed that one day he would end up in a wheelchair.

He put off examinations; it did not matter. Another operation was unthinkable. At a hospital in Houston he had almost died on the table. No one was going to cut on him, ever again.

Once, years ago, he drove to Corpus Christi to visit the last hospital where he had stayed. The buildings had been razed, but he roamed the old grounds. In his mind's eye he could still see the operating suite, the dayroom, the recovery barracks. He could still see his ward mates too, some with one arm or one leg, some half blind, some worse. He stood there in the emptiness and began to shake. "I've got to stop this shit," he said to himself. And never went back.

He tried to hunt and play golf, but, with his mangled hand, could not steady a club or a gun, and gave them up. He liked to travel but could not walk far without stopping for a break. Small chores gave him trouble; it took great effort to bring a hammer home to a nail. His balance was gone; he hated ladders. And now a light bulb needed changing, a gutter had to be cleaned.

Still, he could invent, take flight. He dreamed of hiking the Rockies, rising at dawn and climbing past stands of aspen and white birch to walk along the snow line and the sky. He dreamed too of driving a truck, a semi-trailer with eighteen wheels, on long hauls across the plains and through the Great Divide. Such were his rambles.

We had been talking for hours. Jean slipped into the kitchen to refill her glass. In a bedroom down the hall, a child coughed, then dropped back to sleep.

Craig leaned forward and sighed heavily. We had been headed this way all night and now he could not stop it.

"You know—" He was sobbing. "I've wept so many— The hospitals— You see, I'm getting new memories and—

"You know, I saw the look on your face when I told you earlier how lucky I always felt. I've been thinking about this for sixteen years. The pain—the God-awful pain is always going to be there. And I don't mean the wounds—"

Tears sluiced down his cheeks and into his beard. His body began to shake.

"It's going to be okay— Be okay— Promise you."

He fell silent for a moment. Jean was standing in the doorway, weeping.

"It was terrible for me to sit there those last days before the country fell watching what we fought for become undone and think about what had been sacrificed there," he continued. "I was so torn. There was no sense in more people being killed, but, my God, we were just going to pull out? I said to myself, 'That's what all this has come to?'

"It made me crazy, not for me, but for the others—for Payne, for Gonzales. They paid the awful price for nothing.

I couldn't believe it. It made me crazy that I didn't have any answers."

He wiped his face with a handkerchief.

"It's just like it kind of never happened. But it did happen. It happened—happened—"

It has been written that men like Belknap, men who have been savaged, have lost the capacity to feel. That is wrong. They feel too much.

Saturday morning came sunny and hot: 102 degrees on the clock by the bank in the small shopping center near his home. We were running errands, beginning a day together.

"Take a deep breath," said Craig. "Smell something?"

"No."

"That's horse shit, boy. What's the matter? Your sinuses clogged?" Then he threw back his head and howled.

We stopped by his office, a low, flat brick building on the edge of Oak Lawn, one of the city's posh residential districts. "The facility"—his word—was a sixteen-bed home for female alcoholics and drug addicts. The staff gave them structure and counseling and taught them to stay clean. Many made it; some did not. Policy was set by a volunteer board of Dallas businessmen and socialites. Craig was the executive director, a kind of manager and point man rolled into one. One minute he was checking floors, the next lobbying the legislature.

He made his way with moxie and charm, the handsome war veteran in the Turnbull & Asser shirt and the blue Bill Blass blazer.

His salary and disability pension let him live comfortably. Shopping was his recreation; he had subscriptions to the fashion magazines, and the clerks in the men's shop at Neiman Marcus knew him by name. His closets were bulging. "I'm the best-dressed cripple in Mesquite," he said. And laughed.

He had thought of moving on, perhaps to a bigger facility, maybe work for a corporation or go into government. But he could be stubborn, difficult, short-tempered—serious liabilities unless one was the boss. So he stayed put, no doubt sensing that, for the time being, he was well-placed.

That afternoon, we stopped at an espresso shop with wrought-iron tables, bentwood chairs, and carnations dangling from tiny glass carafes. We sat in the cool of that place for hours, talking about our wives, our children, our jobs, all the details of all the years we had been away from each other.

The next afternoon Craig took the children to the movies and Jean and I were left alone.

"There was something you wanted to tell me?"

"Yes," she said, "I wanted to tell you about the pain. He underplays it, downplays it."

"How much pain is he in?"

"Have you noticed the way he sits down? He throws himself onto the furniture."

"I hadn't noticed."

"The only signal he gives, even to me, is a groan or a grunt. In the morning when he gets up, he'll shove his hand into the small of his hip or he'll grab at me to get his balance."

She rose from the table to brew another pot of coffee.

She was still as petite, as thin as the teenager in her old pictures, a hummingbird living with a broad-chested peacock. They plan no children. Amy and Barrett on weekends were enough, she said.

The affair and her divorce rattled her. The idea of a backstreet romance seemed so seamy, even if the paramour was her high-school sweetheart. When he suggested that they simply live together in their apartment, she became depressed. Then he proposed and they settled into a house in Mesquite, outside Dallas.

She thought the war had changed him, opened him to the world, made him "more sensitive." She loved that in him, the side violence rendered so soft. And she was proud of him, too. To her his weals and welts were medals; sometimes, when she looked at him in bed, she thought: how brave he was to fight while so many stayed home.

Beyond this, however, much of his past was impenetrable. She could see his frustration; she knew he was looking for answers and could not find them. But she could not feel, as he did, the weight of war—although once, a few years back, he had tried to give her a sense of it.

In a cardboard box of medals and photographs, he had kept as a souvenir a pair of sheer black pajama bottoms peeled off an enemy corpse. "Try 'em on," he said one day, holding them forward.

Was he joking? "I didn't know what he wanted," she said. "I was scared. I thought, maybe he wants me to model them because I'm short. But, still, it was odd. He had not been telling war stories or having dreams. I thought to myself, I'm not wearing any black pajamas. Then he said it again, 'Here, put 'em on, see if they fit.' I thought, I can't turn him down. That would be cruel and disrespectful, just like a slap in the face.

"I took off whatever I had on. I looked them over good before I put them on. I looked to see if there was any dried blood on them. I remember thinking, I don't want to be squeamish about this. Here is a person who has seen all of these horrible things. How can I be squeamish about a pair of little black britches? Actually, I didn't want to wear them because they represented the enemy to me. I wasn't his enemy."

That was the end of it, but the moment sometimes comes back to Jean. It frightened and bewildered her. Later, when I asked Craig to explain himself, he laughed. "Aw," he said, "that was nothing."

Monday came too soon. We were up early and out to the A&B Cafe for a breakfast of eggs, biscuits, and gravy. The Southwest was still sweltering. Even the flies swirling around the sugar bowls seemed listless.

We headed out to the expressway and made for the city and the airport. "These last three days, I'm drained," said Craig. "I don't know what else to say."

The night before, we had been up late, making inquiries of old occasions.

"I used to think a lot about the guy that shot me. What was he like? It scared me when I realized that it was just some asshole picking me out of the crowd, so to speak. It happened so fast, so fast. Whose bodies were we going to get, anyway?

"I know that I will probably never be able to walk down that road again. I also know that is something I wish for more than anything else in the world. I don't care where or how, before I die, I want to walk down that road. The bridge is such a great part of who I am, yet I can't touch it. I wonder, where does it end?''.

(1)

It is said that in ancient tombs in certain parts of Italy and Greece, there have been uncovered thin gold plates inscribed with directions to the underworld. According to the myth of Orpheus, these plates were left so that souls bound for the lower regions, souls who one day hoped to return, might distinguish between two springs—Mnemosyne and Lethe, the waters of memory and forgetfulness—and know from which to drink.

Sometimes, when I am lonely, I find myself in a long-remembered room looking out between the mullions at the cold gray river of my youth.

It might be a birthday that takes me back, makes me hear again the footfalls from the sprawling estate that was once a posh boarding school for boys. It is easy to drift back to those stone buildings that looked out on the Hudson River from atop a steep slope of green, back to that day more than thirty years ago when my mother and first stepfather drove off through the stone gateway and left me alone on the gravel drive in the shadows of the porte cochere.

They were newly married and I, an only child, was an interloper in their pas de deux. My mother, a model busy chasing a career, had often sent me to live elsewhere, but there, at Nyack Boys School, I was indeed on my own; there, between a stone fence and the river, I first learned of longing and sought refuge in the company of men.

The property was stunning: rolling grounds of tall pines and paths that wandered through the woods. I was one of the younger boys, a fourth-grader and resident in the school's main building, a Tudor mansion with stone arches and casement windows. Behind the mansion were broad green playing fields that ran almost to the tree line along the main road. In front was a great lawn that swept down majestically to a stone balustrade above the gray river.

We wore a uniform at Nyack, a blue wool blazer with red piping; many years later, in the very same colors, I stood on a boot camp parade ground waiting to graduate. In fact, as I look back now, everything at Nyack prefigured that day. We slept in rooms of four, barracks-like; before dinner, we formed ranks for inspection in the main hall; when we misbehaved, we were beaten; and, across it all, we came under the icy eye of an unyielding martinet, the headmaster.

I was sent to Nyack at the suggestion of my first stepfather: he thought me soft, ill-mannered, by his standards even lawless. Nyack would give me discipline, "make a man of you," he said. I was nine years old.

My mother assented, quietly. "It's only for a year. Anyone can go away for a year."

The message was unmistakable: this was a test; there was no coming home without passing it.

So I went. At night, on the second floor of the mansion, Bok House, I would sit in my room and look out between the mullions into the darkness at the bridge that led to the city where my mother lived; I learned the deep ache of loneliness at Nyack, an ache I would come to feel again and again.

But there, behind the stone fences and rows of tall evergreens, I also felt the first stirrings of comradeship. My model in those days was a Titan of a man, Mr. Wotasick, an English teacher and table master at Bok House.

He was tall, broad, and powerful, with a thick, rectangular face, square glasses, and a deep, sonorous voice. The other masters were often sharp with us, ready to cut and wound, but not Mr. Wotasick. He never took seriously the behavior of small boys. It was as if he had seen enough of the world to know better; or perhaps he saw himself in the faces at those small wooden desks. In either case, he was a generous teacher who gave his students his best. From the others, it was the jackboot, from him always the gentle hand.

He reveled in Kipling, so we too read the barrack-room ballads, the poetry of men: "Tommy" and " 'Fuzzy-Wuzzy' " and the "Screw-Guns," but most of all, his favorite:

> 'E put me safe inside,
> And just before 'e died:
>   "I hope you liked your drink," sez Gunga Din.

We only half understood its message of self-sacrifice, but from that poem and the teacher who introduced it, we learned the meaning of the word *comrade.* To a young boy who saw himself forsaken, the notion of fidelity had great appeal.

We set to work memorizing "Gunga Din," practiced it for weeks. Then, one Sunday after dinner Mr. Wotasick picked a few of us to perform, and we stepped to the front of the great hall and said our verses before the entire school. When we had finished, our master was beaming.

I never forgot that poem. Years later in a fighting hole a world away, I met a tough captain of Marines.

One night, full of himself, he bragged about his Kipling.

I listened obediently while he finished the "Screw-Guns." Then I reached back across the years.

It was "Din! Din! Din!"
With the bullets kickin' dust-spots on the green. . . .

TWO

A CONDITION
OF COMPLETE SIMPLICITY

He began the letter again.

Dear Mike,
  After sixteen years it was quite a trip talking to you,
Troy, and Belknap last night. The amazing thing is that
my wife and I had just discussed the possibility of once
again seeing someone from my outfit. Damn, it's just
unbelievable. . . .

He had been at it most of the morning. His tablet was
almost empty; his false starts littered the table and floor.
He wanted to give a good account of himself, but there was
so much to say. Memory mobbed him. Nothing sounded
right. He started, stopped, threw down his pen.

"All right!" said his wife, breaking her long silence.
She'd been sitting nearby with her needlework, watching
him struggle for hours. "Look, you just have to tell him
what you want to tell him. You just have to write it down;
write what you are thinking, just like he was here and you
were talking to him. Okay?"

. . . My wife, Georgia, advised me to write you and just "ramble on." You will like Georgia when you meet her. She has helped me to put my life together. This lady seeks the beauty in life and the beauty she finds she always shares. I suspect that you will find that behind the success of each one of us is some good lady. . . .

. . . I am anxious to spend some time with you this summer, to sit down and talk. It's kinda difficult to write a letter when it's been sixteen years. . . .

You are the first person from Golf Company I've written since the war. I don't know why exactly, but my vivid memory of things ended on April 19th. That day has never escaped me and I believe that everyone there that day changed in significant ways. After April 19th you secretly went into the field praying that you could avoid combat. . . .

Officially, he came aboard as Michael Tom Williamson, but everyone called him "Squeaky." Tall and bean-pole thin, from Bethany, Oklahoma, he was eighteen years old when he reported to Golf Company in early December 1967. He was so thin for his height that his uniform billowed and sagged, as if, by mistake, he had donned another man's clothes. His helmet rolled round his head like a mixing bowl. He had a long, narrow face and ears that stuck out, especially when he smiled. His hair was dark brown and straight; an unruly forelock swept down from the summit. His skin was slightly tawny, colored with a trace of Choctaw, his mother had said. Finally, there was his voice; surgery for polyps had flattened its timbre and raised its pitch. He was sandpaper on soft pine now, a hiss and a squeak.

Squeaky was a city boy; his father was a baker, his mother a file clerk. But his dark, deep-set eyes gave him the hard-scrabble look of the hills and backcountry. In fact, he seemed oddly at home in the bush, one of the best men to break trail or scout a hilltop.

Over all, he gave the impression of youth—the baggy

uniform, the shock of hair, a pubescent sense of humor. If Belknap was our wit, then Squeaky was our joker, the maker of mischief and pranks, the kind of guy who held reveille by hooting and banging on a metal tray.

He selected as his best friend a man who shared his sense of humor, a shoe clerk from Beeville, Texas, Tommy Gonzales. They joined the company the same day and both were assigned to Charlie Squad of the 1st platoon—Belknap, Troy, Payne, Doc Hefright, Louie. . . .

Gonzales was a short, dark man, twenty-two, older than Squeaky, married, and the father of a baby girl. But when he discovered the madcap in the Oklahoman, he instantly took to him. They bunked together and arranged to pull the same watches and patrols. Soon they were inseparable, always off plotting something absurd.

At the battle for the bridge, Squeaky had been ahead of Gonzales in the line of march and did not see the explosion and gunfire that caught the Mexican and Belknap in the open. By the time Squeaky doubled back to see what had happened, Gonzales was dead, his body sprawled on the road.

. . . For many of us, April 19th was the first taste of death on a personal level. You and I had seen men die but they had not been that close. We lost brothers on that day. . . . I remained close to those I knew on April 19th but I never allowed myself to become close to anybody else after that day. Somehow I think that happened to all of us.

I want to tell you of two distinct memories I have. The first is of Tommy Gonzales and seeing him dead after Louie and I came back from the bridge. Snow and I threw Gonzales' body up on a tank. Then Ciappio ran over and laid rosary beads on Tommy.

The second vision I have of April 19th is the face of Jim Payne. I saw Payne being driven away but I knew he was dead. I see that white-ashen face in many a dream. It's strange but when I dream of you, Louie, Troy, Belknap, or anybody that was in that original group, they grow older in my dreams. Even when I dream of Tommy Gonzales he has aged with the years. But when Jim Payne comes into one of my dreams it is still the ashen face of death. . . .

Within a week, I had booked myself a flight to Tulsa.

Squeaky was right. Until the bridge, we had been lucky, charmed in fact. From December, when a handful of us came aboard, through April 19, no one in the squad had been hit. The longer our luck held, the more we came to believe in it. The other platoons were cannon fodder, not us. We were going home.

"I thought at one time that we were almost a touched group, that somehow all of us were going to make it through," said Squeaky during one of our first conversations. "We seemed almost invulnerable to what was happening there. You knew you could count on that small select group, that with the brotherhood we had, we would make it. It was almost mystical."

But the war broke through our circle, just as it did all others. And after the bridge, those who survived clung to one another, wide-eyed, with a darker kind of wonder.

Squeaky had a new sidekick now, Louie Tartaro, a streetwise kid from Queens, New York. Louie was sure that the worst had passed. "All the way to the end," he said to the survivors of the bridge, "we're gonna get all the way to the end." He was a poor oracle.

In May Lieutenant Ciappio was medevaced with malaria. A short time later, I, too, was delirious with fever and ended up in an Army hospital in Okinawa. In mid-September, when I was shipped back to the war, Squeaky was gone.

The platoon had been under the command of a new lieutenant, very green and very desperate to prove himself. At a battle at a spot called the Twin Peaks, he had been told to take his men up a hill to a landing zone to pick up supplies. He ordered Charlie Squad to take the lead.

Squeaky, by then a lance corporal, was in charge. Midway up, his point man found fresh footprints on the trail.

Squeaky called for mortar fire; he wanted to soften the way ahead. But the lieutenant intervened. No mortars, he said. The corporal had misread the signs; the prints were old.

Not so, said Squeaky; he had seen signs like that before. But the shavetail, too green and too proud to accept counsel, told him to move. Now, more sure of trouble than ever, Squeaky assumed the point. He was leader of the squad, the one to take the risk.

He walked slowly, delicately. The enemy was near; he could feel it. Then he spotted a mine sitting on the ground at the head of the trail; a wire attached to its base ran off behind it into the brush. And now that wire was wiggling . . . wiggling. . . . "Sweet Jesus," Squeaky said to himself, "the gooks are trying to set it off."

"AMBUSH!" And he turned to run.

He might have made it to safety, but he stopped on the trail, wheeled toward the enemy, and fired his weapon. Perhaps instinct made him turn back. Perhaps he was trying to protect his squad. In either case, as he turned, the mine exploded.

The blast blew him from the trail; he landed on his back by a tree. He shook his head, tried to get his senses, looked for his helmet, his rifle. His face was warm and wet; he saw blood. His left eye was swollen almost shut; the vision in the other was badly blurred.

By the time they rolled him into X-ray back at the battalion hospital, the morphine had taken hold. He was beginning to drift. Someone was turning him over now, shaking him. "Corporal . . . Corporal . . . hit in the head . . . brain damage . . . have to operate. . . ."

Medical history: shrapnel wounds to head. Exploratory craniotomy performed to clamp bleeders; subsequent NOP vision in his left eye due to transection of the optic nerve and optic atrophy. Blind in left eye secondary to wound.

In Guam he went into convulsions. The seizure struck as they were wheeling him into the hospital. It sent him into a wild dream, one so vivid he was able to recall its details years later when he began to keep a diary.

I caught sight of military equipment stacked against the walls of the [hospital] emergency entrance: helmets, flak jackets, M-16s, grenades; all the equipment that had been the mainstay of the past year.

Then the doctor informed me that war had broken out in Guam and I was to take out a patrol. I looked over, and there were the men who had died and been wounded in the war: Payne, Gonzales, Belknap, Hefright. Gonzales had a bandage around his head and Payne had a bandage on his gut. It was the old squad.

I led all of them out of the hospital into the smoky jungle. I smelled the stench of war. We engaged in a firefight again. People were wounded and people were killed. When it was over, I returned to the hospital by myself.

I lay on the stretcher for a while watching the drip from the I.V. bottles and trying to figure out what had happened. I thought I had been wounded—again.

Had he put on weight, I might have missed him, but he was still lank, even more bare-boned than I remembered. His hair hung down to his neck and a thick mustache spilled over his lip. His skin was dark, deeply tanned. His eyes were the eyes of an old man: deep caves surrounded by shadows. He walked with his head tilted slightly to the right; he did this to give his left retina as wide an angle as possible, but it was a slightly bizarre stance. The effect of all this—the cadaverous frame, the Stygian skin, the cock-eyed posture—was to give him an aspect of foreboding. He looked—there is no other word for it—haunted.

Georgia was at his side—bright blue eyes, a round face with red cheeks and an even smile, long blond hair neatly piled into a bun on the back of her head. She was much shorter than her husband; he was just over six feet, she less than five and a half. Yet the two seemed attached. Their arms touched even as they moved forward.

"Hey, Mike!" It was him, no mistaking that high-pitched

rasp, that squeak. "How's it goin'?" He said this almost casually, as if only weeks had passed between our meetings.

We stopped for hamburgers, but he was really hungry for news. I gave him all the details, all I knew so far of Belknap and Troy, Ciappio, Louie, and Hefright. "Damn," was all he said, when I had finished. "That's somethin'. Damn."

After lunch we piled into their small blue pickup truck and headed south to Route 59 and Cedar Lake, where they were camped. Georgia drove; it was not safe to let the man with one eye behind the wheel. His depth perception was bad, his vision in the other eye sometimes blurred.

The lake was two hours away, nestled in the Ouachita National Forest in the shadow of Winding Stair Mountain, some eighteen miles from the Arkansas border. Even in early August, the foothills there were cool and green, filled with hickory and oaks and an understory of wild dogwood.

They had lived alfresco since they met, pitching their tent or pulling their travel trailer from campsite to campsite. They had wandered east to the Great Smoky Mountains of Tennessee and south to the swamps of Florida, but they preferred the west: Montana's great blue vault and the glittering canyons and winding brown arroyos of New Mexico.

They worked when they needed extra money, painting barns or cutting hay on Georgia's family farm, but, for the most part, they just wandered, away from Oklahoma and back, then away again. They lived on Squeaky's government disability pension, more than a thousand dollars a month, and they were careful with their money.

They had saved enough to put a down payment on a patch of scrub land just outside Bengal, a blink of a town a stone's throw from Cedar Lake. Their land was raw, "unimproved," the agent had said, but it was just what they wanted, ten acres they could shape to suit themselves. When I first saw it, Squeaky had already cleared some brush just off the macadam road as a place to set their trailer. The land was to be their compass rose, beginning and end.

He had been a long time getting to that spot. His circuit

had been wide and aimless. And yet, as such trips go, he was more or less on schedule. Odysseus, after all, was ten years reaching Ithaca.

From Guam, Squeaky was shipped to Memphis, Tennessee. On Christmas Eve 1968, he left the Naval hospital there and headed home to Bethany, Oklahoma, a district of Oklahoma City. Bethany—two barber shops, a gasoline station, a clothing store, a bakery, and a drug store with a soda fountain and marble-top counter—was more small-town than suburb.

The family, his mother, Doris, and sister, Gayle, lived in a red-brick house not far from St. Joseph's Orphanage. His father, Pascal, had not been in residence for some time.

(Pascal's story is a cheerless one: Raised in the orphanage, he ran away to Houston when he was fourteen, and, two years later with a forged birth certificate, joined the Navy. He served in World War II as a cook and, afterward, married Doris, his high-school sweetheart. They settled back in Bethany, where he became a baker. Not long thereafter, the marriage went sour, and Pascal left home and joined the Army. A year and a half later, as he was crossing a street in Fort Worth, Texas, an automobile ran him down. The accident left him brain-damaged, without a short-term memory: he could not remember his doctors or his ward mates; he could not hold on to the day-to-day. He lived in a compound at a veterans hospital in Colorado. Sometimes he was given a pass to visit his son and daughter. Sometimes they drove west to spend time with him.)

Doris had supported the family; she had been a seamstress, a laborer on an assembly line, a file clerk in the police department. When Squeaky was fourteen, he too went to work, at the Windsor Bowling Lanes as a dollar-an-hour concourse boy. He cleaned ashtrays, collected empty glasses, swept the floor, worked every day after school for four years. At the Windsor he took his first drink of whiskey. "You might say I grew up there," he said.

In his senior year of high school, he enlisted in the Marine Corps, and after graduation took a long train ride west to boot camp at San Diego. He had nothing to prove by signing up; he suffered no boredom or discontent. He just wanted to be in the fight. His countrymen were waging war and he was drawn, as many were, by its danger and its mystery.

SEPT 21 68
GOVT PD FAX
THIS IS TO CONFIRM THAT YOUR SON LANCE CORPORAL MICHAEL T WILLIAMSON USMC WAS ADMITTED TO US NAVAL HOSPITAL GUAM ON 16 SEPTEMBER 1968. . . . HIS DIAGNOSIS IS MULTIPLE SHRAPNEL WOUNDS TO THE HEAD, LEFT LEG, LEFT FOOT, WITH TRAUMATIC AMPUTATION OF THE FOURTH TOE OF HIS LEFT FOOT. AND BLINDNESS OF THE LEFT EYE.

In September 1968, at the Naval hospital in Memphis, a Navy doctor noticed that Squeaky had shrapnel in his surviving eye, but he assured him that the shreds of metal were so minute, they were harmless. None of this, however, not the examination or the findings, was put on paper.

A year later, his vision began to blur. He went to the Veterans Administration Hospital in Oklahoma City where doctors found cataracts and removed them. But no one spotted the small shreds of shrapnel, and Squeaky, eager to be discharged, said nothing.

He had enrolled at Oklahoma City University, majoring in politics and civil administration. War had left him a skeptic. He distrusted government, wanted to know how it worked, how to force it to change.

One day in the student union, he met a girl with a lyrical name, Ladayna. They sat and talked for a long time. Then they strolled across the campus. Four months later they were married.

From the first, there was trouble. He was a renegade and social malcontent, a "hippie," as iconoclasts were called in those contentious times. His hair fell to his shoulders; he smoked marijuana and hashish; and he refused to take seriously anyone or anything—except the war, which he was determined to stop, and the government, which he wanted to prosecute.

Ladayna, as he remembers it, had suffered his excesses silently during their courtship, but after they exchanged rings and established a nest, she tried to reset his track to the straight and narrow. The hair had to be cut, the drinking and smoking stopped, the protest abandoned for a job and a paycheck.

They quarreled for eighteen months; then they parted.

He stayed in school and planned to become a professor, a specialist in foreign policy and the Far East. Before long he had more than enough elective credits for a master's degree, but near the end, just three easy required credits—a Spanish course—away, he left. Maybe the prize had lost its value or perhaps, in the cause of nonconformism, he had simply been shortsighted and unwise. At all events, he began to drift.

He worked at different jobs—once for the state employment service as a counselor to unemployed veterans—he traveled, married again, divorced for a second time. He roamed the dry rocky tracts of Idaho, then lived with a woman in Portland during months of incessant rain.

In December 1978 he came home to Bethany for the holidays. On New Year's Eve at the house of a friend, he finally found love; he met Georgia.

"Hey, Mike, lemme ask ya somethin': Do you think they'd've given you the Purple Heart if I'd've blown your leg off?"

Squeaky was having a good time. I had almost forgotten the night he sent a grenade shell glancing off my right calf.

"I can't say, Squeaker, but if you had blown my leg off, I can guarantee you our meeting would not have been as amiable as it's been so far."

"Damn." And he laughed.

We had just passed over the Arkansas River, slow and brown under the afternoon sun. Georgia had been quiet so far. As we drove through Poteau, Squeaky tried to draw her 'out. He pointed to a pawn shop. "I've only used a pawn shop once in my life; pawned my first wife's wedding ring."

Georgia swung her head around. "While you were still married or after?"

"Still married," he cracked.

Soon we were at the state forest at Big Cedar Lake where they had camped with the trailer. Georgia took off her "city clothes"—a print blouse and black linen pants—and donned a yellow top and bib overalls. Squeaky cut kindling and built a fire to cook a supper of pork ribs and corn on the cob.

It was dark by the time we had finished and cleaned up camp. A bright half-moon threw a silver light on the small hollow of aluminum campers and tents. Georgia sat inside the trailer near a tiny black-and-white television, embroidering a shirt. Squeaky and I settled into lawn chairs next to the fire to watch the embers. Beyond us, in the darkness, crickets and tree frogs sang their raucous night songs.

"Do you remember the last time we were together?" I asked.

"Nope. Do you?"

I took out a photograph: we were standing bare-chested side by side looking directly into the lens. I switched on a flashlight and illuminated the picture.

"When was that taken?" he asked.

"On Route Nine a few hours after we finally kicked the gooks from above Bridge Twenty-eight."

"Damn," he said.

Across the years, he steadily lost sight. That "harmless" shrapnel in his eye had been insidious, though the doctors—with no evidence of it—still believed that the damage was being caused by cataracts. By the spring of 1978, he needed a new cornea. Using him as his own donor, doctors removed the undamaged cornea from his left, or sightless, eye and used it to replace the one that was failing on the right.

After the operation, for the rest of that year, Squeaky

stayed close to Bethany. It was that New Year's Eve at a party that he met Georgia.

Their encounter had been a piece of matchmaking by Georgia's sister, Zelma. She thought Georgia might like this peripatetic veteran. Both had been twice divorced; neither followed an itinerary or a schedule. Who knew what might grow from such peculiar symmetry.

Georgia, however, was not a woman easily won. The mother of two, one child from each marriage, she had lost custody of them in a long and venomous court struggle. In the years since, she had been on her own—a bookkeeper, a real estate agent, a truck driver—resourceful and independent. She had just freed herself from a long affair and was wary of another attachment.

And yet there was something about this strange, scrawny man now standing in the warmth of Zelma's kitchen, chatting with her. She liked him. It was the eyes, she thought; his look was penetrating, direct. They spent the night together, then the week, then the month.

By the spring of 1980, they were on the road, cruising across the West in a gray-and-white 1968 Oldsmobile and living in a seven-by-nine-foot brown tent. It was the most contentment both had known in years. Then Squeaky began to have trouble again.

His eye filled with fluid and swelled; his vision blurred. He and Georgia shortened their circuit to stay within reach of his doctors. When they needed fresh air, they made for a state or national park somewhere close, within Oklahoma, never more than half a day's drive away from the clinic.

It was at one of these spots, Lake Tenkiller on the eastern border of the state in the land of the Cherokees, that he began to make regular entries in a journal.

He wrote with a plastic ballpoint pen in a spiral-bound notebook. The entries begin in April 1980 and end in January 1983. He has since insisted that the dates have no significance. It is only coincidence, he said, that the impulse to write parallels the appearance in his life of great love and the threat of great loss.

* * *

His sight now was the worst it had been since the war. Days were better than nights, but even in the light he was surrounded by fog or thick gray smoke. He squinted to make out details—a dirt road cutting through a meadow, a stream sliding down a hill. Colors came in fractured rays, kaleidoscoped. Darkness was the worst, hard and impenetrable; it trapped him; he could not move against it. Some nights he would try to flood the campsite with light, switch on every hand lamp and beacon they possessed.

In their first months together, Georgia was bewildered by all this. Then she hit on an idea: she would be his eyes.

"I wanted to be as accurate as possible. I wanted him to have the picture of the golden eagle circling the mountain, the rivers, the power and magnificence of the rivers, the delicacy of the flowers. I'd spot something and say, 'Michael, we've got to stop here.' He would tell me how much he could make out, which was usually minimal, and then I'd say okay, within that frame this is what is there. And he would say, 'Oh, I see what you're saying.' "

Tuesday, April 22, 1980
Lake Tenkiller

Night falls quickly with little evening, as the sun disappears behind the island, throwing an orange hue in a sky now tinted blue. As the lake is the sky's mirror so it reflects and swims in the sea of colors, gently whispering a beat against the shore. . . . The sparrow's song remains.

Everything upbeat. Dog going into heat, acting foxy. The birds are in mock-fight, quarrelsome song. The sky is changing, falling deeper into gray. Darkness is but a thing of the past, something created in the mind of one who fails to see. Now we welcome the night.

Thursday, April 24, 1980

This is [the journal of] a recluse dropping from the mainstream long enough to grasp the meaning. . . . This is stepping from defeat into victory and discovering that there was never no defeat. This is the real beginning.

Two weeks later they moved slightly north to Fort Gibson Lake.

Hot showers, flush toilets, and a concrete table, all at the right price—free, free, drag out the "e". Two fish caught this week and I caught neither, but tonight should be a good one fishing bottom. Yesterday first real swim of the summer.

May 10, 1980

The wind, both last night and today, has made fishing the feat of only the courageous and fool-hearted. . . .

The weekend crowd has appeared on the scene, armed with sound which not even the wind can drown, a true conflict to nature. Weekends are just a part of this trip, something to remind us that there is still a world out there.

May 14, 1980

Early morning. Deer skirt the edge of the forest, and a Tom-turkey fans his tail alongside the roadway. Slowly the various birds join the chorus, some in song, harmony, while the crow stands alone in song. Fish break the mirrored water and shad rush the shore leaving a trace of white foam.

Georgia is now cooking up a couple of catfish we caught yesterday. Seems that every time the catfish really start biting we run out of worms. Everywhere they are out of the big Canadian worms, so we bought a few dozen of the native, really skinny, worms, but the catfish don't really like 'em all that well. If a worm don't catch fish then it is totally worthless. . . .

. . . Last night sat around the neighbor's campfire and laughed like hyenas. No one but me realizes the courage I displayed . . . when Ron, our neighbor, set the park afire starting his camp fire. I jumped up and kicked the can [of fuel] away then smothered the flames with my foot.

I cannot figure out why I am suddenly becoming so brave and courageous. Just the other day, Georgia got tangled up in the rocks and I waded out into the breakers and freed her. I wonder if there are any spots open at the Roundtable?

May 17, 1980

Saturday morning, and the lake buzzing with boats, kids from a Baptist church swimming. No one walks on water these days, not even Baptists.

Awakened 'fore dawn by noisy people who talked about ugly. "When you were born they put you in the corner and fed you with a slingshot."

May 18, 1980

Already we have overstayed the 14-day limit and the friendly ranger told us that this limit is strictly enforced, so now we must find a new home, maybe Taylor's Ferry, two miles down the road. . . . Altogether this has been a pleasure trip, except for the leaks in the tent.

May 27, 1980
Lake Eucha

Yesterday we drove up to Grand Lake for a swim. Found the water very refreshing. I did not even have to threaten Georgia with splashing to get her in.

June 1, 1980

So we end another stay and are ready to move on to some other place; considering Missouri, the Table Rock, Bull Shoals area. Met Wayne and Jean, a couple in their sixties, who have been the highlight of this trip. Wayne was on his annual two-week vacation from "Ma Bell" and they camped here in high style, fifth wheel and a boat. Like Georgia and I they started camping poor-man's style and gradually worked their way up. Soon they will take a six-month vacation twice a year. Fortunately we are already full-time vacationers.

That month, with Squeaky's sight slightly improved, they drove north to Idaho to visit his sister, Gayle. Afterward they stopped to camp and were so taken with the Clearwater range in the Rockies, they talked of staying in Idaho.

After considerable thought, we decided against settling here in North Idaho. Somehow, there is something missing, although I cannot say what it is. . . .

So much of America left to see—I feel no need to plant roots yet.

On the way back, they made for Wyoming and Yellowstone National Park to see Old Faithful, then headed south and east along two-lane roads through Medicine Bow and Laramie.

We witnessed the desolation of barren mountain tops. . . . A certain beauty in desolation that holds one in awe.

By early July, they were back at their temporary base, a white farmhouse in McLoud, near Oklahoma City, that belonged to Georgia's sister, Zelma.

Squeaky's eye was still swollen and filled with fluid, so his doctors put him on steroids, but the physician who wrote the prescription was careless and wrongly issued instructions for four 20-milligram tablets a day, quadruple the usual dose.

Even in recommended amounts, steroids sometimes leave a patient euphoric. In Squeaky's case, 80 milligrams a day sent him flying.

He was lost. For days at a stretch, he lived in the empty space between reality and fantasy, not knowing day from night, not awake, not asleep. Georgia would find him wandering absently around her parents' house or out by the barn; she was afraid he might get sucked into a baling machine and had to keep a constant eye on him.

His dreams were bizarre. One, in particular, returned night after night, a dream so graphic, so real he thought himself transmogrified.

"Well . . . I was a duck. I was up in Canada and I was a first-year duck. We were all sitting in a lake up there, just swimming around, and it was starting to get colder. I was talking in English and when I did this, it scared the ducks around me, and some of the older ducks came over and started plucking tail feathers from my butt. So I learned quickly not to speak English. They started quacking about how we would be flying south soon. A large number of us had not made the journey, but we knew the path we would fly. We flew for hours and my wings ached like hell. Night after night it was the same thing: I would pick up with that damn migration. I hated going to sleep because it was just tireless flying and all you could see was the ass of the Goddamn duck in front of you.''

Georgia, too, was growing weary of this migration. "He would quack in his sleep and he would flap his arms like they were wings. For Christ's sake, I had bruised ribs."

Then, three days in a row, he dreamed he was a cabbage. He described the dream to Georgia. She thought, "This is getting serious," and called the clinic, at which point the mistake was discovered and the doctors cut back the dose.

His wits were quickly restored, but his sight was still blurred and his spirits began to flag. Tethered to the city by clinic appointments and surrounded by Sheetrock and paint, he had nowhere to look but inward.

July 21, 1980

I see the world so differently that words fall short to explain. Could I explain the fear of night dark, night upon day without images? Could I explain the ceiling swirling in ether, the dripping of the liquid through plastic tubes, the masked faces of the doctors and nurses? My eye spins a web before me, somehow my words seemed gagged.

I must continue to search for the meaning, no matter how hidden. To do this I must overlook the things I see, see beyond the shadows. Scribbling one's experiences out into perceptions . . . to paint the total picture.

Perhaps the loss of detail will lead me to look deeper into the people I meet, the things they say, the way they laugh.

Sometimes one of the tiny shreds of shrapnel suspended in the fluid of his eye would float forward in front of his pupil.

A large black butterfly dances before my eyes, wings motionless in flight, a ballerina caught in slow motion. The reflection of a tiny piece of metal, a vision into a future not known. Angel in black, looking into the past as it comes alive.

He tried to laugh at his liabilities. He told his friend Billy that he was glad his blind eye could not be restored because, with his luck, it would work like a movie projector that had been stopped in mid-reel. Someone would suddenly flip on a switch and "I'd start seein' again in 1968. Then I'd be right back in the damn war."

Often during this period, he thought about his father.

. . . trying to understand such a waste of life and why did it happen. He must have been thirty-two or -three when hit by a hit-and-run driver down in Ft. Worth. Since then he has been living in memories always fading.

As a child I never understood why my father drank in the bars behind the painted windows of Reno. One time my mother took me to see my dad's skid-row hotel room, and I stared out the wiremesh window to the brick wall. I think my dad died that day.

Through all of this, the black humor and the melancholy, Georgia kept silent. She, too, felt the weight of what was coming, but she did not want to be the one to give it voice, to put it in front of them. When he was ready, he would tell her; then they would talk.

Last night Georgia and I discussed for the first time the inevitability of going blind. I cannot say for certain that blindness is inevitable, but most of the indicators point in that direction. Fortunately, I have not resigned to marking time, but have decided to see as much as possible. To do this I call upon my memory, remembering the beauty of better sight and painting in my mind the colors of reality. My mind must become a picture book of color, detail and beauty, the eyes behind the eyes.

They lived on his government disability check, a monthly payment for his wounds. When he first started drawing the money in 1969, he felt a twinge of guilt, as if he had not earned it. Now, facing the prospect of great loss, the money seemed to mock him.

One thousand dollars sounds like a lot, but it's not, and lately it don't seem so free anymore.

As his vision got worse, he began to lose strength and self-assurance.

I have an appointment in the eye clinic one floor up. Not only must I ascend a flight of stairs, but I must climb to a high mental level. Despite myself, I must deal with this examination as if a normal person. A lot of years have passed since I was a normal person. It's a matter of knowing you have something to do and doing it. It's like being back in the war, taking out a patrol, being responsible in a life and death situation. What the hell is wrong with me, anyway?

In late August they drove south to Lake Texoma for a few days in the wild.

Must learn to find new meaning, unseen beauty, in the morning. Perhaps I can erase the haze and see in memory. Strange, however, that I cannot remember what it was like to see perfect. I wonder if people who go totally blind forget completely what sight is all about.

For a year or more I have waited for my sight to clear, now I know that will not happen. Must accept this reality.

When he returned to the clinic in Oklahoma City, the doctors, at last, spotted the shrapnel, but the splinters were so tiny, they could not get hold of them. Three times they put him on an operating table, rolled him on his stomach, and waited for the metal to drift forward. But each time they flipped him back to work on him, the splinters retreated and disappeared. "Finally," he remembered, "they just said, 'The hell with it,' and sent me home."

He was told that the shrapnel would cause the cornea to deteriorate until it was so clouded, no light would reach the retina. That would be the end. Five years, said the government doctors, probably less.

But the portion of a man who survives combat always carries some luck.

On one of his trips to the clinic, Squeaky stumbled on an old ally, the surgeon who had performed his first eye operation, the cornea transplant. He had gotten on well with this man, a private physician, a specialist serving as a consultant to the Veterans Administration.

When Squeaky laid out his case and the government's prognosis, the specialist took him quietly aside.

"I can help you," Squeaky remembered him saying. "Don't worry; we'll get government insurance to pay for it. Come see me."

A few weeks later, using a new technique he had developed and practiced with success, the specialist drained the fluid that lubricates the eye and filtered out the shrapnel.

The cornea, however, was so damaged, Squeaky needed another transplant. He put his name on a waiting list. The call came at the end of the second week in February 1981; the transplant operation took place a few days later at Presbyterian Hospital in Oklahoma City.

In the months that followed, his sight was still muddled, but if the eye did not reject the cornea within a year, the doctor said, his vision would clear.

He had survived an enemy mine, endured the ineptitude and miscalculation of his own government, found love, and escaped blindness. At last his case had an end. Then came the letter from Washington.

Squeaky had filed an insurance claim for the operation with the Department of the Navy. Now, in an astonishing reply, some hollow head told Squeaky that he refused to process the claim unless the corporal could supply the name and address of the person who had injured him.

A more orthodox man might have fired back in anger. But a salty iconoclast would never waste such an opportunity. Squeaky sat down with his writing tablet and pen. He respectfully reminded Washington that he had been injured in a rather large government enterprise that involved an unusual number of actors, many of whom were unknown to him.

"I said as far as identifying the fella, all gooks looked alike to me, but that they might write Hanoi and ask who it was. I added that if Hanoi should write back with the information, please send the man's name to me; I'd like to pin his ears to his head."

That summer he and Georgia quarreled about money. She thought they needed extra cash and should both find work. When an outfit that made custom T-shirts offered her a job on the rodeo circuit, she took it. The separation would not be long or painful, she told Squeaky.

He hated the idea. They argued. She left. He fumed for a while, then lit out after her.

Sitting on the shoulder of Highway 10 hoping for a ride to San Antonio. Did not bring my sleeping bag for this trip so last night was pretty uncomfortable and wet. Fortunately I did have a poncho which gave me some protection from the moist ground. I really never intended to sleep alongside the road but I just don't see well enough for night hitchhiking. . . .

Some damn drug-crazed kids got me this far, and I had just as soon crawled on hands and knees. They were throwing beer cans alongside the road, driving dangerously, flashing knives and bragging of pistols tucked under the seat. This is not my cup of tea. What happened to the hippie and brotherly love?

It is a beautiful day, early morning before the rising heat. Fortunately I came upon a truck stop, purchased a cup of coffee, and am feeling awake. Rides are few and far between, a sign of the times, I guess.

Was hoping to be in San Antonio sometime today and possibly catch Georgia before she begins the show. Attempted to call yesterday but failed to make a connection. I hope I have not lost Georgia, for now alone I realize how really precious she is. How I miss our times together, the camping, the traveling, the strolls through secondhand stores. I wish I could say, "I love you," and she could feel the desire of my heart. Did I throw away all that beauty for dreams that had already come true? Another chance?

Well if I continue at this rate of 100 miles a day I shall make San Antonio by Tuesday, July 7. Won't I be feeling chipper by then.

> July 3, 1981
> San Antonio
> About 10 P.M.

A lady named Theresa picked me up about 9:30 A.M. this morning. I think she wanted someone to talk to about her rather dire situation—she is due to give birth on July 16 and just left her husband in Phoenix.

Right now I'm leaned against the wall, somewhere, at some kind of festival. All kinds of booths selling all kinds of food and beer and I'm broke. Kerouac couldn't have done it any better.

No one can tell me how to get to I-35 North and I'm sick of this valuable road experience. I'm alone and I guess it's just what I deserve. Damn VA check up in Idaho. Home really nowhere.

Georgia is down at the King ranch enjoying her own life and I have a feeling her life will never include me again.

I'm sick of trying to see my way through these dark nights, squinting at road signs and fighting the glare of lights. Life is slowly clawing my eyes out.

As I was feeling about as miserable as a slug worm in salt, a policeman chased me down, told me to sit tight until midnight and he'd take me out to I-35. Good people still left.

He went back to Oklahoma after that, just as Georgia, bouncing from one town to the next, was beginning to relent.

At a state fair in Sedalia, Missouri, she sat down on a bale of hay to think: she was weary of the road and missed her man. That night she called Squeaky and told him to meet her a day or two later at Zelma's house. "I said, 'We're gonna be together and that's that and to heck with anything else.' "

Three months later, on December 29, 1981, they were married.

The first ceremony took place on a cool but sunny afternoon in the county courthouse by the town square in Madill, not far from a house they had rented near Lake Texoma.

Georgia remembers that the judge wore a dark three-piece suit and performed a simple "Do you take this man" ceremony.

Then the couple, accompanied by friends and family, returned to the rented house, where they again stood side by side. This time they began by reciting the history of their courtship and the highlights of their travels. They faced each other, held hands, and promised to be inseparable.

Georgia wore a hand-embroidered dress, Squeaky a cotton peasant shirt; the best man and matron of honor were in homemade buckskin. The wedding cake was whole wheat, the wedding wine Cold Duck. Georgia said it was a hell of a party: some of the guests slept where they fell.

We were up early, brought out of bed by a riotous gang of starlings and sparrows. Georgia and Squeaky had spent the night in a tent and given me the bunk in the trailer.

The quarters were close: the bunk was barely double-size and not more than six and a half feet long; it was opposite the galley, which consisted of a stove, a counter and sink, an icebox, and three storage cabinets; forward was the sitting area, which consisted of a small couch built into the bulkhead, a tiny table that could be collapsed, and a chair on a metal pedestal; aft was a small bathroom with a shower stall. In all, twenty-four feet stem to stern—about the length of two church-hall tables with a chair on either end—and eight feet wall to wall.

Georgia tried to give this aluminum box the look of a home. She pinned some lace doilies to the valance above the front window and put down a striped cotton throw rug in front of the sink.

They had a small black-and-white television and a radio and tape player. Squeaky liked to fish and sometimes stayed at it for twelve hours at a stretch. (It was Georgia, however, who always came home with the catch. "She's got the luck," he said, dismissing her success.) They read; he liked humor and political history; she liked sagas and Indian lore. Sometimes they played Scrabble or chess, sometimes did beadwork and embroidery for Christmas presents.

Sometime around 7 A.M., Georgia came stumbling into the trailer and put on a pot of coffee. Squeaky followed, puffing on his first Marlboro of the day.

After breakfast Squeaky and I climbed into their truck and set out for Heavener, the nearest town, to pick up some fresh fruit and supplies and to make airplane reservations for a trip to Texas in a few days.

We were going to Mesquite to visit Belknap and Dave Troy, who was scheduled to be in Dallas the same time on business. It was to be a small reunion, the forerunner of a much larger gathering a few of us had begun to discuss.

"Hey, Mike, you remember the time Tommy and me came into the bunker banging metal trays?"

"Yeah, Squeaker." I was at the wheel. It was a hot Southwest morning and the air rushing in the open windows felt good. We came down out of the foothills into the valley past a convenience store and a roadside restaurant.

"You think about Gonzales a lot?" I said.

"I did think a lot about the injustice of it. Here's people like Tommy Gonzales, with a wife and a child, getting killed, and here I was with no attachments; I struggled with that for a little while. I used to have a lot of remorse when I thought about Tommy, but maybe the years had separated me from that or taught me how to handle it. Tommy Gonzales was the first person who died that I ever really cared for, that I loved. It makes me so bitter because it was so needless."

We stopped to pick up the groceries, then lingered in the parking lot for a while, leaning against the back of the truck. He asked about Belknap again: What was he like? Did he think a lot about the war? I had told him how Craig had spent years looking for answers to impossible questions and how, failing, he no longer listened to any voice that claimed to speak with moral authority, especially the Church.

Squeaky nodded. "Yeah, I was a Christian—until the bridge. I can remember that night: I just kept thinking, 'Maybe I ought to pray about this stuff,' and then saying, 'Fuck the whole thing; there ain't no God; otherwise this stuff wouldn't't've happened.'

"I thought about Tommy Gonzales and Payne that night, over and over again. I tried to grasp the idea that so many people had been killed and wounded that day, and that the next day it was going to start all over again. It seemed never-ending. I got to the point where I never wanted to find the enemy again. I never wanted to kick ass after April nineteenth."

He let his foot drop from the chrome bumper into the dirt and dug into his pocket for a cigarette. His inquiries were more political than Belknap's, but he seemed driven nonetheless by a need for imperatives, something final and concrete.

"You have to come back and look at what you did and make a judgment on it, right or wrong. You're not a kid anymore who knows nothing about the war and the issues it raised. You have to ask yourself: Did I really look at the choices I had? Did I really have a choice?

"Then you get back and you start looking at the political side of it. You start looking at the moral issues. You never asked yourself: Is what the United States doing right? You just assumed it was. Well, anybody who studies the war is gonna find out that what the United States was doing was completely asinine. You ask: Who is morally responsible for this? Me or the government?"

He had finished his cigarette now, so we climbed into the Dodge Ram and left the question hanging there in the hot Oklahoma afternoon. When we arrived back at camp, the sun was baking the park and we stripped off our clothes, put on our swimsuits, and made for the deep blue water of Cedar Lake.

Out beyond the rope line, I thought I discovered an underwater spring; the current there was faster and refrigerant. I stayed in that place quite a while, treading water and gliding back.

The company was encamped on Hill 37, a small knoll off Route 1 that the enemy blasted every day with its artillery and mortars. One morning, Charlie Squad was sent on a patrol into the mountains. The men were happy to leave that torrid hill and escape the danger, if only for a moment. Halfway up the mountain, we came across an icy stream rushing over rocks; its water was clear and sweet. At first we were content to fill our canteens, but it was not long before some of the men were soaking in the stream. We took turns cooling off and keeping lookout.

From the stream, we could see down the mountain and over the road, about a mile or so, to Hill 37, our base, and as we watched, the enemy began to rake the hill with fire. We could hear the pop of the big guns and mortar tubes in the distance, then the scream of the shells slicing through the air, then the crack and crunch as they ripped into the rocks and earth and the bunkers full of men. Then the shooting stopped and the gray smoke lifted. The corpsmen rushed from their holes, and litter bearers struggled down the hill with the casualties. A line of flatbed trucks arrived. The litters were loaded and the trucks headed south toward the battalion aid station and the battalion morgue.

We saw all this, but did not feel it, not up there on the green mountain in the cool stream, up there where the war seemed so small and distant, as if, already, it was part of the past.

Later that afternoon I went for a walk in the woods with Georgia.

"How was Squeaky when he first heard from us—me, Craig, and the others?"

"He was extremely apprehensive, agitated," she said. "Then after he spoke to y'all, he was very quiet-like, and I could tell he was thinking about a lot of things that he had not allowed himself to think about."

"Was that new to you?"

"Well, in a way. When he talked about the war, it was mostly to joke about it. You know, off-the-wall stuff. And also, Michael's finally at peace with himself. He's been at war with himself and society and the world in general for so long that finally he's at peace."

She paused and lit a cigarette. We had stopped in a small

clearing with a picnic table. Georgia looked older than at first glance. The hair was blond, the cheeks round, the eyes buoyant and blue, but beneath this country-girl countenance was an aspect that admitted no one. She was voluble, except when it came to autobiography. She said it was enough to know that there had been two unhappy marriages, a child-custody battle she had lost and not appealed, a period of bitter disaffection from her family, a welcome reconciliation, and, finally, a long and unhappy period with another man who, at times, lived on both sides of the law and made her feel as if she had gone through a war of her own.

"Has contact with his comrades brought the fighting back for Squeaky?"

"We live with it daily, of course; all you have to do is look at him," she said. "I get angry about the war: it's personal; it breathes; it lives at home; there's no way to get away from it. But to tell you the truth, there's too many other things that are more important. But you brought some of it back for him."

"How?"

"The first night, talking about Tommy Gonzales; his death has never been settled in Michael's mind; I doubt it ever will be. Of course, I had heard the story of the bridge many, many times. But he rarely spoke of Gonzales. He was angry at him for dying, for getting killed, and he still is. Gonzales died on him. Gonzales wasn't supposed to die. Gonzales had a family. When we go to funerals, Michael will not view a person in a casket. There is still something in there and he won't let go of it."

"You mean forget?"

"Won't let it go."

The next day the three of us climbed into the truck and headed for his land, the rocky, tangled, ten-acre patch that was Squeaky's concession to convention, as close to ambition or career as he was ever going to come. The land was a sign that the rebellion was over. He had a mortgage; he was finished with the Age of Aquarius.

They closed the deal on the land July 4, 1984, with a down payment of five hundred dollars. They were short on groceries the rest of that month, but they had what they wanted—a home, ten acres of sandstone and hard soil with a southern slope in the foothills of the Winding Stair Mountains.

The property was just outside the town of Bengal, which had not been a real town since a coal mine there had closed many years before. It was little more than an intersection now, a crossroads with a green-and-white sign that said WELCOME TO BENGAL, a convenience store built from railroad ties, an auction shack, and an old one-room schoolhouse used now for town suppers and Christmas parties and meetings of the Water Board, which was a bit of wishful thinking since no utility company had shown any interest in running a line to those hardscrabble hills.

Squeaky and Georgia planned to clear a part of their tract and establish a building site on which, at first, they would set their white Globestar trailer.

Yes, they would still roam the green arcades, looking for golden eagles and large-mouth bass, but their circuit now had an end and beginning.

"It is a place to start to build a home base," Squeaky said on the drive from Cedar Lake to Bengal. "You could say it takes the place of having a career. It's something to accomplish. I really don't have anything else to accomplish that'll make me happier by accomplishing it."

Perhaps they would put up a house, perhaps not; nothing pushed them that way; from their union, they said, there would be no children. In the main, all Squeaky was after was "a real peaceful, real calm life," which to him was just as worthy a pursuit as selling stocks and bonds or drying out drunks or planning logistics for the armed forces—the labor of some of his comrades. The difference was the others were doing someone else's business; he was doing his own.

It was as Georgia had said the day before: "I think that he was worried that you would look down on our lifestyle, that you would think he was a failure because he does not have a real prestigious job or so forth. For me that was the main apprehension, too. A lot of people think he's lazy and ambitionless, but we have our own goals."

We turned left before the BENGAL sign and a quarter mile up the road found access to their land. They had already started to chop out some of the briars and blackjacks and small cedars. The meadow grass in the clearing was knee-high. We walked from one section to another as they pointed out their favorite spots: this was where they might build a house, this was where a corral could go. It was quiet. Over a hillock, a rooster called out in the afternoon.

We set lawn chairs under the scrub oaks and sat down to cold drinks. Squeaky had on his blue-denim bib overalls and around his head had tied a red bandanna.

"This is gonna be nice," he said, sweeping his hand across the scene before him, "but I'd still like to have some land in the mountains of New Mexico and . . ."

They had not lost their wanderlust. Land titles and tax bills aside, it was a good guess that one day soon they would take to traveling again. They would hike and fish, swim in the blue water, brew tea in big jugs under the afternoon sun. And Squeaky would record it all, just as he had so often along the road that had led him home.

July 10, 1982
Fifteen Springs,
New Mexico

We arrived here mid-afternoon yesterday. Our camp site is at the base of a mountain which is covered with spruce. A small stream runs within ten feet of the camp providing drinking water. . . .

So far we have not heard a sign of civilization. Last early evening heard the coyotes howl. I have been told that when you hear that sound the coyotes are going in for a kill.

. . . The streams here are very cold, and Georgia is out there somewhere bathing in them. She is chunked full of the Pioneer Spirit.

Well I have chores to do even out here in the wilderness. I must cut up some logs for a nice fire before it is dark. I can only guess as to how fast the sun will fall tonight.

July 11, 1982

The flying insect population is completely out of hand this morning, with the pesky little mosquitoes dive bombing and flies scurrying across the page as I write.

At this very moment I can hear the stream babbling and only wonder where it is going. "To the Gulf of Mexico," you say.

July 12, 1982

Man can never escape the long arm of civilization and we are no exception. Yesterday a Forest Ranger called on us, explaining the rules of fire safety and informing us of the fourteen-day camping limit. To make it all official, he left us with a contact notice, and I gave him a can of grapefruit juice to show my good intentions. . . .

July 13, 1982

My right hand has swelled up like a watermelon and the cause I can only guess—a spider, bee, or horsefly.

Yesterday black clouds rolled in and it thundered for all it was worth but not a speck of rain.

July 14, 1982

Georgia drove the old truck back to camp last night and did a quite exceptional job of maneuvering down those primitive roads.

Had a breakfast of corned beef and hash browns prepared by camp cook Georgia Lee.

July 20, 1982

It is surprising how well we eat considering that we are without refrigeration. For instance, we started the day with fried potatoes and ham and finished up with spaghetti and green beans.

Took a bath in the cold stream today using a french clay soap which is made for oily skin. This soap is safe to use in streams as it contains no detergent and is biodegradable. I feel clean as a whistle.

July 23, 1982
Rio Grande Park

We went to Taos for the last big splurge of the month. Dos Equis beer! Georgia had some wine mixed with club soda and a twist of lime. What a life.

July 29, 1982

It rained throughout last night and this morning the Rio Grande is flowing muddy. Georgia was sick all day yesterday with what appeared to be a stomach virus but is much better today. . . .

The first of the month is around the corner and I am anxious about my V.A. check. Anymore I never know when and if it will arrive. Someday in the future, perhaps after the mule trip, we can go to work and not have to depend on my disability for a livelihood.

August 2, 1982

"We're in the money." What a great song. Went to Taos today to call Texoma bank and verify our deposit. Then knowing we were no longer poverty stricken we ate a fine breakfast at Michael's kitchen washed down by a Dos Equis from Oglevies. Then on to Safeway where we purchased sirloin steaks for tonight's supper.

Evening

Those steaks tasted mighty good, cooked over an outdoor fire. We made a resolution this evening to have steak on the first of each month, and what more deserving couple. Tomorrow we break camp and head to Albuquerque for restocking at Kirkland Air Force Base PX. Then back to the mountains.

August 7, 1982

This journal has not been kept up to date and for that I take all the blame. I have yet to write of the frantic tear through Santa Fe, the tourist dance of rush 'n shove. All this and we're beating the sidewalks of the plaza for food, reading menus with prices only the rich can pay. We left Santa Fe hungry only to stop at the La Something Roadside Cafe and pay $3.00 for a cheeseburger.

August 12, 1982
Coronado State Park

Today we are going to Kirkland AFB Hospital and find out what has been making Georgia feel bad. [She began to tremble and have blackouts.]

This park is not one where a person would want to camp for any extended period, but it is convenient to Albuquerque, about 11 miles away.

August 13, 1982

Yesterday was split between the base hospital and the hot streets. Georgia did not find out what is causing her to feel bad, but the heart was pretty much ruled out. All the blood tests came back normal so the next step is an EEG or brain scan.

After a tiring day we returned to camp only to be hit by a strong dust storm followed by rain. (I was wounded today, a deep gash in the ring finger of my left hand. I bled like a Truman Capote book.) Georgia is busy scrubbing our table but here I sit writing in this journal.

August 19, 1982

Georgia had an EEG at KAFB and one is only allowed four hours' sleep the night before, so starting out the day, without coffee nonetheless, at a hospital makes for a bad day.

August 24, 1982

There is a new addition to our family, a six-week-old Australian Shepherd/Alaskan Husky mix. A twenty-dollar investment, he should be able to repay us with a year of work. Now he is a pleasant drain on our resources. Lakotah is the name we finally decided upon after narrowing it down to Waylon, Jessie or Lakotah.

Sept. 3, 1982

Had breakfast with Dale and Kay this morning over at the EM club. They are from Illinois, he retired from the Air Force. They are especially nice people. Visiting Georgia; she is at the hospital [where she was admitted for more tests and treatment—still no formal diagnosis].

Here it is the third of the month and we still don't know if we've been paid or not. Damn bank seems to be in cahoots with the V.A. Slowly whittling away at my senses. Sometimes I think it might be easier to take to the factories. . . .

Sept. 4, 1982

Sure is nice to have Georgia out of the hospital. Sure hope the Dilantin gets her back on the road to feeling better.

Dec. 22, 1982
[McLoud, Ok.]

Home for the holidays ... Georgia said last night that it is difficult to deal with the many different personalities and life-styles in our two families and we have quite an array of them. Perhaps our life-style is the most removed from the norm. Society has put us on the fringe and I hope we spend our remaining years on the outside only occasionally making a visit.

Dec. 28, 1982

Enjoyed two days with Georgia's children and ended the visit with a game of dominoes.

Jan 10, 1983
Lake Murray [Ok.]

In my dreams I am never in my own boat but rather a borrowed one. I am out on the lake and the motor has died. The waves are rocking the boat and a thunderstorm is approaching. I look to the faraway shore and suddenly my glasses fall off and sink to the bottom. With one oar I row the boat in circles. Such are my dreams.

Today in pleasant weather, we strolled over to Tipps Point, about one-half mile south of here. Our faithful dog, Lakotah, followed us on his leash.

Jan. 28, 1983
[Last entry]

I wonder if vanity keeps this journal, for surely I am but a common man, still I am on an uncommon journey.

(2)

In Philadelphia, where I was going to college, the owner of a sandwich shop near campus hung a hand-lettered sign on the greasy wall above his cash register. AMERICA—LOVE IT OR LEAVE IT, it read. He had always seemed an amiable man, but the politics of the day filled him with a strange and menacing passion. Back then, everyone was choosing sides; even short-order cooks were ready for a fight.

The streets in those days seemed to be filled with men in uniform. In the late spring of 1967, you could see them riding the buses that used to make the long hot trips up and down Broad Street.

One day, two Marines got aboard. It was rush hour; all the seats were taken and they had to stand—two ramrods in tan and green, clear-eyed and clean shaven. They stood silently, their eyes fixed on the bulkhead in front of them. At a stop down the line, they turned smartly in the aisle and disembarked. I twisted back in my seat by a window to watch them until they were out of sight. A week later, in the basement of a red-brick post office in Bloomfield, New

71

Jersey, near my home in Montclair, I signed the papers to enlist.

I had done badly that semester. It might have been liquor or drugs—each was at hand—or the courses, business and accounting, dry loaves that dragged out the days. Who can say?

The failing grades upset my mother and second stepfather. They complained, but I kept silent—after all, they had paid the bills—and waited for the storm to pass. Once their anger was spent, that would be the end of it. But no judgment is as withering as the one that comes from within. I had not expected it, but the bad odor of my failure followed me that summer. It trailed me to dates and parties; it hung heavily in the spaces where I tried to hide.

There was also a girl. Call her Brit. The year before, though not yet at the age of majority, I had gotten into a discotheque. My partner that night spotted two girls at a nearby table. Pairings were arranged; mine was plain, but not unattractive, something about her lips. She said she lived abroad but had come to work in the States. She was there to dance; I had something else in mind.

Months passed. We saw each other often. We were circling; I guessed—hoped, really—that she was no less amative than I. Then one night on a brown corduroy couch, we finally commingled. When I went to raise myself, she grabbed my arm. "I love you," she said.

At first I did not understand, then when I did, I tried to free myself, but she held on, hard. The finish was bitter, filled with charge and countercharge; at the very end, we could not meet face to face. The last message between us was passed through a go-between.

She had been hurt; I felt responsible; and the feeling only made the weight of my failure at school harder to carry. So that summer, in the cool basement of a red-brick post office, I enlisted.

The recruiter was a young sergeant with short blond hair, from somewhere down South. He was slow and clumsy with paperwork, so I bumped him from his chair and typed out my own enlistment contract. "Where will I be going?"

He smiled a tight smile. "I'm not gonna bullshit you; you're goin' across the big pond to a shootin' war."

"Good." It was the answer I wanted.

I had read the newspapers and watched television news; the sights and sounds of battle were irresistible. History was unfolding and I had an urge to be part of it, a Henry Fleming hoping to "mingle in one of those great affairs of the earth."

"Shit, you just have a Hemingway complex," a friend said. And that was true as well. I needed to prove myself; I wanted to pass the test. And I had a fantasy too. Maybe some day hence on Broad Street, a college freshman aboard a bus bound for City Hall would spot me standing in the aisle, a ramrod in tan and green, and wonder to himself if he too would ever be that untouchable.

THREE

TOO MUCH TO TELL

Squeaky was short-tempered, on edge. It was the night
before our flight to Dallas to gather with Belknap and Troy.
We had just come back to the trailer from the shower
house. Georgia was helping him lay out his clothes and
pack his kit. He could not find his favorite shirt and now,
for the first time in days, there was suddenly a snap in his
voice. Georgia tried to calm him. "Here," she said, "have
a cup of hot chocolate." But the remedy did not help. He
crawled into the brown tent and zipped the flap behind him,
restless and out of sorts.

I was sure he had not cooled to the trip. In the shower
house while we shaved, he had talked about our "strong
brotherhood" and how "amazed" he was at "how little"
had really changed. "The feelings," he said, "are still the
same."

So I reckoned that something old had unsettled him, and
from his silence I thought I knew its source.

He had gone to our reunion table early, was there now,
even as he slept, holding a place for Tommy Gonzales.

*　　*　　*

Semper Fidelis. Loyalty was the lifeblood of the Corps.

It was stenciled on the squad-bay walls, written in the manuals, and inscribed under the scarlet-and-gold bas-relief emblems. Marines had always answered the country's call, and the proving grounds of their fidelity were legend—Tripoli, Cuzco Wells, China, Santo Domingo, Belleau Woods, Wake Island, Iwo Jima.

The Corps was a family, its bloodline as old and honorable as the Republic itself. Its ancestors were its heroes, and recruits were told that to wear the uniform of Marines was to inherit this brave patrimony. In every sense, it was brotherhood bought with blood, surrounded by the greatest mystery of all. If a man did not come into the Corps with a strong sense of clan, he almost always left with one.

To be sure, there were cowards and braggarts and criminals in the ranks, but they were not suffered lightly, not, at any rate, during the summer of 1967, when the training centers at Parris Island and San Diego ran full throttle to service the war.

The emphasis was on survival. When the drill instructors had us alone, away from the watchful eyes of officers, they cut through the myths. Under fire, they said, men are not moved by the call of country or the rhetoric of a cause. They fight to survive; they fight for their comrades. This, they said, was the real lesson of Tripoli and Chapultepec and Iwo Jima's bloody slopes. And war proved them right.

We lived and fought in small units, squads of ten to fifteen men, three squads to a platoon, four platoons to a company. We shared rations, slept under the same wet ponchos, marched for months at each other's side. It did not take long for strangers to turn into comrades or for two men, finding in one another a vein of humor or decency or raw courage—some moral handhold to steady themselves on the uncertain field of battle—to pair off and make friends.

Wounded or dead, comrades were never left behind. Whatever the cost, no matter how many men were killed or cut down trying, we went after them. Payne, Gonzales, Belknap, Hefright, and half a dozen others were hit as they moved to pull just *one* body off Bridge 28. And they marched out into that killing zone not because they were ordered to do so; they went instead because each believed that if his had been the body on that bridge, other Marines would have come for him.

This was not true of every man, of course; some were bound to wither; some did. But for most, Semper Fidelis was more than a hollow motto. It was a promise they were prepared to keep.

And that is part of what set me on my search and what now was drawing the others to Dallas: a chance again at comradeship, a communion as intimate as lovemaking and as liberating as the finding of faith.

We were up before dawn and across the border to Arkansas and the airport at Forth Smith. It was a cool morning. The black vault was flecked with stars, the beginning of a clear day. Along the way, we sipped hot coffee from a silver Thermos.

At the airport, Squeaky gave Georgia a long, tender kiss; this would be their first time apart since their marriage.

The flight was a propeller-driven Convair 580 with polished brass fittings and plush seats. Squeaky read a magazine. I leaned back and it was not long before the vibrations from those old motors had put me to sleep.

At the Dallas–Forth Worth airport, we boarded a bus that took us to the center of the city. Then we hailed a cab for Fairmont Street and Belknap's office.

He had not expected us so early, and when Squeaky ambled through his door, Craig was stopped by the sight of him—the shoulder-length hair and dark-eyed countenance—but in less than a moment, he had pulled the Oklahoman into an embrace.

"Hiya, Hoss," he said warmly, patting his shoulder and rubbing his back.

We went to lunch at a wood-paneled watering hole with antique sideboards and hanging plants, an oasis for dark business suits and button-down shirts hunched over avocados stuffed with crabmeat salad and white wine in long-stemmed glasses.

The more Squeaky took in, the more he kept shifting on his seat.

"I haven't worn a tie since February 18, 1975," he announced, with obvious pride. "I remember the day because it was my birthday and the last day I worked for the state unemployment service. After I quit, I took all my ties and suit jackets and gave them to the Salvation Army."

Belknap loved it. "Say, Squeaker, how long you and Georgia been married?"

"About two and a half years." Then, as if such dalliance demanded a defense, "Ah, she's a real easy woman to be with."

After lunch, we drove east, twenty minutes, to Mesquite. Jean Belknap was waiting, full of welcome. Craig took us into the kitchen, poured himself a cup of coffee and gave us cans of Pearl beer. Squeaky looked at the can and smiled; he remembered.

" 'Beer from the Land of Eleven Hundred Springs.' Damn," he said.

"Hey, Squeaker, c'mon in here." Belknap was standing by a bookshelf next to a stone fireplace. "See these?" He pointed to several shelves of picture books about the war. "I been buyin' all these pictorials thinkin' that I would turn the page and see one of y'all. All these years I been tryin' to find you in these books."

That evening Belknap got down to business. He was determined to fill in the empty spaces and wanted to know what Squeaky remembered about the bridge.

Craig sat on the carpet. In front of him was a hand-drawn map of the battle scene from an official Marine Corps account of the action. He wanted Squeaky to help him place each actor in position and replay the fight—right up to that moment when he was knocked backward onto the road and out of the war.

Craig had been changed at the bridge, literally reshaped there. The moment of his transfiguration had been so violent and so quick, his mind had either missed it or, mercifully, locked it out. He was creeping forward one moment,

77

down and bleeding the next. And he could not remember how it happened.

Now he wanted those details: Who, exactly, had been near him? Where were they standing? Who was the man who helped Doc Hefright tend him? What time of day was he hit? From which direction were the shots fired? Across the river? To the right from the hills? Whose was the body on the bridge? And so on and so on.

He was determined to dig for this detritus, as if in sifting it he might discover something that would explain the man he had become, his second self.

Squeaky was patient. He had mined the same hole; I guessed the others had too. That short, flat, open bridge was potent ground. Nothing before had been as real, nothing after as elusive.

The door bell rang and in walked Dave Troy.

An insurance executive now, he had managed to juggle his schedule so that business brought him to Dallas in time for the gathering. He had arrived the day before, so he and Craig were well caught up.

I had found Dave months earlier in Putnam County, New York. "Well, I'll be a son of a bitch. Mike Norman. My mother-in-law called and said you were trying to track me down. How are ya?"

He told me about his family and his job in the insurance division of a corporation that leased cars and trucks. We talked about the old squad, of course—Craig, Squeaky, Ciappio, and a few of the others. Then I brought up the bridge.

"Oh . . ." His voice trailed off. "Mike, I—uh—didn't make the bridge. I was on R and R. Don't you remember?"

The day before the battle, he had gone to the battalion rear at Camp Carrol to pack for five days' leave in Hong Kong. The next morning the camp awoke to alarming news.

"I got to a radio receiver and all I remember hearing

were the names and numbers of the dead and wounded . . .
Belknap, BWC 4691 . . . Cobb, CVL 2472 . . . Gonzales,
GT 1841. . . . It sounded like the whole world had come to
an end.''

He kept his flight date, but had a desultory leave; drunk
for most of it. When he returned to Golf Company, half his
former messmates were gone.

Troy was a corporal by then and after the bridge, he
became the leader of Charlie Squad. It was not like the
old circle; most of the men were replacements; just new
cannon fodder to him. ''I'm not going to make any
more close friends,'' he promised himself. ''It just isn't
worth it.''

He spent his time with Squeaky and me and, once a
month or so, sent a letter to an old friend.

> 5 May 68
> Calu

> Dear Craig,
>   . . . Things are relatively quiet here. The platoon is
> new of course and all changed around. . . . We have
> beau coup new people and God knows why but we got
> a new Redheaded Californian. Please God he has bet-
> ter luck than the last two. [Payne was the second
> redheaded radioman from California killed in seven
> months.]
>   Be good and write when you get a chance.

He also kept up with his journal, a kind of chronicle of
that spring and early summer.

> 23 May

Woke up to find out Lurch [Lieutenant Hagan, the commander
of the First Platoon] had returned from R&R, and rumor has it he
is still a virgin.

Squad leaders' meeting proved interesting. We are now prepared
to move within 5 days.

Lurch resents my being squad leader but there isn't much he
can do about it without causing a scene. He has made a few

snide remarks but I must admit I've kept up with him on returns.

Stood last roving watch.

25 May

Louie woke me up to tell me Lt. Ciappio [now executive officer of the company] wanted me ASAP. Cap told me Louie fell asleep on watch—big hassle over nothing—Cap wanted to burn Louie and I told him No. Now I've got to stand watch and check lines every night.

Lt. Hagan is as bad as ever. He hates the thought of me as squad leader.

By the beginning of June, with less than three weeks left on his thirteen-month tour, Troy was a genuine "short-timer," even more diffident and wary than was his reputation.

We knew him as a cautious man. In the late fall of 1967, he had been hit in the throat during an enemy mortar attack. The piece of shrapnel entangled itself deep in the muscles that control the tongue, and even after five hours of surgery, doctors still could not dislodge it. The operation left two long parallel scars, one on each side of his windpipe; these pink tracks and a weathered Irish face gave him a grim look. I had never seen someone so tried, so ready for battle.

I was fresh from boot camp then, full of fight, and when Dave turned out to be less than his image suggested, I scoffed at him. He was gun-shy, a turtle who rarely peeked from beneath his shell. Under fire, he stayed deep in his fighting hole and held his weapon high above his head.

Then came Bridge 28 and I began to understand the uses of fear.

Furthermore, by then it was clear that Dave Troy was a counterfeit coward. A month after the bridge, during a fight by the sea at Cua Vet, Dave held together a badly mangled squad. "You do what you have to do," he said later, "then you go clean your pants." Even his chief antagonist was impressed.

June 1

Lt. Hagan is still full of compliments for me and my job out in the bush—all psychological—tell them you're a shitbird then anything you do right is an accomplishment. I'll have to tell him I'm not a garrison Marine. I'm a field Marine.

After that he simply marked time. He had only twenty days left on his tour.

June 2

Didn't sleep much last night, thought about home and mainly about Sheryle. Anticipation is not the word for it.

Squeaky had L[istening] P[ost] and borrowed his tapes. Mike Norman told me he had a chance to get an office job through Ciappio—I hope it works out for him.

June 4

Got a new man today—he rotates home June 17, 1969—God help him. He's a full blooded Navajo Indian. Juan Wilson.

June 6

Completion of one year—Good feeling but a nervous one. I don't like the sounds of the words "saddle up." Maybe with the Help of God I won't hear them anymore.

June 13

Woke up at 9 a.m. to give Norman some money for his R&R to Australia. Said my good-byes to him as it might be the last time I see him 'till Dec. when he comes home.

June 19

Lt. sticking to his belief that there is no such thing as a short-timer. Unofficially, I'm letting Squeaky take over the squad. I'll do the admin., he'll do the rest. Ambush tonight. Not anxious to go. Sweep [back] to Bridge 28. . . . Brought back memories for a lot of guys. . . .

June 22

Came in at 0700—Slept and washed—At 10:00 Lt. Hagan yelled up and told me to get out of his sight—My field time is over.

He headed home, of course, back to the family—his mother, Eileen, his sisters, May and Ann, and his father, a remote and irascible Irishman. The patriarch was forty-four when his first child was born. For most of his life, he kept his kin at arm's length.

David Joseph Troy came from the old country, the village of Ardmore, County Waterford, one of thirteen children. When civil war broke out in 1921, he joined his brothers on the republican side. The cause lost, they were branded criminals by the British and forced to flee, ending up in Westchester County, New York, where he found work as a grocer's apprentice, then landed a job with the city of Yonkers driving a trolley and a bus. He led a narrow life. During the week, he worked; on Sundays he would wander down to Coyne Park and gather with the men around a keg of beer at the horseshoe pit. With his family, he is said to have been dry and uncommunicative; he rarely kissed his children, never played with them or walked them in the park. His most obvious virtue was his raw mettle. One winter the old man broke his ankle alighting from his bus and, disdaining help, walked the four miles home in a snowstorm. He likely loved his son, his namesake, David Joseph Troy, Jr., but never showed it and, as the boy grew up, the gap between father and son widened.

Dave was reckless, a beer drinker who smashed up the family car. By the time he was a freshman at college, his father had written him off, a burden to be endured. Even when he joined the Marine Corps, the old man barely took note of it. But Dave lionized him nonetheless, and when he returned from boot camp, he finally got his reward.

"It was my first day back. My father wasn't home yet. I went down to the bus depot where he was working as a dispatcher and saw him at the desk being the supervisor, in all his glory. Then I walked in where he could see me and my uniform, and it was the first time I ever saw my father smile at something I did in my entire life. He actually turned around and said, 'Now you're a man.' I was twenty-one years old."

So he went off to war and landed in the thick of it, and

one sodden night the enemy rained mortars on his position and he was hit.

Back in Yonkers, the news was delivered to his family in the middle of the night by two Marines in dress-blue uniforms. His mother answered the knock at the front door.

"Then she went into the bedroom and woke up my father. He was sleeping soundly and she shook him hard. 'Get up,' she said. 'David's been hurt.' My father sat up in bed. 'Hurt,' he went. 'How can David be hurt? He doesn't have the car.' "

I saw David often that spring in 1984, the first time for dinner at my house in Montclair.

His company was reassigning him from New York to New Jersey and he and his wife, Sheryle, had spent the day house hunting. They arrived at Wildwood Avenue on a soft spring night just before dark and parked at the curb. Sheryle emerged first: auburn hair cut short at the neck, large glasses sliding down her nose, and a look of either petulance or worry; there was no telling.

Dave came around beside her from the passenger side: a brown wool herringbone jacket, a button-down shirt and club tie. He had put on weight since the war; there was the beginning of a spare tire. His hair had started to gray at the sides and the years had lined his face. His collar was unbuttoned; he still had tracks straddling his windpipe.

He smiled broadly and warmly; we shook hands, embraced, patted each other on the back.

Then, almost immediately, and taking me quite by surprise, he launched into a war story . . . then another . . . and another. . . .

He paused only long enough to take a forkful of food or a sip from a tumbler. The incessant monologue lasted for hours, through dinner and dessert, down the front steps, across the lawn, and back into his car.

David had rewritten history. The war was now a series of comic skits. Sometimes his stories were accurate, sometimes not, but in either case the actualities did not matter.

Death, pain, dismemberment—no matter how stygian the event, it ended in a laugh.

He even made light of the morning he was wounded.

". . . See, I didn't know I was hit—it didn't hurt—then the blood comes spurting out and someone looks at me and says, 'Hey, Troy, you're hit.' And I said, 'Oh, yeah.' Ha, ha, ha."

He pumped out his stories like buckshot, one blast, then another. There was just no escape.

". . . I'll never forget the time at Cam Lo that I was out on the LP and an ARVN [soldier of the south] walked into our LP by mistake. I remember saying, 'Shoot the mother-fucker,' but Pace said, 'He has a red bandanna on, which means he's friendly.' I didn't give a shit. He wasn't sup-posed to be there and we should kill him, so we're all fumbling for our rifles and Pace grabs his and chases the ARVN up a hedgerow and all of a sudden I see a real gook right down in front of the fifty [caliber machine gun], and the guy on the fifty starts locking and loading and everyone on the other side of the river starts locking and loading, and I'm going, 'Forget him, we gotta get outa here 'cause those bastards are going to be firing right at us. . . .' "

There was the story of starving men spreading mayon-naise on leaves, the story of a corpsman falling off a tank, the story of Louie at Cua Viet so nervous they had to give him tranquilizers, the story of the burning latrine, on and on and on.

Sheryle could not bear it a minute longer. She slipped into the kitchen, where Beth was fixing coffee. "I'm tired of hearing his stories," she said. "He'll corner anyone—friends, people at work. He met this one guy at a wedding, didn't even know him and he started up."

That spring Dave was at the house twice more for dinner, both times alone while he was on business in New Jersey. Each occasion began pleasantly enough; we would sit in lawn chairs under the thick canopy of pin oaks in our long backyard, drink cold gin or beer, and catch up on each other. Then we would climb the back steps to the screen porch, light the kerosene lamps, and sit down to dinner. Not long after that, however, the stories would begin.

By the end of June, I was sure I had heard them all. And I was puzzled; I did not remember Dave that way. What had made him so voluble, so full of foolish chatter about events that had left most of the others speechless?

Sheryle thought the war had changed him.

They had met at a mixer at Westchester Community College. He asked her to dance; she liked his manners. He might not have fit her fantasy—a professional football star with a horse farm in Kentucky—but he was a good dancer, full of fun.

After that they were part of the same lunch crowd at school and saw each other often. He was easy to talk to, so approachable, so attentive. Soon he was among her suitors. And one night he told her she would marry him.

She laughed; how could he know? And yet the idea of it stayed with her.

"He wanted to be like Mr. Del Grosso, to teach and be the dean of students," Sheryle said. "I knew the Del Grossos. They had a nice little house and were well-liked. I said to myself, 'That's a fine life for me.' "

One day Sheryle was sitting at the lunch table with the rest of their crowd when Dave wandered in and announced that he and a friend had enlisted in the Marines. "We all looked up and said, 'Why?' All through school, we had no idea about the war. In 1966 I couldn't've even told you we were there."

After Dave left, they wrote to each other regularly. She sent news of the family and the lunch table; he told her about Charlie Squad and his comrades. At the end of every letter, he made a point of saying how much he missed her.

He came home in June 1968 and, at the beginning of the next year, enrolled at Hunter College to finish his degree. That summer, on the Sunday before Labor Day, Dave and Sheryle were married.

He had long ago lost his ambition to teach and be a college dean. For a while he thought of being an FBI man or an agent with the federal bureau of narcotics. Then along came a job as a claims investigator with a large insurance company. And it was not long before inertia had quieted any notion of another adventure.

As for the marriage, at first it foundered. He spent his weekends drinking with his old chums. Sheryle felt abandoned and pressed him to stop. At last, out of desperation, she threatened to leave. She was angry and frustrated; there was nothing left of the man she had met years before at a college mixer. He did not dance anymore. She could not get him to sit down and talk.

Suddenly, his parents took ill simultaneously and this crisis of family brought him home.

By now they had begun to have children; first a daughter, Taryn—named by Sheryle to honor her heartthrob, Tyrone Power—then David Joseph Troy III, and, finally, Courtney.

In 1973, David's mother, Eileen, died of emphysema. Soon after that, the family patriarch, who was suffering from the same ailment, moved in with his son and daughter-in-law in their new house in Mahopac.

There was still a distance between them, but, at last having something in common, combat, they found a way to be with each other—they told stories. The father delighted in recounting his early life, his days fighting with the IRA. Soon his son became his most faithful audience.

"My father had an iron-trap mind. He remembered it all, facts and dates; chronicled it all; put it all in perspective. He told some great stories, especially about the war, like how one day the IRA might come into a town to the cheers of the people and the next have porridge thrown on them— the glories of war.

"Yeah, he told some great stories, but I don't think he understood how much I loved him because as cold as he was, I could be cold back, so it was one of those relationships where there was respect, but no feelings. They weren't allowed.

"We argued right up to the end, to the day he died—but he told some great stories."

* * *

Dave was coming through the door now. I was sitting on the rug with Belknap and Squeaky, huddled over the map of Bridge 28.

"Hey! . . . Hey! . . ." Dave had just caught sight of Squeaky. "I thought you would have a beard. You didn't get any fatter, though. You look good, skinny as ever. I get a kick out of the hair."

Squeaky came right back. "You look good too, Troy," he said, conspicuously eyeing Dave's spare tire.

Belknap looked up from the map. "We've been listening to Hank Williams, shedding a little tear, passing around some bullshit, so you arrived just in time."

Among the black-and-white photographs with curled edges resting in the plaid satchel in my attic was a picture of those three and Tommy Gonzales. It was taken on a cold day in February at Camp Carrol, the large battalion fire base on a hill near Dong Ha. The men in the picture are wearing field jackets; their hoods are pulled up over their helmets. Tommy is taking a long drag on a cigarette. Dave is staring at the camera. Squeaky has his head down and his hands shoved deep in his jacket pockets. Belknap, out of character, wears a sad, almost mournful face.

The five of us slept in a small bunker constructed from wooden ammunition crates. As I recall, I took the photograph just after sunrise. We'd had a difficult night: the bunker leaked; rats ran over us as we slept. At first light, we were up and outside, more comfortable in the rain than huddled in those miserable quarters. I cannot remember why I wanted to record that moment, but I reached into my pocket for the tiny Minox I carried and stepped back to take the measure of my comrades.

Even the most murderous and pathological of men, those who held themselves apart, wanted some companionship. The group was the fire in the cave; no one survived long away from it. To be part of such a circle was to surrender the smallness of self. Each man lived in the others. As long as one survived, we all made it home. When the shooting started, that knowledge was our only comfort.

Of course, we did not speak of such notions. The attachment, this strange feeling for other men, was new and bewildering to us. Even later, each time I thought of a night of rats and rain and a morning together, I remembered the wonder of it.

Troy was telling stories again.

"Do you remember the day the ARVNs came across the bridge at Cam Lo? They were supposed to be a blocking operation and they came across the Trace in APCs like cavalry, and they were on the east side of our position and we sat up there and watched them all day—they wore red scarves. This was the way they were going to win the war. . . ."

Squeaky wandered into the kitchen to get another beer and stayed to talk with Jean. I tried to listen over Dave's voice.

". . . Your wife . . . Shirley? . . ."

". . . No . . . Georgia . . ."

But I could only catch pieces of their conversation.

Dave drummed on, putting loyalty and forbearance to the test.

Dinner was a feast, ribs and brisket. Craig had been tending his portable smokehouse all day. After dinner Dave returned to his hotel and the three of us reconvened in the living room over the map of the battle at the bridge.

That night I was up for hours, scratching chigger bites around my waist, souvenirs of the trip to visit Squeaky's "unimproved" ten acres. I was still scratching the next morning when Belknap wandered into the kitchen.

"What's-a-matter?" Craig was watching me, a crooked smile on his face. "Chiggers, heh? I'll tell you what: when those critters bite you, they burrow into the skin and then lay a bunch of eggs. If you think you itch now, boy, you just wait till them eggs hatch."

He howled so hard he almost stumbled backward.

Squeaky joined us, freshly scrubbed. "A hot shower—damn! Wait till I tell Georgia about this."

After breakfast we went for a drive. Craig was behind the wheel, Squeaky beside him.

Belknap: "I didn't get to hear much about Squeaky last night. Tell me about yourself. How long did you spend in the hospital? Were you blind in the other eye too?"

The Oklahoman told his story—the threat of blindness, his troubles with the V.A., his rebellion and political disaffection. "You ever get involved with the antiwar movement?" he asked Belknap. When it came to politics, Squeaky was like a bird dog, always trying to flush out someone's point of view.

"No," said Craig, "I was too involved with my own problems, and quite honestly, I couldn't see any shades of gray. My world in those days was black and white; either you were for what the Marines were doing or you weren't."

"So when did you get to the point when you knew the war was hopeless?"

"Toward the end," Craig went on. "I thought, 'How could they operate that way?' I kept thinking, 'What a terrible, terrible waste.' "

"Yeah, nothing good came out of the war . . ." He stopped himself here. ". . . 'cept what's happenin' between us, right now."

That evening Dave met us in Mesquite. Belknap had made plans. "All right, boys . . . saddle up! We're going to dinner."

We ate at a gourmet Mexican restaurant, a sprawling place of art deco trappings, cool and elegant on a hot Texas night. Jean Belknap took a seat between Dave and me. She had been silent for most of the visit, watching our interplay from a distance, but now, finishing the last of a frozen daiquiri, she leaned toward me and whispered, "I feel real close to Squeaky. Tell me, what's Georgia like?"

Later Craig wanted to show off his war buddies to some friends. No one minded much. The friends had plenty of beer in their refrigerator and a game room with a full-sized pool table.

"Whaddaya say, Squeaker?" Belknap pointed across the

game room to where I was standing with Dave. "You think a cripple from Texas and a one-eyed Okie can beat those Yankees?" The Oklahoman nodded. "You do, huh? Okay, you make sure you keep the right eye open, y'hear?"

Hustled by the handicapped, Dave and I fell quickly. It was well after midnight when we finally put the pool cues down and headed back to Mesquite.

Jean went off to bed; we took seats around the kitchen table. Belknap brewed himself a pot of coffee and poured the rest of us a drink.

Here was Charlie Squad again, part of it, at least. How long had it been? Fifteen—no, sixteen years since we'd sat in such a circle.

". . . so there had to be a point when you knew the whole war was lost." Squeaky was kicking the thickets again, this time trying to force Dave into the open.

"I got to the point where I didn't give a shit whether we won or lost," Dave said. "But you had to protect the people who were there, our guys, and if you were not, then get them the hell out."

"We lost it anyway." At this point, Squeaky had a lot of beer in him. "There would have been less Americans killed if we'd just gone and surrendered."

Dave was provoked. "*We,*" he yelled, pounding his chest and pausing on every word, "we . . . didn't . . . lose . . . the war. The government never wanted to *win* it."

"Aw . . . shit . . ." Squeaky was slurring his words. "We were doomed from the beginning. . . ."

"Bullshit!" Such talk was treason to Dave. "We would have walked from Danang to Hanoi in six months."

The Oklahoman backed off. "All right, all right, but I got a question." He took a long pull at his bottle. "If we could turn back the hands of time, would you go again?"

He looked at Dave.

"Yes."

He looked at me.

"You can't bring back the dead—" I began, but Belknap cut me short.

"Look!" He leaned forward and laid his arms on the

table. "I want to bury all those people. I want to stop crying about them. I want to put it to rest and get on with our lives, pick up with us, the living."

Dave and I had booked seats next to each other on the flight back to New Jersey, and Squeaky's airplane to Arkansas was scheduled to leave from the same terminal, so the next morning the three of us rode together to the airport.

I thought we might have a few moments over coffee before the departures, but after we turned in Dave's rental car, Squeaky said, "See ya," and sprinted off to his gate.

Dave looked surprised and wondered if there was any ill will left from the night before. Not likely, I said. Georgia was waiting at Fort Smith and I guessed that Squeaky could think of little else but getting back to her.

The day was clear, good flying weather. The aircraft departed on time and we settled back in our seats.

"I gotta tell ya," Dave began. "I felt a twinge when I first saw Craig again."

"Oh?"

"But it was good to hear that laugh of his. He was looking so well. The weekend was just so smooth. I don't know whether I expected it to be overwhelming or what."

He lit a cigarette and looked out the window. "I'll tell you something I told Craig." A pause, a drag, a spout of smoke. "I used him for years as a crutch. Whenever I was feeling bad, I used him. I thought, 'There's always somebody worse than I am and he's handling it.' The time I came down here after the war, 1970, he was hobbling around on crutches with a bottle of bourbon. I thought a lot about him after that, thought it should have been me on that bridge with that team of his. Had I not been on R and R, it could have been my hand and my hip."

What was this? Sober thought from the storyteller? Suddenly, the men he had served with were no longer comic burlesques, the inventions of a garrulous witling. We were his comrades.

Why, then, all the tall tales?

"The stories are an escape," he said softly, "a release. I

don't bottle it up. If I had, I would have exploded fifteen years ago. You had to find humor in it. You couldn't live at a hundred and ten miles per hour for thirteen months. So I make jokes about the war. I never shut up. Sheryle is bored to death by them. It got really bad when one of my friends came to the house and I would begin to tell a war story and he would finish it."

And finally I began to see. It was not the substance of the stories but the act of telling them that seemed to say the most about Dave. Perhaps the stories were his way to fill the silence; such tales, after all, had once helped his father cross that space. Perhaps too, as with some of us, the war sometimes seemed unreal to Dave, more fata morgana than memory. Maybe he was simply trying to convince himself. Maybe all those stories across all those years had really been directed at an audience of one.

A tone sounded; a light came on overhead; the aircraft began to descend. Dave smothered his cigarette in the ashtray and snapped on his seat belt.

"I got the car; you'll come with me."

"Sure," I said.

"Great trip, wasn't it?"

"Yeah, Dave, it really was."

The wheels touched the runway and the plane taxied to the gate. We collected our luggage and found his car in the parking lot. The Turnpike was crowded; we'd be a while getting home.

"Listen," Dave said, "do you remember the time at Cam Lo when one of the gooks in the river threw a grenade at Tex and he . . ."

(3)

By September 1969 I was out of the Corps, convinced the war was well behind me. I had been lucky: I'd gotten my adventure and come home whole. I was headed back to campus, in Newark now, not far from Montclair, where my parents then lived. Instead of market reports and balance sheets, this time I took up literature. My family thought this a worthless pursuit and urged me to study something more serviceable. But it was too late; I'd been bewitched by words. I wanted to be a poet.

I did not set out to create art or to make myself a man of letters. I had neither the vision nor the voice. I only meant to get my experience on paper. And I was sure that poetry was the one form capable of conveying the awful power and deep mystery of what I had seen. I wanted work that was self-revealing; I wanted to explain and understand myself.

I wrote terrible poetry, one day throbbing with sentiment, the next leaching blood. My adviser, a brilliant woman, a poet for twenty years, told me to stop. I was not ready, she said. The past was still too incendiary. Now was the time to study, to learn the discipline of meter and form.

Years hence, she promised, I would see the wisdom of emotion recollected in tranquility. She said this knowingly, as if she, too, had felt the fires.

It was a belligerent year at the academy. Opposition to the war had widened. "Moratoriums" were being staged. And there was hardly a campus that did not have a "peace committee." Newark's protesters were encouraged in their peevishness by the very look of Rutgers: gray stone buildings—designed in what can only be described as the fortress style of architecture—surrounded by an equally gray concrete plaza; to the east and south was a dying downtown, to the north and west, a simmering ghetto.

Most of the students were locals: children of the suburbs who couldn't bear, or afford, to leave home. Some were candidates for nursing and law degrees, some city kids with low test scores admitted to special programs. Here and there were those scholarly eccentrics who wanted to blend erudition with the raw meat of experience, the kind of learning possible only in a hard and gritty place like Newark.

Early in the fall term, I joined the main organizing committee of the peace movement. At that point, it was run by young professors and graduate students, reasoned and well-mannered. We talked about "creating a broad base of support," of drawing in all those middle-class homes and businesses in the suburbs. The militants, the longhairs among us, urged "raids" on government buildings and wild assemblies in the streets, but at that point no one listened.

It was hard to resist the spirit of those times. Again a great event was at hand. Again adventure was in the air. And I hated the war; its cost left me half crazed.

We made earnest speeches and sang civil rights songs. We marched and rallied and rode buses to Washington, D.C., where we swarmed on the Capitol steps and slept in sweaty knots on the floors of college dormitories. We mixed passion into our politics: the girls and boys from the suburbs cast aside old notions of propriety. The rules changed and changed again.

But the war went on.

The next term, with disobedience no longer a novelty,

there were only half as many on the organizing committee. We met in the basement of the law school now; we were a cadre, conspiratorial and menacing. The militants had taken control of the meetings. One night a wiry girl with dark eyes got to her feet. "If you're not willing to die for the movement," she said, "then get the fuck out!"

I had not, until that point, thought much about my Marine comrades. I was convinced that the protests would shorten the war and thus save lives; to me, it was an act of loyalty to take to the streets. But now, with "The Movement" turning dark and mean, I felt I was betraying the spirit of an old circle.

There was no longer a sense of kinship, political or otherwise, and no shared purpose on the committee. This was no close company; it was a loose gathering of lone wolves. Each week they came together with their tin drums, whipping one another up and beating one another down. "I'd like to cut Nixon's balls off . . . Fuck a boycott of Dow . . . We ought to drop a bomb on the fucking Pentagon."

The fury and hollow bombast left me cold. Suddenly, I was thinking fondly of the past, taking more pride in the service of a corrupt cause than a noble one. I was as wary now of those who challenged the war as I had been of those who prosecuted it.

So I walked away, into my books. I decided, simply, to forget.

FOUR

THAT CERTAIN
SOUNDNESS OF MIND

We went to the sea that August, to a large green clapboard house rented with friends at Rehoboth Beach, Delaware. I needed leave from memory, at least for a while, and some time with Beth and Josh.

Each morning we hopped across the hot asphalt toting our beach chairs and blankets to a crest of sand near the water's edge. The children played in the surf; gulls rode the currents overhead; the tide came and went, offering the cool appeasement of the sea, then pulling it back again.

The search had gone well. My comrades were talking about a full-scale reunion in the fall and were pushing me to round up the rest of the men on the list. At that point, I had met with five of the eleven and had scheduled visits with two others, Mike Caron in West Haven, Connecticut, and Lt. Col. David Nelson Buckner, stationed at U.S. Naval Headquarters, London.

I sat with Josh by the sea making sand castles. After a while we climbed aboard his blue-and-red rubber raft and floated side by side on the cusps of the waves. He was five then, blond, blue-eyed, ebullient. At night, after he had gone to bed, Beth and I played cards or board games with David and Linda, old friends with good instincts. They knew I'd opened the past, but did not question me about it.

When I got back to Montclair, a letter was waiting from Squeaky.

. . . I never thought that the flight from Dallas to Ft. Smith would cause jet lag, but such is the case. I guess after a short rest I will be able to continue with this vacation.

Reluctantly I dragged my butt from bed this morning, gulped down two pots of coffee, and began the dismantling of our camp at Cedar Lake. . . . It is a very smooth operation and this morning was no different, despite the intermittent rain.

. . . We drove through the mountains toward Talimena Park. Low gray clouds cloaked the mountain tops, bellowing fog into the valleys below. I remembered the monsoon clouds, but now, sixteen years later, I could see the beauty of nature's endeavor. If there was beauty in the war I was blind to it.

Then Belknap called. "Where the hell have you been?"

"Went down to the seashore."

"Well, I figured it was something like that after about the third shot at trying to get you."

He said he had news: he had just spoken with Doc Hefright, the corpsman from central Pennsylvania who had saved his life at the bridge. Belknap was worried. Hefright had suffered a nervous breakdown several months before. He was still depressed, Craig said, "still hiding behind a lot of false laughter."

I had been talking regularly with Doc. He had quit his job as head of a prison infirmary and had been in the care of a psychiatrist. His depression sounded acute.

Craig told the Doc that he would be coming east in October for a conference in New York, that he would link up with me, and that we would then swing west to Pennsylvania for a visit. The prospect seemed to cheer the Doc, Belknap said.

The gathering in Mesquite had left Craig full of camaraderie. He wanted to see Squeaky again, too. "I told him in a letter that we need to talk and walk. I'm not sure if it's our mutual wounds, common part of the country, or just a sameness of spirit, but we need to visit with some quiet time included and catch up on each other."

"Mike Norman, how the hell are you?"
"Fine, Frank."
"I tried calling you; you been away?"
"Yeah. After I got back from Oklahoma and Texas, we went to the shore for a week. I was going to call you and fill you in on Squeaky."
"Hey, how was the Squeaker? Did you guys do some drinking without me?"
"Uh-huh."
"You shitbirds."
Frank Ciappio, formerly First Lieutenant Ciappio, had been the salty, wild-eyed commander of the First Platoon and later executive officer of Golf Company.

Frank was a mustang, an officer who had risen from the ranks. He was proud of those roots and, with his brother officers and superiors, made no secret of his sympathy for the men—"my family," as he often called us.

Demo Dan was his *nom de guerre*—"demo," short for demolition, because Frank loved to blow things up. His pyrotechnics were a kind of performance, an unbridled and public expression of the inner man. He was impatient, he was precipitous, he was explosive. War suited him well; every day had the potential to be the Fourth of July.

I met Frank on Christmas Day 1967 at Camp Carrol, one of fifteen replacements who had come up from Dong Ha and had been assigned to Golf Company.

It was cold and raining; I was sitting in a tent watching my new shipmates celebrate the holiday when Ciappio ducked under the flap. A few of the men looked up.

"Hey, Lieutenant, wanna beer?" one of them said.
"Nah. Where's the new man?"
He looked around for a moment, then spotted me and

came over. "Hi, I'm Frank Ciappio. Hear you're from New Jersey. Me, too. Where you live?"

Here was a landsman, a friendly face. He had olive skin and jet-black hair, weighed roughly 180 pounds, stood about six feet two inches, but carried himself taller, chest out, ramrod straight. A thick mustache spilled over the sides of his mouth, a decoration that made him look at once silly and sinister. There was, however, a complex man behind that preposterous mask.

The side he liked to show most was the reckless, unpredictable incendiary, the petroleur who went fishing among the sampans on the river with plastique and blasting caps. Some of the men thought him unbalanced, a "flake" whose wild ways would one day get them killed.

The other side, however, was unaffected, always approachable, considerate. He took seriously his obligation to the Marines in his charge. The Corps advised its officers to "protect, shelter, and feed [the men] before you think of your own needs. . . . Never let them down." In that, Frank went by the book.

He thought of himself as more than our military overseer and whip. He did not lead so much as he sought to harbor and shield. "My kids," he called us. He was twenty-two years old.

When I came aboard that wet December in 1967, Ciappio pulled my file. When he saw that I could type and had two years of college, he took it upon himself to make me a clerk in the rear. He was going to do his landsman a favor and move him out of harm's way.

"You're out of here," he said one day early in January when we were set in at the bridge at Cam Lo. He was smiling broadly.

"What do you mean, sir?" I had no idea.

"I got you a job in the rear, asshole. You're gonna be an office pogue. You're outta here."

I had joined to fight, not spend a year on a hard chair in a musty tent filling out pay forms and sending home death notices. At that point, I had seen little of the war and did not recognize the humanity in Frank's gesture. Only a few of the men had been killed and wounded during my first few weeks, and these were strangers from the other platoons, just unlucky, I thought. My comrades, my new messmates, were just beginning to accept me. They were shaping up as good companions—the Texan who could sing, the scrawny Oklahoman, the kid from California with the red hair and freckles.

No, no office job, I told Ciappio. If the lieutenant really wanted to help, he could recommend me for sniper school.

Ciappio sighed and shook his head. "Listen, asshole." He was patient, still smiling. "I'm trying to do you a favor. That job in the company office is a ticket home."

But I did not hear him. "If it's all the same to you, Lieutenant, I'll stay where I am."

The paternal smile was gone. "All right, dickhead, go on and get your ass shot off—while you're at it, clean up this fucking area."

A week later Ciappio was named Golf's executive officer—XO, we called it, the second in command. And into the compound at Cam Lo came the First Platoon's new commander, Second Lieutenant John Robert Hagan.

It was no surprise that Ciappio and the new man did not get along. Hagan was red-haired and fair, a Protestant from the South with a measured and deliberate manner. Ciappio was Catholic of Italian stock, dark, quick-tempered, intense. Hagan had gone from boarding school to Vanderbilt, Frank from one year of college to the Corps. They were antagonists from the start, but no one expected the trouble that followed.

There was no missing Bob Hagan: six feet, six inches, 240 or more pounds, alabaster skin topped with that red cap. He was so big a man that one nickname was not enough; "Lurch," the men called him, because his long legs gave him an ungainly gait, or "Feed Me!" because the canned rations that sustained other men barely made a dent in his hunger.

Hagan held a degree in civil engineering and, in the way of an engineer, he liked things orderly and neat. During his first days of command, he called together his coadjutors and subordinates and gave a little speech. Most of the details of this impromptu address have been lost across the years, but on one point several of those in attendance agree: Bob Hagan announced that he wanted to win the Congressional Medal of Honor.

Marines are gamecocks; they like to preen before they fight. Lots of young officers would fluff their feathers and crow. But no one ever boasted he was going to win the CMH. So many of them had been awarded posthumously, for action under the most desperate and hopeless of situations, that there was something spectral, almost hallowed about that medal. To actually seek it was either to have a death wish or to be the most dangerous kind of fool.

Word of Hagan's little speech spread quickly across the perimeter. An officer bent on collecting medals usually thought little of spending the lives of his men. "Goddamn asshole," said Belknap. "He's gonna get us killed."

Ciappio, already disaffected, now burned to get back command of the First Platoon. His campaign to unseat Hagan spilled into the ranks and began to undermine the new lieutenant's authority.

A few of the squad leaders and sergeants rallied to Hagan. They dismissed his boasting as meaningless, nothing to cause worry; one encounter with the gooks was usually enough to curb any man's vainglory. And they resented Ciappio's interference, too. It was not his platoon anymore, it was theirs; they would run the unit, keep things together, until Hagan was seasoned enough to take control.

Finally, Frank backed off. In the months that followed, I did not see him much. He kept busy as XO, shuttling papers between the encampment at Cam Lo and battalion headquarters at Dong Ha.

In mid-spring a spot opened up in the Second Platoon and Frank, eager for another field command, took the job. It was in this role that he led a rescue column, two tanks and some forty men, down Route 9 on April 19 toward Bridge 28.

*   *   *

I remember seeing Frank just once during the battle. It was on the afternoon of the first day as our platoon was forming up to try once more to move on the bridge.

Medevac helicopters had finally arrived to take out some of the wounded. A line of stretchers was waiting on the road. Ahead, the company was crouched in a column against an embankment. The sound of gunfire and mortars echoed up and down the river. A thick curtain of dust hung in the air like a layer of noxious gas. One chopper had come and gone and another was about to descend. The aircraft eased along the river, then set its skids on the road. The corpsman and litter bearers began to move forward with the wounded when, all at once, one of the men from our column, a sergeant in the Third Platoon, tossed aside his weapon and bolted toward the chopper. The man was panicked—he did not want to make another assault on the bridge—and now was trying to push aside the stretchers and muscle his way through the aircraft door. Out of nowhere came Ciappio, beside the man now, one hand locked on the scruff of his flak jacket, the other holding a cocked .45 caliber automatic to his head.

Though I wished for it then, I am glad now that Frank did not dispatch the coward. Every Marine on the road came to know the fear and panic the fugitive felt. It was impossible to crawl past a certain point near the bridge that day without being soaked by another man's blood.

After the battle at the bridge, Dave Buckner, a new Skipper, took command of Golf Company. For a while he left Ciappio in charge of the Second Platoon. Frank did not fit Buckner's idea of the perfect officer; he was not fastidiously military, "squared away," we used to say, and, to the captain's way of thinking, was much too close to his men. But he was seasoned and, his penchant for pyrotechnics aside, he was steady, too. A few weeks later, the Skipper even moved him up again and made him the XO.

It was early May and the company was on a huge battalion-sized sweep at Cua Viet by the sea. The second day out, we were caught in the open by the enemy's big guns and were getting pounded and taking heavy casualties.

Ciappio shuttled from one group of men to another, trying to get them under cover and keep them dispersed.

At that point, Frank had been in combat for nine months—three months more than an officer's tour required. At first he stayed to win back command of the First Platoon, his old circle. Then Buckner, in need of experience, asked him to extend. Finally, Frank hung on for his "family," "those kids" he believed it his duty to protect.

In the end, he stayed too long. During one of his dashes across the battlefield at Cua Viet, he came upon his old radioman from the Second Platoon. The man was dead, a corpse with half a face lying in the hot sand.

The sight filled Frank with fear, and that fear finally overwhelmed him. He lost all sense of duty and responsibility. He no longer felt proprietary; his kids were on their own now. Terror had stripped him of the self-imposed assignment. His mission had been simplified. He looked down at the dead radioman and he wanted out; he wanted to survive.

Chance was kind to Frank Ciappio. He contracted a severe case of malaria and was flown from the field. On the hospital ship *Repose,* he called one of his doctors aside. "Look," he pleaded, "I'm scared, so I'm finished; I can't lead men any longer. I've only got two months left in country, a little time left. I don't want to go back." And that day the doctor signed a set of papers that sent Frank Ciappio home.

"Goddamn, Mike Norman, it's good to see ya."

He was taller than I remembered. The bandit's mustache had grown into a full beard, a black mask immaculately clipped. He still bounced and rushed about, energy barely contained, Demo Dan.

He was a stockbroker now, working in a regional office of a national firm in suburban New Jersey, not far from his home in the hills around Lake Mohawk.

The first time we met, I went to his office to pick him up

for lunch. I gave the receptionist my name; a few seconds later, he came bounding out to greet me.

"You haven't changed a bit," he said. He was smiling broadly, pumping my hand. "Listen, c'mon back to my desk for a minute. I've got just one more call to make."

He worked from a large cubicle on a back wall. While he was on the telephone finishing a deal, I took inventory of his chamber. Chief among the decorations was a large Marine Corps flag—a gold eagle, globe, and anchor resting in the middle of a deep-scarlet field. He had positioned this standard directly behind him and overhead, so that it was impossible to walk by Frank's cubicle without being struck by the sight of it.

I had found Frank through his parents, who still lived in Dumont, not far from Montclair. The first time he called, we exchanged histories, then started to run down old names.

"There were kids in that company I would really like to find out how they are doing." So, we were still his kids. "You remember Jim Parsons, the AO [artillery officer] who was shot in the head? We were tight. He's on the memorial, down there in Washington—" Suddenly, silence. " . . . Look . . . in all fairness, I'm not handling it well. I don't handle it well at all. It's one of those periods of my life I'm very proud of, but I don't handle it well. It's—I don't know—You live with it."

Frank Ciappio, the son of a millwright, grew up in the suburbs of New Jersey, went to a Catholic boys' school, worked on a construction crew, then took a job as a page in a pavilion at the 1964 New York World's Fair. When the season was over, he enrolled at Iona College in New Rochelle, New York, but left before the next semester and joined the Corps.

He had wanted to be a flyer. Color-blind, he ended up in the ranks. One day a notice went up that the Corps needed officers. To improve his lot, he applied. By the spring of 1967, he had been commissioned a second lieutenant. His father was so proud, he paid for Frank's dress uniforms and his officer's silver sword with the gold Mameluke handle.

After the war, he got married, then divorced. "Politics," he said, explaining it; he was a hawk, she was a dove. Of course, the roots of their disaffection ran deeper than that, but on the issue of the war, he would brook no dissent. Before he was anything else—husband or lover or friend—Frank Ciappio was a Marine. The Corps was his axis; everything else turned on that.

Then, as now, he considered himself distinct. "There are damn few Marines in the world," he told himself, fewer still who had seen combat. "I'm one of the *select* few," he often thought, a blooded member of a society of bold men.

Not long after his discharge, he tried to recapture this cache and signed up with a unit of reserves back in New Rochelle. But these weekend warriors—accountants and Ph.D.s looking to dodge active service—were ersatz Marines, to him mocking and unworthy.

He re-enrolled in college, Fairleigh Dickinson in Teaneck, New Jersey, and earned a degree in business, then passed through several jobs in manufacturing before landing at a brokerage house. He settled down and built a book of clients. When Wall Street went bullish, he began to prosper. He remarried—a tall, elegant bank officer named Karen—bought a house in Sparta, had a son, Frank Jr. Then, suddenly, at the beginning of 1984, four months before we made contact, Frank began to lose his balance.

He started drinking heavily. The binges began after work and went late into the night. Sometimes, in the bars, he did crazy things: got down on all fours and barked, set fire to the hair on his chest. He left these romps at reckless speeds. One night he lost control of the wheel and his vehicle jumped a curb and was badly damaged. Then, just before we met for the first time in late April, he had a dispute with a colleague and put his fist through an office wall. His co-workers thought him a wild man. He cursed, he drank, he destroyed the decor. Demo Dan, it seemed, had reprised an old role.

We went to lunch at a local watering hole for white-collar climbers—stained glass, hanging ferns, a horseshoe bar.

"Hey, sweetheart, how ya doin' today?"

"Okay, Frank," said the barmaid, seeing him and reaching for a bottle of gin.

"No, no." Frank wagged his finger. "I'll just have club soda with a twist of lime. The wife's on the warpath; I'm on the wagon."

Karen had given up her job in the bank to take care of their five-year-old son. The family was busy that summer making arrangements to receive a child from a New York ghetto, a visitor delivered to New Jersey's cool woods by the Fresh Air Fund.

"The gods have been good to me," Frank said. "Why not share a little bit?"

We finished our sandwiches and he ordered another club soda, then, finally, his first gin.

A week later we met again. Meanwhile, Frank had been to a psychologist at a nearby Veterans Administration psychiatric hospital. "I felt like I was off my feet, off my stride," he said. "I wanted to get my life and business back together."

He arrived at the hospital early one morning before work and was sent from one gray building to another until he found the right office. The wards in the buildings were open to view and during his wanders Frank got a good look at the hospital's eccentric inventory.

"There are guys walking around screaming, talking to themselves, holding conversations all alone, guys with real problems down there. Looking at them, at first I felt like I had done something wrong, like I had violated the place and had no right to be there. I mean here I am in a business suit, driving a good car. Then I said to myself, 'No, if I got a problem and if I'm gonna find an expert anywhere, it's gonna be here with the rest of the crazies. So that's who I am.' "

To the psychologist, he put his case more casually: "I think I essentially have my shit together. I just want to clear up some thoughts in my own mind."

He talked to the man for an hour and a quarter. Afterward the psychologist leaned back in his chair and said, "You have Post Traumatic Stress Disorder."

"And I said, 'Disorder? When somebody says you got a disorder, that sounds severe. I just wanted to talk to someone.' "

By the lights of the American Psychological Association, Post Traumatic Stress Disorder, "PTSD" as clinicians call it, is "the development of characteristic symptoms following a psychologically traumatic event that is generally outside the range of human experience." Though it is possible to argue otherwise, given the frequency of organized bloodletting in the current century, war is one of the events that the writers of this diagnosis had in mind as something outside the range of man's endeavors. Victims of PTSD were said to suffer symptoms of depression, including nightmares, daydreams, feelings of depersonalization, dissociative states, and, in general, an abiding anxiety. It was also said that they often drank in excess or took drugs, acted on their feelings of anger or helplessness, resented authority, had high divorce and suicide rates, and so on. Only rarely was it suggested that it might be reasonable to expect this kind of behavior from anyone who had seen heavy combat and had been lucky enough to crawl off the battlefield. Nowhere was it written that perhaps the real disorder, the true sickness, might be found in the man who, after surviving a year of bloody campaigns, returns home and acts as if nothing at all has happened.

". . . But who do you talk to besides the guys? Other people have no concept—you didn't take a bath every day or you didn't get a hot meal every day—and they have no concept. I've even talked to veterans of World War Two and they say, 'Oh, *that* was a guerrilla war and you guys weren't really in the shit. I don't know what you're upset about. *That* wasn't a real war.' So where do you fit? So who do you talk to? Half a million men went to war with us. How many of them were on that bridge?"

He saw the psychologist three times, then stopped the visits. "That's for guys who are sick," he said. "I just wanted someone to talk to."

* * *

107

Frank grew up a shooter. It was in the thick woods and rolling green hills of Bergen County that he first learnd the feel of a gun stock against his shoulder and the unequivocal sound of a rifle's report.

When he moved to Sparta, he joined a club a short drive from his home. The club had a range, and one gray Saturday morning a few weeks after our first lunch, I met Frank for a day of target practice. I had not fired a weapon since the war and suggested to him that I just observe, but he insisted I shoot. "You can't come to a firing range and just stand around and watch. You'll be bored to death." So I put on a shooting jacket and took my place on the firing line.

For Frank, shooting was more than just sport; it was an escape, his release. He said that he always felt better after a day on the range. The report of the weapons and the smell of spent powder was peculiarly reassuring to him.

The range was cut into the side of a hill and surrounded by thick green woods. The shooting parties—mostly men—aligned themselves along an asphalt strip two hundred yards from a row of targets. Several wore camouflage, bookkeepers and sales clerks aping the real thing. Frank brought along a weapon for me, an AR 15, a version of the black rifle we had used overseas. I got down in the prone position and locked my arm in the sling. I had promised myself never again to shoulder a rifle and now had the feeling that I was somehow breaking the peace.

"Okay there, Sergeant." Frank handed me a loaded magazine, then slapped me on the shoulder. "You're all set."

I held the stock so tight to my cheek, the recoil bruised my jaw; it was a week before I could chew food without pain. Rifle fire was louder than I remembered, but I had not forgotten the unmistakable odor of spent powder that used to hang in the air after a fight.

Frank was beaming. "This is what I call fun."

After lunch Karen and Frank Jr. stopped by the clubhouse to say hello. Ciappio had been trying to get young Bud, as he called his son, to take up shooting, but the boy, tall, lean, and blond like his mother, was frightened by the noise.

At mid-afternoon the rains came, a drizzle at first, then a downpour. The sky went gray, dark as asphalt. Frank was in the butts pulling targets when the deluge began. I turned and spotted him coming up a long muddy path.

For a moment, seeing him like that, wearing boots and wrapped in a poncho, took me back.

"Yeah, know what you mean," he said. "It's funny; sometimes I can smell it—the buffalo shit, the humidity. Do you ever smell it? Then something clicks and you start to . . . what? The adrenaline starts to pump and then . . . *whack!* It's gone. It's a fleeting moment. You're there, and then not there."

Late in the afternoon, the showers turned to torrents, so we drove down the highway to a small roadside tavern on Route 23.

It was an old and comfortable place, built, I guessed, before World War II, with a low ceiling, walls of wide pine planks with several coats of varnish that had yellowed with age, bar stools covered in red Naugahyde, and, on the counter, huge jars of pickled pigs feet and real beef jerky.

The barmaid was middle-aged. The beer was served in pony glasses. The conversation belonged to Frank.

". . . Take my boy. If he could be a Marine Corps officer, I'd be very proud of that because I think that says you're better than most. I don't know what it is, but it never leaves you. It's yours and nothing they can ever do will take it away from you. . . ."

Outside in the gravel parking lot, two men emerged from a pickup truck and sprinted through the rain toward the door.

". . . I love my son; I love that little fucker. I call him Bud. I want to give him values, the right to make his own decisions. But if soniebody in ten years, fifteen years, says to him, 'We want you to go to Nicaragua, Israel,' they're not going to get my son. I'll give him the money to go to Canada. I'm not going to watch them kill my boy. I don't want to lose him. . . ."

He drained his glass and ordered another.

". . . Golf Company was a family, Mike. That was two hundred and twenty kids that had a job to do. They were twenty years old. They were eighteen, nineteen. They were kids. I had to protect them. Somebody had to protect you guys. When somebody died in that platoon, a piece of you died with them. After a while, there were no more pieces left. You couldn't give another piece, because the moment you gave another piece you were going to die with them. Then you began to come apart.

"Look at me." He lifted his arm from the bar and held it out in front of him. "Talking about the damn war, I got goose bumps."

The rain was still heavy, splashing against the windows. We had been talking for more than two hours.

". . . After Cua Viet, it wasn't fun anymore. Cua Viet, there were rounds coming in and I was scared, and I said to the Skipper, 'I want out of here. You get me out of here.' And Buckner said, 'Okay, get back to the command post.' I didn't have another firefight left in me. I was finished. I had been in the field nine months. I was scared. I'd lived through it. And for fifteen years, I've felt like I did something wrong."

I put down my glass and turned to face him. "You thought that being afraid was wrong?"

"Yeah, as God is my witness. Yeah. I've lived with that for fifteen years."

"Who did you think you were?"

"I don't know, but I shouldn't have been frightened. Gung ho Marine, that's me. But I was scared; I was so— But you see I wasn't allowed to get scared. When you got scared, you were supposed to come to me and I was supposed to say, 'You do this.' And I didn't have it anymore. You understand that, Mike? I didn't have it anymore. I was done. I was washed out. I was finished. When I saw my radioman with no face, I laid in that paddy dike and couldn't move. Mike, you were all my children, as absurd as that sounds. Everybody that I could've gotten home, I did. For fifteen years, Mike, I felt badly about the fact that maybe I didn't do every—I was—Mike—"

He stopped, cleared his throat. "It's just . . . it goes with you . . . it goes with you every day of your life."

A few days later I sent Frank a copy of the first letter I'd received from Squeaky. I underlined the following passages.

> . . . *Snow and I threw Gonzales' body up onto the tank. Then Capio ran over and laid rosary beads on Tommy. I had always liked Lieut. Capio (probably misspelled) but on that day I saw Lieut. Capio as One of us and realized how his bars must have been more of a burden than a privilege. No, it wasn't even a burden it was a compassion for life. I can say that I served under Capio and somehow he always made it serving beside him. . . .*
>
> *You know Mike, I believe Capio was the only officer I ever really trusted.*

Not long after that, Frank called.

"That was one of those letters, you just kind of read it and you sit there and look out the window and the tears are rolling down your face and you pray that no one wants to talk to you because you don't want the people in the office to see you, because all they know is you're one of those crazy people."

(4)

She was nineteen when we met, a nursing student in white and blue: long dark hair, hazel eyes, all innocence and freshness. She was, by all lights, lovely. A young man's fantasy. A heart's paradigm.

We sat and talked. She had a boyfriend in Philadelphia, "a biker" was how she described him; I imagined hobnailed boots, greasy blue jeans, a black leather jacket with brass studs. No matter. The boyfriend was there and she was here, still distinctly sweet, so ingenuous.

That Christmas I invited her home for a visit; I had not sought the family's sanction since well before the war. We sang carols in the snow and walked the village streets till our feet were numb with cold. I no longer felt so tough and grizzled. She softened me, helped bring me back.

A year passed. At first I wooed her constantly. Soon the biker was sent packing. I could relax now—the field was clear—and returned to my books. That semester I encamped in the library. I was weighing the merits of graduate school and wanted to get the feel of the scholar's life; days and nights with Milton, Dryden, and Pope.

She was patient; she waited. When I emerged a few months later with perfect grades, she was talking about "someone else." During our interregnum, she said, she had often dated a medical student, "a rich guy" with a private plane who flew her to dinner in exotic places. She made it sound innocent, but I knew this flying philanderer and did not want to lose her, so at the end of the semester, over a cup of coffee in a greasy spoon, I asked her to marry me. She cried; I paid the check.

A friend helped me make the arrangements. The man was a true stoic; he assumed nothing. "Why are you getting married?" he asked as we went to fetch the liquor.

I had to think. "We want to live together, and her father is a devout Catholic." That, of course, was only the smallest part of it. But even if I could have summoned the language, I would not have talked of love. I felt something else, quite apart from fidelity and trust, affection and devotion. Even now I do not know exactly what to call it. She had an aura that seemed incorruptible, a simplicity so fresh and pure, I wanted to live forever in its light.

FIVE

THE LONG ROAD
FROM LICK RIDGE

Ours is a town of trees, long colonnades that line the streets and bracket the parks. Behind our house are four huge pin oaks, several stories high. Their roots run deep, their trunks are pillars, majestic. In the spring the upper branches grow together like fingers locked in prayer. In the summer a broad green bower keeps the yard cool and in shade all season long. Well before the first frost, the leaves begin to turn: russet and hammered gold at first, then brown, like chocolate or dark coffee. They fall slowly, littering the long narrow yard, giving it a mottled look. By mid-October the oaks are bare, the grass hidden beneath a crisp, foot-thick coverlet.

Craig Belknap had never seen such leaves, four-foot piles spilling across the tops of his shoes. He had come north from Dallas for a week-long visit and we had put him to an afternoon's work. The day was overcast and cool with the first snap of fall.

He stopped for a moment and leaned on his rake to catch his breath. "This is great. Dallas was still warm when I left. I couldn't even break out my corduroys yet."

With Beth, we made a work party of three, raking the leaves into piles, hauling the piles to the street. The children loved those deep mounds of autumnal down, and between trips to the curb we stopped to watch their frolic.

I had missed Craig. Our meeting in Dallas in the spring had been much more than just a reunion of two old pickets from the same battered line. We had stayed in touch, talking on the telephone at least once a week, and now he had come north for a long visit.

He seemed to enjoy the afternoon's labor. We still worked well together, more naturally in tandem now, beneath the pin oaks, than ever.

I had quietly planted the seeds for this trip for months.

Craig's hip and knee pain were growing worse. Jean had pleaded with him to seek help, but she could not move him. He refused to take painkillers or regular analgesics; he feared addiction, he said.

He thought an operation futile as well. To him the pain was a sign that his joints were deteriorating, that arthritis would cripple him and put him in a wheelchair. He would not listen to talk about new drugs or dramatic advancements in orthopedic surgery.

In truth, he simply was afraid. As he remembered it, the last time on the operating table had almost left him dead. "Everything was okay until they started to put me out. For some reason, I was real anxious about going under the knife. During that little surge before you go completely under, I could feel that cold surgery and I just thought, 'Oh my God—I'm not gonna wake.' "

When he revived, his mother was at his side, her face worn from worry. He had gone into cardiac arrest, she said; he had been lucky to make it off the table. And that, he promised himself, was the last time he would let anyone lay him open.

Now Jean ached from watching him. In the mornings he seemed to take longer to get moving. In the wet and cold he was especially sore and stiff.

I relayed these reports to Squeaky and Dave Troy, and

when the four of us gathered in Mesquite in August, both men tried to get Craig to talk about his health. But he dismissed their questions and mine.

Then, one Thursday night in late August, several weeks after the trip, he called me at home.

He began casually enough. "I just wanted to see what you were up to and check on if you'd heard from Squeaky or anything." We chatted for almost half an hour. "Well, take it easy," he said finally; then, just as I was about to put the receiver in its cradle, he blurted out, "Oh! Oh! The most important news—I forgot—I've got an appointment in the morning for a physical."

He said he was going "to get a real good rundown" from an internist and then planned to see an orthopedic specialist.

What had changed his mind?

"When you guys were down here, y'all just looked so good physically, I gotta do everything I can to compete," he said, laughing, and leaving the real reason, whatever it was, unsaid.

The next night he called again. The internist, he reported, had given him a clean bill of health. The orthopedic man, however, was booked for several months and could not see him.

When he hung up, I talked to Beth. She was a nursing professor at a large university and had good contacts. She suggested that Craig come to New York to the Hospital for Special Surgery in Manhattan, one of the foremost orthopedic facilities in the world. After some checking, we had a referral and passed the information to Craig.

Three weeks later he called back, buoyant. He had made an appointment for October 22 in New York with a hip specialist. "I've been living with this for so long and have been so reluctant for anyone to chop on me that I've resigned myself that it would get to where you can push me around in a wheelchair. But now the time is right. It's all coming together."

He arrived on a Friday. Josh rode with me to the airport. I wanted my son to meet this man who had once been my comrade and now was becoming my great friend.

The boy was six at the time. As we drove along, I explained that Craig had been wounded, that he limped now and had a mangled hand; I tried to describe how it happened and why the battle had been fought, but it was hard to say how much the boy understood. To him, war was still play, a bloodless backyard game.

The flight was late. Belknap was among the last to disembark. He limped down the Jetway with a garment bag slung over his shoulder and a hardwood cane in his bad hand.

"There he is," I said to Josh. The boy stood very still.

"Well, what's goin' on," said Craig cheerily as we embraced. Then he stepped back and looked down.

"Hi ya, Hoss," he said, holding out his claw to Josh.

The boy, wide-eyed, fixed on those twisted fingers. Finally, he grabbed the claw and gave it a shake.

I think he'll long remember that moment.

For months afterward, he asked often to hear the story of the bridge.

Belknap's visit was a celebration of the season, a weeklong whirl of shopping and dining, museums and concerts. On Saturday we took him to Rockefeller Center, showed him the skating rink guarded by the gold statue of Prometheus, then we walked across Fifth Avenue to the great Cathedral of St. Patrick, then up the east side of the street in the swell of shoppers toward Central Park, past Gucci's and Steuben Glass and FAO Schwarz, and, finally, to a rooftop café, where we stopped for a rest and a cup of cappuccino.

That evening we drove back into Manhattan, first for drinks in the staid and storied lobby of the Algonquin Hotel, then for a light dinner at the Parthenon on Eighth Avenue and on to the Imperial Theatre for a performance of *Dreamgirls*. Afterward we took a cab uptown to the Palm Court in the Plaza Hotel for strawberries and whipped cream, Sacher torte and coffee.

Craig tried to be casual about it all. This was not, he said, his first time among the bright lights; Dallas too had its moments. But it was easy to see that Gotham had stirred him and that we would soon see him again.

On Sunday we drove out to Ciappio's house near Lake Mohawk, about an hour from Montclair. Craig and Frank had not seen each other since the war and now both were on tenterhooks, impatient and wondering what would take place between them.

When Frank set eyes on Belknap, he bounded up to him and pumped his hand so vigorously I thought he was going to hurt him, then he almost pulled him off his feet into an embrace.

They passed the afternoon trading stories. Frank hauled out his collection of handguns and rifles and military posters. Later that evening we went to dinner together at a local tavern.

"I'll tell you something," Craig said over coffee. "There's just something about us. It's like a bolt of lightning that hit a bunch of guys. There's just something about us that I'll never have with another man. But you know what, just getting back together is not going to be enough. I want everybody in this happy little circle to dance. I want them to dance."

The next morning Craig had a few hours to kill before his meeting with the orthopedic man, so I brought him along to the newspaper on 43rd Street. I was scheduled to take part in a debate that morning between two candidates for the U.S. Senate. The incumbent was well ahead in the polls and, at that stage of the campaign, had begun to ridicule his opponent. Craig watched them bicker for a while, then slipped out of the debate room and made his way on his own across town to the Hospital for Special Surgery.

By the time I joined him an hour and a half later, he was with the hip specialist, Paul M. Pellici.

"The joint itself is still in pretty good shape," the doctor said. "So really you should not be considering any kind of replacement. Your knees take wear and tear because of the deformity of the hip. This is nothing to worry about, yet. I recommend anti-inflammatories, drugs that are aspirin-based, and slow repetitive exercise to lose weight."

Pellici was young—in his mid-thirties, I guessed—soft-spoken and genial, with a good sense of humor. Belknap appeared to trust him.

X-rays taken that morning showed shrapnel still in his hip. "You were hit by a high-velocity bullet which has a shock wave that tends to damage the whole theater of the hip," the doctor told him. "There are things you could do surgically that would correct the deformity, but I don't think the benefits are worth the risks. If you can live with your symptoms, I would. You've lived with this deformity for sixteen years now. At this point the only thing that might make you say, 'Go ahead,' is constant pain."

Belknap said nothing. Pellici closed his file and turned off the light on the X-ray display. "I tend to be conservative," he said. Then came a smile. "If I weren't a surgeon, I'd be a faith healer."

Just as he was about to leave, Belknap thrust out his right hand. "Hey, Doc, take a look at this, will ya?"

Pellici eyed the claw. "I don't do the hand, but wait here a minute." He returned a few moments later with another man in tow. "This," he said, turning to the second man, "is Dr. McCormack. He does hands."

Richard R. McCormack Jr. was taller than his colleague, somewhat stiff, harder to read. He took hold of Belknap's right hand and began manipulating his two fingers and talonlike thumb.

"It's not much," he said, icily and flatly. "But it's better than a steel hook. Right now it's just a claw, not much good for anything except holding a briefcase or a suitcase, but I think there are a lot of things that can be done. Why don't you come back in a few weeks and see me."

Belknap was off the table and on his feet. He faced the physician squarely. He had long ago abandoned the notion that it might be possible to reclaim what the past had taken. But now . . .

"Look, Doc." Craig took a step forward. "I'm from Dallas, you see, and I'm only up here for a week."

McCormack stopped him. "Come back at three-thirty today. I'll see you then."

We ate lunch in the hospital cafeteria. Belknap made small talk; I pushed the food around my plate.

The examination began on time. For almost an hour the doctor palpated the hand and made detailed drawings of the bones and tendons.

"There's nothing that's going to make your hand look normal," he said finally. "But right away we can improve its function by at least a hundred percent."

He proposed two operations: one to straighten the fingers and reattach the tendons, a second to cut wedges from the bones of the thumb and wrist, bringing them from their current posture, curled downward like a hook, up to a more level plane.

"How we do this is very important," he went on. "What you want is the least amount of surgery and the most amount of function." Then he sent Belknap downstairs for one last set of X-rays.

I called Beth, spinning, barely able to deliver the news. I was sure I had found that little lesson, that sliver of light, I was after. If McCormack could straighten Belknap's hand, remake his maimed flesh and help him recover a little of what had been lost, then perhaps every man who had served with Belknap might, in some small but significant way, be redeemed as well. Time and distance aside, we were still a circle, our places held by memory, each a part of each. To redress the wrongs of one was to make amends to all of us. I ached for that operation.

Dinner ran late and Belknap looked exhausted, but he wanted to stay at the table and talk.

At first, he was filled with wonder. "I could see that McCormack wasn't shooting his mouth off. He didn't say, 'You can play the violin in six weeks.' It wasn't that kind of bullshit promise. I'm very excited. This is not at all what I expected. It's kind of like you were getting ready to go up in a hot-air balloon and all of a sudden they say, 'No, we're not gonna do that; we're gonna sky dive.' "

Then, all at once, came doubt. He saw "logistical problems." Where would Jean stay? he asked. And who would run the halfway house while he was away? What about money? Suppose gvernment insurance did not cover enough of the cost? On and on, round and round, until he arrived back where it always began. "The surgery has to be *my* decision. It is elective surgery and I am scared of it. I'm *scared* of going under."

I took the rest of the week off work and on Tuesday, early, we set out for central Pennsylvania to visit Doc Hefright, the corpsman at the bridge who had saved Belknap's life and now seemed so troubled.

Belknap and the Doc had kept in touch after the war, but it had been many years now since they'd talked. Craig and Squeaky had called him in the spring. In July Doc wrote me a letter.

What do I tell my brother. . . . Can I tell you that like Craig, Squeaky, Louie and Tommy, I have carried you in my memory all these years.

Squeaky gave me your address after he and I talked about the war for a short time, I have talked with Craig over the years but it would appear we have not talked with our feelings. . . .

My wife, Judy, and I have been married for twelve years and have a boy, Matthew, who is ten. We have a house on eleven wooded acres in the hills of south central Pa.

In the last sixteen years I have, let's see, gone to college for two years, been a police officer for three years, an infirmary supervisor in a prison for nine years, and I am at present off of work and have been for nine months with a "Nervous Breakdown." Look out, I'm still crazy after all of these years!

Mike, please write and let me know how you have been and maybe all of the guys can get together sometime.

Eric Hefright

The day was cool and gray. We drove west along Route 80, then turned south along the Susquehanna River, winding our way through the small hill towns of Beaver Springs and Painterville and Mill Creek.

Doc's woe, of course, was a large part of what had brought Belknap east. He wanted to see if he could give aid to the man who had once rushed out under fire to help him.

Eric Karl Hefright grew up in Huntingdon, Pennsylvania, a river settlement of seven thousand set against the steep hills and ridges of the Allegheny front. Doc's world had been circumscribed and safe. As a boy, he fished and hunted on the shores of Raystown Lake, sang in the choir at St. James' Lutheran Church, lolled with buddies over the pinball machine down at Skeet's newsstand.

In his junior year at high school, he told his mother and father he wanted to leave. "There's a shootin' war going on and I want to see what's happening. I'm gonna find out." A year later, after graduation, he enlisted in the Navy.

He thought he'd find action as a demolitions expert or as a gunner on a river boat. Instead, the Navy made him a medical corpsman, which, as it turned out, suited him well. Doc Hefright was a Christian man who believed strongly in the ethic of service. To him, there was no action more ennobling than "to help people, to take care of someone."

Navy corpsmen served as hospital aides and combat medics attached to the Marines. They supervised sanitation and disease control; they rushed out under fire to comfort the wounded and console the dying. Most were fearless and, as such, they suffered terrible casualties. At one point during the savage fighting of 1968, their ranks were hit so hard that Marine headquarters urged field commanders to lecture their corpsmen against taking unnecessary risks. The two Docs assigned to Golf Company ignored those warnings. When someone yelled, "Corpsman up!" they always came running.

Hefright got hit at the bridge helping Belknap. In Doc's version of the story, meant to needle his friend from Texas, Belknap was "a baby yelling about a little scratch."

"Christ, you should have heard him," Doc said. " 'Don't leave me here! Don't leave me here!' he goes. I say, 'Goddamn, Belknap. I told you, we're all gonna stay or we're all gonna leave.' '' Then the Doc grabbed Craig and started to run. One, two, three steps . . . an explosion . . . and he was hit in the foot. The two went down hard on the road. Blood began to pour from the corpsman's boot. "Oh, Lord," he thought to himself. And just then, help arrived.

[April 21, 1968
Island of Guam]

Dear Mom and Dad,

Well it looks like my luck ran out, not all of it, just some. . . . The squad was pinned down, one of my men was hit in the butt and I went to help, the gooks set off a claymore and broke my thumb all to shit. I fixed up my man and then myself. I just got his butt fixed and my hand when the gooks set off another claymore, it got me on the top of the foot. . . . I am coming state side in the next few days and will probably go to Philadelphia Naval Hosp. as a patient.

I am real fine, a little pain but I will make it with the help of the Lord, you should have gotten a telegram from the government.

I will see you soon and take care.

Love,
Rick

[September 1968,
Naval Hospital,
Philadelphia]

Dear Craig

Well, how are you doing? I thought I would drop you a line just to see if you were still around. It has been five months since we were hit, so you should be getting a little better. I am still a patient here in Phila. I may get a medical discharge. I only have ten months left anyway. I have received a few letters from Norman and the other[s] . . . we had about 17 KIA & 29 WIA and a few missing that day out of the company, some shit, huh!

How is your hand, you still have it I hope. It looked

*good the last time I saw it in Guam. I guess your hip is
the main thing though.*

*. . . I hope I will hear from you, until then take it
easy.*

*Doc
Hefright*

About a year later the Doc went to Waco to see for
himself how his former patient was healing. They had a fine
time together—what each remembers of it. "We got into
some bottles," said Belknap.

After that they exchanged a letter or two, but did not see
each other again until that wet October day when Craig and
I turned off the main road out of Huntingdon and made our
way up a dirt and gravel switchback through thick woods to
an isolated rise of land called Lick Ridge.

Doc was suffering from acute depression and was being
treated by a psychiatrist. He had not worked for over a
year. He slept most of the day, came awake after dark.
When Matthew and Judy were asleep, he would settle into
a big chair in the living room, alone in the still watches of
the night.

I guessed that much of his trouble went a long way back, and
yet both Craig and I were sure that we could hear in Doc's
voice the unmistakable echo of war. Here was the guilt, the
sadness, and, most telling, the anger; a fury that gathered
unseen, struck without warning, then quickly disappeared.

His "breakdown," as he called it, began on a quiet evening after a day at the prison infirmary. He was sitting in
the big chair in the living room, nursing a cup of coffee,
when his son, Matthew, came wandering through. The father said something to the son; the son answered back.
Then came the explosion.

Doc picked up a paperweight from the table next to him
and hurled the heavy missile at the boy's head. It just
missed, slamming instead into the Sheetrock. Doc looked at
the gash in the wall, then at the quivering boy. In that
instant, the corpsman knew he was sick.

*   *   *

124

Belknap and I checked into a motel in Huntingdon, then called Doc, who gave us directions to his house. The maples and oaks had dropped most of their leaves; Lick Ridge was covered with a dry and brittle drugget.

The house was one story, a modular unit set on concrete and cinderblock, with white siding, black shutters, and a brick front. Catercorner to the house, among the trees, was a flagpole with Old Glory flying from the top. A black cat sat on the front porch staring at the ground.

Doc heard our car and came ambling out of the house. He was a great bear of a man now, six feet, two inches, 260 pounds, up at least a hundredweight since the war. He wore blue jeans and a flannel shirt with the sleeves rolled partway up his forearms. He had added a mustache since the old days and a pair of tinted aviator-style glasses as well. His hair was neat, short on the sides, slightly longer on top, the signature of a small-town barber. The weight had rounded and softened his face. Perhaps what I knew of his recent troubles colored my sight, but at first glance, out there in the open among the bare trees, the big man who had been so brave now looked vulnerable.

"You haven't changed a bit," he said, wrapping his huge arms around me.

"And you," he said, embracing the man he had saved, "you're not limping that bad." Then they both laughed.

Doc made me feel like a coward. I wanted to see him, stand by him, but I did not want to do it alone. Of all the men on the list, we had the least in common, yet in no other voice did I hear more of myself.

Several years before, I too had an unwelcome break, a dark interposition. About that period, I do not remember much. It began after Christmas and lasted a long time. I know I felt hollow at first, then weak, then full of rage. Beth called a professional, a small man with large eyes and an unnerving gaze. I sat in a chair in his office session after session watching him watch me. When the silence was finally broken, the first words between us were about war; I

125

could, of course, go back to other unhappy venues, but nowhere else had my spirit been more dispossessed.

Once a week for three years I went to see the little man with the large eyes. One summer day there was nothing left to discuss; I finally felt restored, full again. But I never forgot the penetrating emptiness of those first days, and when I heard about Doc, I remembered the rack of my own melancholia, and was afraid.

Belknap's suffering was easier to confront than Doc's. What had happened to Craig was part of the past; it held no danger for anyone but him. Doc's wounds, on the other hand, could easily at any moment be visited on the rest of us.

Supper was venison smothered in country gravy, and fresh vegetables. Then Judy brought out homemade peach cobbler and poured coffee and tea. After dinner we gathered in the living room. The wind was blowing hard on the ridge, whipping the leaves up against the windows. Belknap and I sat on a couch. Doc settled into his big chair.

In the years immediately following the war, he had earned an associate's degree at Harrisburg Community College, married Judy, a widow whose first husband had died of leukemia, and signed on as a patrolman with the nearby Lewistown Police Department.

The job, too, had its travail, but he liked the work.

"One night my partner and I were on foot patrol in different sectors and he heard this baby crying inside a house. He didn't think too much about it. Couple of hours later, I went by the same place and heard the baby. I knocked on the door. No answer. Well, we found out it was a woman's house. She was divorced. She drinks a lot. I beat on the door some more. My partner knew the grandmother and called. They said she had been known to leave the house and the baby alone and go to the bar. Well, this kid was in there just raising hell. I found an open window and went in. The kid was standing up in the crib. The milk in the bottle was curdled, his diaper was overflowing, the house was a wreck. I took the kid into protective custody.

Judy and I gave him a bath. We go back to the house and I've still got the child in my arms. Here comes the mother, who's drunk, with her boyfriend. We had to give her the baby. [Later] she sued child welfare [and kept custody of the child]. But it was worth it."

He stayed a policeman for three years, "starving to death" on an annual salary of $6,700. Then one day his father called. Richard Hefright was a supervisor at the State Correctional Facility at Huntingdon. He had been at the prison almost twenty-five years, first as a guard, then as a manager of industrial shops. He rarely recommended prison work. It was thankless labor, caught as keepers were between the lumbering bureaucracy of the state and the barbaric society of inmates. But there was an opening on the prison medical staff, a job that carried a healthy raise, so against all wisdom and ignoring his father's caveats, Doc took it.

Convicts in a maximum-security prison carry long-term sentences, usually twenty years or more. They are society's slag, its most violent members, a caged assembly of thugs and cutthroats; "your basic murderers and mother rapers," Doc said, "the bottom of the barrel."

Doc supervised the infirmary. "I had maybe twenty inmates working for me, plus I had six or seven officers. I gave out pills, carried out doctors' orders, did treatments. Knifings? Fixed 'em up. At first I liked it.

"Most of the time in the infirmary the inmates were hiding from something: cigarette debts, drug debts, sex debts. Once in a while you'd get somebody with this broken or that broken.

"They all wanted something [drugs]. They'd line up to see the psychiatrist. 'I'm gonna do this' or 'I'm gonna do that,' they'd say. 'Oh, well,' he'd say, 'can't have you doing that. Here, here's some Valium.' They'd really play it.

"One morning I was running this doctor's line, hell of a nice guy, do anything for you. He'd tell the inmates up front if he thought they were lying. This one big guy comes in. Doctor looked at him and said, 'Nothing I can do.' The guy had injured his knee. Doctor said, we've done this and that and now you're gonna have to rehabilitate it. The inmate started calling him all kinds of dirty motherfuckers. So I intervened. I just run him out right down the hallway. The baby-raper murderer got mad and went to see my supervisor.

"The captain of the watch called me in. 'You made this inmate mad,' he said. 'Well, so what,' I said. 'He'll make the other inmates mad.' 'If they want to fight, I'll fight,' I said. They said I incited the inmates. After I got home, I had a nervous breakdown.

"It had been building up for months on end. The superintendent said, 'Give 'em what they want, don't make 'em mad.' I said, 'Wrong. If a guy's sick, I'll take care of him, otherwise . . .'

"I went to see a state psychiatrist. He asked me what I did in the service. I said I was a corpsman with the Marine Corps. 'What did you do?' he asked. 'A little bit of treatment here and there,' I says. 'Oh, that's all?' he asked. Nobody asked me whether it had an effect. I told my psychiatrist I had over my lifetime, since I was seventeen, seen so many people hurt and injured in different ways, terrible injuries, that when I see somebody that's just trying to beat the system and not hurt, I just can't deal with it. I seen too many good men die for this bullshit, just seen too many dead.

"In the end, I just couldn't deal with the malingering. The last year I was there [his seventh on the job], I'd lock myself in my office. I was trying to sort out in my mind how I could overcome a no-win situation. I said, 'I ain't got nothing to give.' Guys would come to me with little cuts on their fingers. . . . It was easier to kill them.

"In my mind, I decided I was going to in fact kill inmates. I'd come to the point where I was visualizing this as happening, really, as taking place."

Psychiatric evaluation, Eric Hefright, October 10, 1984:

Mr. Hefright is a 36-year-old white male who was referred by an insurance company for a psychiatric evaluation regarding work-man's compensation. . . . States that last year around this time he had to leave his job as a correctional infirmary supervisor because of pressure he was under.

Prior to that he notes that he had become withdrawn, short-tempered, would feel fatigue despite increased daytime sleep, diffi-culty with sleep at night, would cry and would have violent thoughts. . . . He would get angry and had difficulty with inmates and his supervisors.

He was treated with a combination of psychotherapy and antidepressant.

. . . Mr. Hefright states that for the past few months he has been living on his pension plan and actually has been having difficulty supporting himself and his family.

Mental status exam: patient was accompanied by his wife. He was appropriately dressed. . . . No thought or perceptual disorder noted.

Diagnosis: Major Depression.

Formulation and recommendation: I believe Mr. Hefright's con-dition has been related to his work and furthermore, at this time, he is unable to return to his previous job. I also recommend that he continues therapy.

_____

M.D. Psychiatry

Lately, Doc had been having trouble with the state, his employer. The prison system had refused to honor his claim for workman's compensation and the claim had ended up in court.

Meanwhile, his money was running out. And he still was not well enough to work. Belknap, speaking for all of us, tried to offer a loan, but Doc wouldn't hear of it and Judy just said, "We'll be okay."

We tried to think of something else. Craig said Doc should have gotten a medal for his action at the bridge and now wanted to round up as many witnesses as he could find and petition the Corps. He was sure a Bronze or Silver Star would help raise the corpsman's self-esteem. I told him I'd help, but I didn't embrace the idea. It seemed to me that the gratitude of his comrades might mean more to Doc than some vacuous ceremony conducted by an anonymous brass hat.

The next morning Belknap and I fetched Doc from the ridge and went to a diner for breakfast. After the meal we sat for a long time filling our cups from a pitcher of coffee.

"If you need anything—" I began to say, but Doc cut me off.

"Nothing," he said. "We're making it right now. We're gonna make it somehow or another. Judy's had it rough the last couple of years. She's stood behind me."

Belknap told him that the men on my list—the original members of Charlie Squad and a few others—were talking about a reunion, that the old circle was going to "link up again."

Doc was listening, but was somewhere else. At length, Belknap seemed to catch on. "You know, Doc, after Mike and I got together for the first time, I felt a little down."

"I was down last night," Doc said.

"Oh," said Belknap, leaning forward, his eyes filled with concern. "Really?"

"Digging it all up again, turning it over again." Doc stopped, took a deep breath, and let it slowly slip out. "Oh, God, it's a wonder we haven't ever found anybody else, the other guys we can't remember for some reason. Hell, we lived with them for months and months, bunkered with them, and yet I can't remember their names."

Doc turned to me. "I was worried he was dead," he said, nodding at Belknap. Then the big man's eyes started to water and he began to shake.

Belknap slid quickly to his side and put his arms around him. "The way you took care of us, you don't know the sense of debt we all feel toward you. I knew when I was laying out there on that road and I yelled for you, I knew that you would come. That's what keeps us tight after all these years."

We left Lick Ridge by the back roads. Doc said it would be more scenic that way and he was right. We said good-bye after breakfast, when the hills were still wet with dew and a light mist was clinging to the bottom of the brown hollows.

Belknap was quiet at first, content to let the hills and empty fields roll by. Then, just outside the town of State College, he said he thought he had Doc "all figured out."

"He's got two sides: the part that wants to be the corpsman and help people and the part that wanted to be a Marine and shoot people. It's just a matter of who you shoot and who you help."

Compassion commingling with rage; in a way, it made sense. The tenderness was easy to understand—men who have been scourged, often have the softest touch. The anger, however, was not that simple.

Psychologists who have studied us have written that our anger was political. They say that as combatants we were angry at not being allowed to finish the fight, to "win." Surely there was some of that. As Doc said the day before we left, "I didn't get enough. I got hit and I figure I owe somebody for that."

And yet men have come home angry from every war. Ours was not the first generation to know bitterness after a battle, to return to peace and yet feel so unsettled. No, it was not the politics of our particular war, maddening as that conduct was, that left my comrades churning. It was the incessant drumming of memory.

To think of the war was to remember the waste, the incalculable loss, and to be brought back to that, to face the weight of those numbers over and over again, was to be left in a rage.

Why would any society send its future to a slaughterhouse? Was it answering some bloodlust? Was it suffering some cyclic madness? No answer made sense. And the questions, as Belknap discovered, never stopped.

Family and friends wondered why we were so angry. What are you crying about? they would ask. Why are you so ill-tempered and disaffected? Our fathers and grandfathers had gone off to war, done their duty, come home and got on with it. What made our generation so different?

As it turns out, nothing. No difference at all. When old soldiers from "good" wars are dragged from behind the curtain of myth and sentiment and brought into the light, they too seem to smolder with choler and alienation.

Every American war has produced disaffected soldiers—the Cincinnati after the Revolution, the Grand Army of the Republic after the Civil War, the American Legion after World War I.

And after every American war, society has been bewildered by their behavior and looked upon these groups with suspicion. Newspapers across two centuries are filled with complaints about the drunken, lawless, self-pitying lot of veterans who seem to be everywhere. What in heaven's name was bothering these men?

In their letters and memoirs, veterans always provided the answer.

"Moral cicatrices," said one Civil War soldier.

"My mind," wrote a World War I Army sergeant, describing the death of a comrade, "is a reel of a thousand such scenes. So is that of every lad who went over."

A generation later, a Marine from the Pacific theater of combat wrote, "It's hard to sleep without seeing men die all over again. My bayonet and shrapnel cuts are all healed up . . . but none of us will be completely cured for years."

All this from doing what one psychologist called society's "death work."

War changes those who are sent to fight, changes them deeply and fundamentally. A group of doctors studying the effects of combat on a small group of World War II veterans well after the war wrote: "They have all changed under the guns. . . . These particular combat veterans cannot blot out their burdensome bloody memories. Of course the man in the street says, 'Forget it—the war was over seventeen years ago,' and therapists have said the same, forgetting that Freud taught us that the unconscious is timeless."

To most clinicians, these men were sick and were labeled as such. After World War I, they were said to have "shell-shock"; after World War II, "war neurosis"; and finally, after our war, "Post Traumatic Stress Disorder."

To be sure, the syndrome of memory has claimed its share of victims, especially in the dislocation of our age where the once safe circles of family, friends, and neighbors seem so distant and so few.

But I did not think of my comrades as victims, not even Doc Hefright, who clearly needed a professional hand to guide him back. We had been hammered, all right, but no more and no worse than any other man from any other age who had faced the fire storm of battle. With this difference: the circumstances of our war—its maddening politics, its sad history, its mismanagement and bungled prosecution—exposed more dramatically than in any other war the lunatic motives that lead to organized butchery and the awful waste that results from it. In our era, it was easy to see that the sacrifice had been for nothing and that perhaps nothing was worth that sacrifice.

So we were angry. Our anger was old, atavistic. We were angry as all civilized men who have ever been sent to make murder in the name of virtue were angry. And our anger was new, too. We were angry for ourselves, for our wounded, for the dead we brought home in bags.

The weather had lifted a bit, but it was still raining along Route 80 east as we headed home.

"Judy told me that Doc's been a lot better," Craig said. "He's not as depressed. I said, 'Well, he may get a little depressed after we leave.' I became depressed after y'all left me in Dallas. But like I told 'em, this ain't the last trip. Don't know when the next one will be, but this isn't the last. We're linked back up. It's not gonna be any sixteen years before we get together again."

Traffic was light. By late afternoon we had crossed the Delaware into New Jersey. It was well before dark when we pulled into my driveway. Beth was waiting, dressed for an evening in Manhattan.

We went to Chinatown that night, ate fried pork and spring rolls, then walked across Canal Street into Little

Italy for cannolies and espresso. Belknap was intrigued with the side-by-side worlds, rice on one side of Canal Street, pasta on the other. He was in especially good humor, roaring with laughter at his own bawdy jokes.

The next day, Thursday, Frank Ciappio drove Belknap out to Long Island to visit Louie Tartaro, the company clown, a loud, ebullient innocent who had survived the war untouched. Everyone remembered Louie. I had been to his home the month before, so I stayed behind and gave Frank and Craig some time together.

It rained again Friday, dark and dank. Belknap was delighted. Summer in the Southwest had been long and hot and had dragged into fall. Here, at last, was the kind of wet and chilly autumn he had hoped for. He broke out his corduroys and Harris tweeds and, with Beth, we set out for another sally through Manhattan.

That fall the critics had lavished praise on an exhibit at the Metropolitan Museum of Art, "Van Gogh in Arles." It had become the thing to see, a New York "event," and Beth had gotten us tickets.

We climbed the broad marble steps off Fifth Avenue to the museum's arched entrance and made our way through the crowds in the grand entrance hall to a suite of exhibit rooms on the second floor.

The show was crowded and the rooms were airless and close, but the masterpieces on the walls kept us there a long time. Here was the "Langlois Bridge," the "Little Seascape at Saintes-Maries-del-la-mer," the "Farmhouse in Provence," the sower, the washerwoman, "The Seated Zouave."

Belknap was dazzled.

I watched him limp slowly along the walls, studying the scenes and faces in each frame. He seemed at ease in that venue. Perhaps it was the promise on those walls or the peace from his company that, at that moment, convinced me to try to keep him close.

"Michael, where's Craig?" It was Beth. Belknap had wandered off. We worked our way back through the crowd to the first of the exhibit rooms and there he was, slumped on the edge of the only bench, his bad leg stretched out in front of him, his cane at his side.

The nurse in Beth had been keeping an eye on him. "He's hurting," she said quietly. "You can see it in his face. Let's go."

Belknap was stubborn. "Y'all go 'head and finish lookin'. I'm all right." But clearly he was not.

We walked slowly east one block to Madison Avenue, looking for a place to eat. Craig's limp seemed much worse. It made me wince to watch him. At a small lunchroom with white walls and butcher-block tables, we ordered a meal of cheese, paté, soup, and bread. We ate quietly. Craig kept shifting in his seat, trying to get comfortable.

The next day, Dave and Sheryle Troy drove over for a visit, and that night, with Frank Ciappio and his wife, Karen, we went to dinner at a Portuguese restaurant in Newark. The restaurant was a small, crowded place that smelled heavily of garlic sausage and paella. We were at the table until well after midnight.

On Sunday we took Craig to the airport. He seemed tired and preoccupied, able to summon little of the bonhomie of our week together. At the airline ticket counter, he waited impatiently in line, shifting his weight back and forth from one leg to the other. At the entrance to the Jetway, he checked, then rechecked, the overhead monitor that listed the departure gates. Finally, when he was ready to board, we embraced quickly and he was gone.

So much had been left unsaid. I had tried, but whenever we were alone, I simply could not find the words. I was drawn to him, but did not know why. He had talked about moving north, but I knew he could not leave Texas and his children, no more than I could suffer such distance from mine. There was no telling what he would do about his hip and hand. He had been lifted by the doctor's promise, but was still afraid of the knife. I wanted him to have that operation; I saw the surgery as a reckoning, a chance to rewrite part of the past. I think I saw too much. But I did not tell him any of this. How could anyone look at his scars and suggest that he endure more pain? How could someone else complain of sadness in front of a man who had suffered so much? Perhaps the silence suited us.

During van Gogh's last days at Arles, he suffered a second attack of delusions and was again hospitalized. He was desperately sick, but, as always, kept up regular correspondence with his brother, Theo. In his last letter from that halcyon place, he wrote, as he often did, of his great companion, Joseph-Etienne Roulin, the railroad postmaster who had befriended him when he arrived in the south and who stayed with him almost to the end. Roulin was exuberant—one can almost see him throwing back his head to laugh—a socialist who argued his politics forcefully and with abiding good humor. The postman posed for the artist, but he was not an easy model to capture. No doubt because Roulin was a friend, van Gogh struggled with him as a subject. "I do not know if I can paint the postman as I feel him," he wrote. And feel him he did, deeply. As he said to Theo in that last letter from Arles:

> Roulin . . . has . . . a . . . tenderness for me such as an old soldier might have for a young one. All the time—but without a word—a something which seems to say, we do not know what will happen to us tomorrow, but whatever it may be, think of me.

(5)

War left me well-suited for newspaper work; it made me a skeptic. I took nothing on its face.

My first job was at a small daily in New Brunswick, New Jersey, chasing after car wrecks and crepuscular office holders. For a would-be writer, the work of turning a muddle of facts into an ordered narrative was a useful apprenticeship. There were no quotas to make, no profit and loss to worry about. My task, my mission—at least in principle—was to get the truth. What risk to the soul was there in that?

I stayed in the newspaper business for thirteen years, long past the point of any useful pedagogy. It was, I confess, addictive labor. The daily byline made the blood rush.

In 1975 I went from New Brunswick to a larger paper in Trenton, the state capital. The paper had just been bought by the *Washington Post* and young, ambitious reporters from across the country pushed to get on its staff. The *Post* promised that if they played "hardball" in Trenton, they might get called up to the "big leagues" in Washington. Someone who wanted to be a writer, who was serious about words, might have taken a warning from such a heavy-handed metaphor, but by then I was hooked. I liked my name in print. And in 1981 I was hired by the *New York Times*.

I had a great run at the Gray Lady. For several years my assignment was to follow my curiosity and roam the provinces outside New York. Sometimes I had to chase a fire engine or detail the last hours of a freshly discovered corpse, but for the most part I was immune to such diurnal chores. I wrote about eccentrics—an old professor who smelled of garlic, a renegade priest who refused to preach—and people who lived off the soil and the sea—boatmen of the Delaware Bay, farmers in the sandy fields along New Jersey's bucolic southern coast. The work was engaging, the tether long, the paycheck regular. Then came a change of command.

The new city editor summoned me to New York. He was a large, garrulous man, recently called in from the field in Europe to try his hand at management. He was gathering in my rope, he said. He planned to restructure the metropolitan staff and wanted me to "volunteer" for the rewrite desk. The executive editor had approved my transfer, indeed, even thought it a good idea. It would be not only impolitic for me to resist the summons, but, he suggested, dangerous to my career as well.

I took my seat at the rewrite desk in January 1986. In November, diagnosed with the beginnings of ulcerative colitis, I typed out a letter of resignation, collected my last paycheck, and bid the newspaper business good-bye. The job, often two deadlines and thousands of words a day, had been impossible, the staff dispirited, the office akin to a cage.

Still, looking back, it was not so much the oppression of that place that sent me on my solitary way. I had been restless well before the transfer to New York. As far back as the spring of 1984, roaming free in the countryside among farmers and fishermen, I felt confined, off the mark. It was then, in fact, at night from a small office in my attic that I began, quietly, to open the seams of the past.

SIX

SAVANNAH: ONE FOUND, ONE "UNACCOUNTED FOR"

Bob Hagan was dead.

Word came by mail, an answer to a routine request for information I had sent months before to the National Personnel Records Center at Kansas City.

July 9, 1984

Casualty report: [First Lt. John R. Hagan was declared] missing in action 6 May 1969 while on a visual reconnaissance mission over Quang Tri Province . . . and failed to return to base. Heavy thunderstorm activity in area at the time.

Wanting more, I called the casualty division at Headquarters Marine Corps in Washington, then checked with a source in the military bureaucracy.

There is very little information available on 1st Lt. John R. Hagan that you do not already have. He was an aerial observer flying in a light plane which was disabled in a thunderstorm . . . somewhere between Vandergrift Combat Base and the Laotian border. The plane went down, radio contact was lost, and neither the plane nor the occupants [Hagan and the pilot] were ever found. Lt. Hagan was designated as MIA and declared dead on 1 March 1978.

Bob Hagan was the commander of the First Platoon through the Tet Offensive and summer of 1968. At the end of the year, he volunteered for a second tour of combat, and after a short leave, flew back to the war, this time as an aerial observer. In his new job, he tracked the movement of enemy troops and supplies. He did this work from the jump seat of a small, slow, single-engine airplane. These craft were easy targets for enemy gunners, and in the winds of a fierce storm, they were as frail and vulnerable as paper kites.

I passed the word to the others.

Troy was surprised. "He's missing? Son of a bitch!"

Ciappio, the platoon commander whom Hagan had displaced, was uncommonly empathetic. "I mean, his parents— You feel for his parents."

Belknap was like stone. He remembered the lieutenant's little speech about wanting to win the Medal of Honor. "What do you think," Craig said, his voice cold and pitiless, "did someone shove the bastard out the airplane door?"

Doc Hefright too did nothing to hide his antipathy. "After the bridge, I wanted to shoot the son of a bitch. You know, when I got back, I had heard somebody killed him. I was in the Naval hospital in Philly, in 'sixty-nine, and I saw this guy named Brown. I'm pretty sure he was from our platoon, white guy missing both legs. We got to shooting the shit and he said, 'Well, did you hear about Hagan?' I said, 'No.' He said, 'Well, they offed him.' I said, 'Who? The gooks?' He said,'No. I'm talking about our guys. Somebody took him out at night on a patrol and just didn't bring him back.' "

This hearsay has a hard edge. Someone *did* try to leave Bob Hagan behind.

* * *

In the months after he took command from Ciappio, the lieutenant volunteered the First Platoon for one dangerous mission after the other: rescues, reconnaissance patrols, night ambushes, listening posts. He wanted glory, and with us as the instrument he now seemed bent on getting it. But we were lucky. Combat was relatively light through the early months of 1968, casualties few.

Then came April 19th, Bridge 28, and the trial Bob Hagan had been waiting for. The company was trapped in a killing zone; the enemy held the high ground on both flanks; it was impossible to move forward or back without drawing their fire; the dead and wounded were beginning to mount; the men were filled with fear, some on the edge of panic.

I was at Hagan's side that day on that narrow road. Just a few hours before, back at Ca Lu, he had made me his radioman. I did not want to leave my comrades in Charlie Squad—and they thought I was crazy to go; "that motherfucker's gonna get you killed," said Belknap—but I wanted the new job and the chance at another stripe.

"Who do you think should take the radio for the third squad?" the lieutenant had asked earlier that morning.

"Payne," I said. "I've been teaching him the codes."

Jim was excited. "Thanks, Norman," he said. "I know all the shit, don't worry."

I didn't. By then we had been together often. I understood, trusted him. I had even promised to visit sunny Glendale when we got home. "We're really close to Hollywood," he used to say. "We can go down there and eyeball the babes." I never got to Glendale, but I came to know a little bit about the place and how it was to grow up there.

Jim's parents said he had to work harder than most boys; he had encephalitis as a child and, after that, nothing came easy. The struggle, however, produced in him a streak of self-sufficiency, and when he took on a paper route for pocket change or decided at Christmas to sell road flares and Styrofoam snowmen, no one was surprised. By the time he was twelve, he was an all-star in Little League and had learned to play chess. He lived with three brothers and a sister, went to Hoover High, and drove a 1950 black Ford jalopy.

Andrew James Payne Jr. dropped out of high school to join the Marine Corps. He never talked to his comrades about this, but after he died, his parents told a reporter from the *Glendale News-Press* that Jim had wanted the "hard knocks, physical challenge" of the Corps.

Several pictures accompanied that article: Jim at six years old standing in front of a Christmas tree in his first baseball uniform; at eight after he had won a potato sack race at a picnic in Griffith Park; as a third-grader in a white shirt and bow tie at Incarnation School; and, finally, standing between his parents in his tan summer-dress uniform, the day he graduated from the Marine Corps Recruit Training Depot—boot camp—at San Diego.

The paper also ran a poem that Jim had sent them in 1967 shortly after he arrived at the war, a forty-four-line sing-song lyric filled with jingo-like conviction.

> We are men who stand alone,
> Twelve thousand miles away from home,
> Our hearts are empty of all but blood,
> Our bodies are covered with sweat and mud.
>
> This is the life we choose to live.
> A year or a lifetime is what we'll give.
> You'll never know what it's like to be here,
> You with your parties, girls and beer. . . .
>
> Pop some pills, roll in the sun,
> Simply refuse to carry a gun.
> There is nothing else for you to do,
> And I'm supposed to die for you. . . .

In a prose postscript he added:

This poem is directed to the people who are burning draft cards and demonstrating. I hope it will inspire students to support their leaders whether in school or in government.

* * *

I don't think he really believed this patter. I suspect he was posturing, his way of pounding his chest in front of his house on Thompson Street. At all events, we never heard his poem. Like the other men, he was dedicated to survival, not the flag, and was left just as pacific by the slaughter as the rest of us.

But in many ways, Jim was the most naive and vulnerable man in the unit. One night we were paired off in a fighting hole when, just before dark, he dug into his pack and pulled out a small Polaroid snapshot that showed him sitting with an Asian woman at a table littered with empty beer bottles. The woman—she was just a girl, really—was staring away from the camera, bored and tired. Jim was kissing her on the cheek, his head half cradled by her arm and outstretched hand. He said he had met her in Bangkok, Thailand, on Rest and Recuperation leave.

"Whadaya think?" he asked, smiling. She reminded me of the bar girls of Okinawa, professional bedmates who drank a concoction of tomato juice and beer while their "dates" poured down whiskey or scotch. "Hey, Marine," they would say, "do you love me?"

I told Jim that the girl in his picture seemed pretty enough and let it go at that. But he pressed the question.

"All right," I said, finally. "What's goin' on?"

"She's my wife," he said. "I married her on R and R. Really, Norman. Whadaya think? I haven't told anyone yet. You're the first guy who knows about this. I haven't even told my folks yet."

He went on to describe the Buddhist temple where they were married and the wedding robes they wore, then wondered aloud about bringing her back to sunny Glendale. I think I mumbled something about a Buddhist ceremony not being legally binding and about how all bar girls dreamed of going to America. Jim said he was not concerned with technicalities and that this wasn't just another whore scheming her way to the States. I think I bruised him a bit that night and he never brought her up again.

The other men were often impatient with Jim. They weren't

Author in late 1968 on patrol with Golf Company.

Craig Belknap, right, with author at Camp Carroll, battalion base, early 1968.

Golf Company's commander, Capt. David Buckner, the "Skipper."

Lieutenant Frank Ciappio.

Mike Caron, without hat.

Doc DeWeese, just after the fight at Bridge 28.

Lt. Bob Hagan, left, in white, long-sleeved shirt, early in 1968 with Doc Hefright, center, and Belknap.

Doc Hefright, February 1968.

Jim Payne,
January
1968.

Louie Tartaro hamming it up, January 1968.

At Camp Carroll after a night of Monsoon rain, left to right, Tommy Gonzales, Squeaky Williamson, Dave Troy, and Belknap.

Squeaky at Camp Carroll.

Charles Whitfield two weeks after Bridge 28.

Reunion of *These Good Men*, August 1985, Montclair, N.J. Left to right, standing: Louie Tartaro, Newton Moore, Frank Ciappio, Charles Whitfield, Dave Troy, Doc Hefright, Squeaky Williamson, Craig Belknap; kneeling: Doc DeWeese, Mike Caron, author. [Lynn Blodgett]

much interested in his chatter about baseball and Ping-Pong tournaments in Griffith Park. But I liked to listen; he made me think of home, the myth of home, at any rate. I think that was part of Jim's appeal. War had promoted the rest of us to the world of men, but, for his own reasons, Jim had decided to stay behind. When I was with him, he always took me back, allowed me, for an hour or two, to leave the battlefield and revisit the safety of my youth.

The day Hagan asked me to join his command post and carry the platoon radio for him, I recommended Jim as my replacement. He wanted the job—liked being in the know and operating the gear—and figured it would give us a link.

So my friend and I shifted. I moved up the column to work directly for Hagan and Jim slipped into my spot in Charlie Squad.

Two hours later we were at Bridge 28.

After Ciappio's men were beaten back, the rest of the company arrived and, with Charlie Squad on point, Golf Company again tried to advance.

Jim, among the first few men in the column, radioed back position reports. I relayed them to Hagan.

For someone who had been so eager for a fight, the lieutenant was strangely cautious. Again and again, he ordered me to tell the point to slow the pace.

It was clear from the morning's events, and the radio traffic, that the men were most exposed on the open bridge. The enemy, earlier, had let them pass unmolested up the road, but as soon as someone stepped on the bridge—bull's-eye in the killing zone—the hills on both sides of the river rained down fire.

". . . Golf-One. This is Golf-One-Charlie." It was Jim.

"Go ahead, Charlie."

"Ah . . . We've got a body on the bridge . . . Ah . . . We're going out there to check it."

Either they did not realize the bridge was a flash point or they did not care.

I tried to get them back. "Golf-One-Charlie! Golf-One-Charlie! Hold your position . . . Golf-One-Charlie . . . Come in, Golf-One-Charlie!"

But he gave no answer, and a moment later up ahead there was the sound of heavy gunfire. Then came Jim's ghostly call.

"No! . . . No! . . . No. . . Norman. Help me! I've been hit."

I turned to Hagan. "We gotta get up there; third squad's been hit, bad."

But he seemed rooted to the road, down on one knee in the dirt staring at an open map.

"Lieutenant!" I was yelling now. "Hey! Lieutenant!"

He didn't move, wouldn't move, just knelt there in the yellow dust, his back turned to the men in trouble, to my friend calling for help.

Hagan was a stone. His look was vacant, his face buried in the map. He was frozen, numbed by fear, indecision, or both.

"Lieutenant! Lieutenant, Lieutenant—"

"Shut up, Norman. I'll move when I'm fucking ready."

But it was too late. By the time we reached the point, Payne had been loaded onto a truck; Gonzales was dead; Belknap was being hauled out in a bloody poncho and Doc Hefright, his foot bleeding onto the road, was seething with anger.

"Man, them gooks is all on the hill!" Doc yelled at Hagan. "You don't need no Goddamn map. Get after them!"

That night the officers gathered in the dark on the road with the company commander. They had counted heads; several men had come up missing. The absentees were from the Third Platoon. That afternoon they had tried to gain the right ridge line and outflank the enemy positions. The effort had failed badly. At dusk some of the survivors straggled out of the bush onto the road, carrying their wounded lieutenant, V. L. Cobb. They had come down quickly, they said, leaving some of their comrades behind. And now the count proved them right.

The company commander asked his officers for a volunteer to lead a rescue squad back up the hill. Bob Hagan stepped forward.

We mounted the slope, groping in the dark up a steep incline. I was in back of Hagan, carrying the radio. Halfway up, we stumbled onto one of Cobb's stragglers sitting in the middle of a small path. He was moaning and babbling to himself like a child.

Then our point sent back word that he had come upon some bodies. I gave Hagan the radio handset to call in the news. And just then the enemy sprang its trap.

"AMBUSH!" the point yelled.

The explosion blew me off my feet and set my ears ringing. Then, above me and to the right, thirty yards away, the enemy opened fire, four muzzles flashing in the dark. I got to my knees, tossd a grenade toward the flashes. All was quiet.

"Let's get the fuck out of here," one of the men whispered.

I looked around. The lieutenant was a few yards away. He was sitting on the ground, his knees drawn up slightly in front of him. He had a hard grip on the radio handset and was holding it near his ear. Most of the others had scampered down the hill.

"Lieutenant." I tried to keep my voice low. "The squad's gone . . . Lieutenant . . . Lieutenant. . . ."

He had frozen again. I tried pulling him to his feet, but the big man was too much to lift. He just sat there, staring into the black.

"Lieutenant . . . can y'hear me? I'm leavin'. You stay and you're gonna get your ass blown away."

But he did not move.

"Lieutenant . . ."

In the still of that moment, I thought of my comrades— Belknap mangled and afraid, Hefright burning with rage, Gonzales face down on the fender of a tank. Hagan! The reader of maps! If he hadn't flagged, we might have saved them, stood by them at least. ". . . Norman, help me. I'm hit. . . ." In the end, I never got to Jim. By the time we reached the bridge, he was in a truck rumbling to the rear. Just before dark, the corpsman who had treated him found me on the road. "I just thought you'd like to know . . ."

He eased down beside me. ". . . Payne's dead. Sorry. They tried. He never made it off the table."

"Lieutenant . . . Lieutenant. . . ."

And then, with the enemy a stone's throw away, I slid down a gully and left Bob Hagan alone in the darkness behind me.

Or so I thought.

All at once, I had hold of one of his arms. We were stumbling down the gully together. Mike Caron, a corporal from the second squad, was on the other side. Hagan was weak-kneed, almost somnolent, on the edge of unconsciousness. He stumbled along, with us half dragging him down the gully, through a narrow break in brush and trees. I remember how unwieldy he was, so big, so heavy, not dead-weight, exactly, but close to it. Suddenly the path became quite steep and the lieutenant's bulk began to carry him forward. By the time Mike and I saw the precipice, it was too late. Over we went, the three of us, tumbling through the air, twenty or thirty feet, to the road below. We landed heavily in a heap.

"Ugh . . ." Hagan began to moan. "Ugh . . . Where? . . ." The fall had awakened him. He looked around, first at Caron, then at me. It was dark, but we could see we were in trouble; we had landed in front of our lines. "Quiet," I whispered, "there's a gun crew down the road. They'll open up on us, so shut the fuck up." Hagan looked at Caron. "I don't know what I'm doing," Mike remembers him saying. "You gotta get the platoon back."

I cannot say exactly what happened that night; it is likely I'll never know for sure. I thought I had left Hagan. I remember looking at him on the hill for the last time, sitting there like a boulder implanted into the side of the slope. I remember calling to him, turning away, pausing for a moment, then scooting down the path.

Caron remembered it otherwise: he said I got as far as the bottom of the gully, maybe fifteen or twenty feet, then turned and went back up the hill with him. Perhaps.

In some ways, the facts did not matter. I *meant* to leave Hagan. I was sure of that.

Even years later, when I knew the lieutenant was blameless—when at last I came to see that he was merely afraid, that his fear was like our fear, just a little more disabling, that's all—and it was clear that all the butchery was simply bad luck, war having its way, even then I was still bitter.

So I set out to confront Bob Hagan, not the man whose essential flaw was being, like the rest of us, unassured, but, instead, the man I'd watched on the road and on the hill, the reader of maps, hero manqué, the man frozen in memory.

Then word came from Kansas City that he was missing, lost, in fact, in the same hills where I had once tried to leave him, the great green anonymous wastes that swallowed so many of our men.

I felt cheated at first; I wanted my reckoning. Then I began to wonder: Why would a man who was so afraid of dying go back to the war? Had we been wrong about him after all?

Savannah was crisp and blue that fall, a city refurbishing itself, especially downtown where the look of the Old South had been brought back in Greek Revival columns and wrought-iron balconies and dormer windows set in gambrel roofs. The side yards were full of dogwoods and magnolias and palmettos. Water oaks lined the curbs along the streets and wide boulevards.

I came to town on Friday, November 9, the day before the Marine Corps birthday, two days before Veterans Day. Newspapers around the country were full of feature stories about hapless or handicapped war veterans. The more haunted the man, the more apparent his wounds, the bigger the play for the story.

I had arranged to stay with Charles Whitfield. After Bridge 28, he became the platoon sergeant of the First Platoon. "Whit," as we called him, was a gentle and quiet man, so

149

much so he seemed almost shy next to his bellicose and swaggering messmates.

Of all the men, he had been closest to Bob Hagan. They both came from Savannah and the lieutenant looked on his townsman as a friend. Whit, furthermore, had the reputation as the most accessible man in the unit; he never turned anyone away.

Hagan aside, I also went to Savannah because I owed Whit. Not long after Bridge 28, he stepped in front of me and stopped a bullet.

In the late spring of 1968, the battalion was on the march by the sea at Cua Viet, pressing forward under an unrelenting sun. We had flushed an enemy force from a village, then, at dusk, dug in and began to set up a watch.

Golf Company had settled in a clump of brush and trees at the edge of a large rice paddy. Whitfield and I had paired off, as we always did after he joined the platoon command post, and were digging our fighting hole with entrenching tools. It was an hour or so before dark and it was quiet.

Whit used his tool as a pick, breaking the ground. Facing him, I scooped out the fill. We dug a long time. The ground was sandy and the sides of the hole kept collapsing and filling it up.

My shirt became soaked with sweat and I removed it to catch some air. We were very near the sea, and now and then an off-shore breeze would sweep across the paddies and into the oasis-like clump where we were digging.

I stopped for a moment to stretch, arching my back and raising my hands to the sky. To the sniper who was watching me, my alabaster stomach must have looked like a square of bright white canvas, a target. He was perhaps three hundred or four hundred yards away across the paddy. Just as he fired, Whit, who was in front and bent over chopping, started to straighten up.

The bullet caught Whit in the back, skidded along his spine, then slammed into the back of his head and laid open his skull before it spent itself in the dirt.

I could swear I heard it hit his head, a kind of heavy thud like a sledgehammer brought to bear against old concrete. And then the sergeant sighed deeply and dropped to his knees in the hole.

Doc DeWeese rushed to dress his wounds, then I half carried, half dragged Whit across the rice paddies to the landing zone.

After the battle, we got word that he had made it home and that doctors had put a plate in the back of his skull to cover the fissure made by the bullet.

I tried to envision what that was like, walking around with a plate in your head.

I called Charles in the late spring of 1984 and we began to plan a visit. His health was good, he said, but he had "some problems" with his vision. Then I brought up Hagan.

"You know, the thing with Bob is a real tragedy," Charles said. "His mother and father were really wrapped up in him and his death just about drove his mother crazy. I went to see them shortly after I got home. I'll tell you, it was more than I could handle myself."

He volunteered to contact the lieutenant's parents, Cora and Jack Hagan, and, acting as a kind of intermediary, help set up my visit. I told him not to press the issue; I did not want to stir their grief and was having second thoughts about the wisdom of seeing them. A month later Charles sent me a note.

I spoke with Bob's mother today and to my surprise and relief she was glad to hear from me. When I told her you would be coming to visit, she made me promise to keep her informed as she is eager to speak with you.

Charles added that he too was eager to get together.

Hearing from you and Frank brought emotions to the surface I thought were buried. Just knowing you made it back to the world alive is comforting. . . .

Thanks so much for sending . . . the photos. I remembered Troy and Belknap and I'm sure there are many other faces hidden in the recesses of my memory. I often try to bring those images forth but I haven't been very successful. I remember events more than faces, probably because I saw so many Marines come and go. . . .

And now here he was, standing in front of his house on Forty-ninth Street, hands in his pockets, a wide grin of welcome on his face.

The house was stucco, tawny, two stories high with red-brick steps, a red front door, and a screened porch. A large water oak, flanked by two sycamores, anchored the front yard. The lawn was sparse; it seemed to be fighting the hand that had been coaxing it. Next door was a large, red-brick elementary school.

"I've really been looking forward to this," Charles said as we held each other.

He had put on some weight—his face was thicker than I remembered. Everything else about him, however—his slow gait, the deliberate way he gestured when he spoke, his utterly confident and easy manner—all else was the same.

There had always been something distinct about Charles, a way he had of carrying himself that set him apart from the others—a whisper of grace, perhaps a vein of unpretentious charm. He was simply one of the most likable men I'd ever met. And it was good to see him again, standing there by the long-leaf pines in the orange shadows of a late afternoon.

"C'mon in," he said, grabbing one of my bags from the trunk of the rental car. "I'll introduce you to Susan."

There was no outward sign of disability from his head wound, no slurred speech, no flickering of the eyes, no paralysis or twitch. He preceded me through the door. His dark brown hair was neatly combed over the spot on the back of his head where the bullet had struck.

The house was comfortable—Persian carpets and Queen Anne chairs in the living room, a thick couch with a bamboo print in the sitting room, brick fireplaces and a kitchen with white cabinets, a polished oak floor, and, on this day, a pot of beans and a pot of potatoes steaming on the stove.

Susan wore large wire-frame glasses. The lenses were tinted slightly amber like her hair, which was neck-length and straight. She wore no makeup, or so little it was not evident.

When we entered the room, she was facing the stove, stirring in one of the pots. She greeted me warmly. "Tell me, Michael, I wonder what it's like to see all those boys again after all those years." Then, firmly, "Charles, didn't you show Michael his room yet? Why, he may wanna unpack or clean up before dinner."

Charles and Susan worked at her father's business, auto-parts supply; she managed the books, he ran a one-man subdivision, a battery distributorship. They had no children; Susan kept cats and rabbits. They had met at a local college in the city and had been married for fourteen years.

We had a long dinner together. Susan laughed at our stories and listened as eagerly as Charles while I talked about the lives of the other men.

After coffee, Charles and I went for a walk. It was a cool night and we'd gone only a few blocks when he began to shiver.

"Wanna head back and get a jacket?" I asked.

"Naw, let's keep going." He shoved his hands deep into his pockets. We walked a long way that night, taking a wide swing away from the house and a long loop back. By the time we sighted the porch light again, it was well after midnight, and many years from where we had started.

The bullet had shattered a knob of bone at the base of his skull. A small plastic plate—a kind of screen, really—had been grafted over the opening.

At first the wound left him blind and, although he knew the condition was only temporary, he worried for his future. Then, at a hospital in Japan, he was placed on a ward full of wounded amputees.

"Ambulatory patients like me helped feed and care for them. You know, you and I had seen guys, good friends, lose arms and legs on the battlefield, but you really don't see how damaging it is and how it's gonna affect their lives. I realized how difficult it was gonna be for them, that the severity of their wounds was incredible. And then I realized how insignificant my own injury was. Sure, I had a big hole in my head, I had brain damage, eyes were damaged, but I had my arms, both legs. I could walk, feed myself. I could act like a normal person. After that, I never considered my injury being very much at all.''

His condition was called "homonymous hemianopsia," or bilateral blind spots. He had a kind of dead zone to the right of center in his field of vision. When reading, for example, he was able only to make out the first three or four letters of any word, then came a blank. To compensate, he learned to read obliquely; using his peripheral vision, scanning for numbers or characters beyond the blind spot. It was a painfully slow and frustrating process. In the end, his reading speed was never better than that of a schoolboy.

In January 1970 he enrolled at Armstrong State College in Savannah. With a severe head wound, of course, he should have delayed school. The doctors had advised a longer recuperation and more therapy. But he wanted a degree and did not see his disability stopping him. He was impatient too, not a man to sit and wait.

Charles Boyd Whitfield was one of four children, two boys and two girls, who grew up in the hot, dry country of norhwest Georgia. For a while his father worked as a policeman, then turned to sharecropping corn and peanuts. It was a peripatetic life; in less than ten years, the family moved thirty times, from one small patch of ground to another. In 1957, seeking a fresh start, they settled in Savannah, where his father found work in the shipyards. This labor, however, was seasonal, marked by penniless lulls, so the family lived frugally, planning a budget day to day.

A dislocated country boy set down in a large city, Charles soon took to the streets. He was twelve then, running with a kind of Dickensian gang "whose idea of something to do was either to hurt someone or rob or steal."

Somewhere along the way, sensing the danger and hopelessness of such enterprise, he broke with the pack and became a model of self-reliance. In high school he worked three jobs, sometimes at once: sold papers on street corners, jerked soda in an ice-cream parlor, hauled sacks of coal up tenement steps. He emerged from adolescence with a plan fueled by a precocious determination.

"I knew that for me to get anywhere in my life I had to graduate from high school. That was the first step. The second step, I needed a full-time job. I got a job. Next step, I had to get my military service out of the way. I enlisted. All along the way, where I had choices to make, I made the choices."

Overseas, the men knew little of Charles Whitfield. I had pictured him as something of an aristocrat: Old South family, Old South money. Maybe it was his gentlemanly ways, his charm and inexhaustible patience that gave him that air.

Now, as we walked and talked, it was hard to imagine him as a boy digging in the dirt for corn and peanuts or hauling coal to cold-water flats.

His parents were divorced and still living in the city, he said, yet he saw them only occasionally. He was in boot camp when they separated; no one in the family had bothered to write him with this and he came home on leave to an empty house. Now, when he talks of his clan, his voice fills with disaffection.

His sisters, married and remarried, had eleven children between them. His brother, in prison, was serving twelve years for armed robbery. All of them, as Charles saw it, suffered the same fatal flaw. "They just let the tide wash over them any which way." They were the victims of fate; he meant to be its master.

Still, they were family and he tried to keep them close. But each time he reached out, something got in the way. Lately it had been religion, "summertime religion," he called it, evangelical, transitory, hard for him to abide.

"Once, we asked one of my nieces to spend a week with us, but my sister would not allow it because we were going to go to the beach and she would not allow the girl to wear a bathing suit. Her religion said she had to wear a long dress down to her ankles to the beach. She was a six-year-old child. But, listen, I don't want you to get the wrong impression from any of this. I love my family."

Along the Atlantic Coast are a chain of subtropical isles known as the Sea Islands. Discovered by the Spanish in the sixteenth century, a few have become well-known: Port Royal is a fishing hub and Sea Island and Hilton Head are posh resorts.

Parris Island, named for colonial settler Alexander Parris, is 7,132 acres of sand, swamp, and salt marsh just off the South Carolina shore in the intercostal waterway, roughly halfway between Charleston and Savannah. The island is hot and inhospitable in the summer, fit only for water snakes and sand fleas and greenhead flies. In the winter, when the wind cuts sharply across its flat, open expanse, it seems a desolate place.

It was on this island that the United States Marine Corps decided to establish its main Recruit Training Depot. Over the years, as the depot's legend grew, Parris Island came to be known as a place of trial and pain, the site where recruits were isolated like inmates and transformed, as an imaginative drill instructor might put it, from gelatinous civilians into a hybrid of heartwood and steel, a U.S. Marine.

From 1915 to 1929, the raw material for this process was transported to Parris Island by launch from Port Royal. After that, the Horse Island Bridge and causeway were built.

I first set foot on the island in 1967. Then, as now, recruits arrived in the dark of early morning when the low country hangs heavy with mist and the air carries the almond bouquet of marsh gas. Then, as now, only the causeway bridge was lighted, leaving the rest of the way from the main gate to the base itself shrouded in darkness and shadow, an eerie passage through the marsh between colonnades of tall palmettos and water oaks hanging heavy with clumps of Spanish moss.

When former Marines return to the depot, as Charles and I did one golden morning that November, it is a kind of homecoming. Parris Island was our alma mater and, in a peculiar way, we were as wistful about its swamps, sand fleas, and malevolent stewards in Smoky-Bear hats as other men were about Gothic towers, gray squirrels, and abstemious professors in Harris tweed coats. Such was the warp of memory that we looked back fondly, sweetly even, on the ten hot and miserable weeks we spent there.

The trip was part pilgrimage too, a return to the source. Parris Island was much more than just a training school for the trade of arms. It was a kind of lodge or temple where a society of bold men gathered its initiates and taught them its hard ways and mysterious codes. It was a school of the self, a place of mirrors that exposed fear and doubt. It was an education in other men too, all kinds of men from all kinds of places, some rising above their backgrounds, others betrayed by them.

As we drove down the Boulevard de France, the main street through the base, I remembered some of those men: Kelly and Kovacs and Lapham and Long, men from Maine and Alabama, illiterates and scholars, hard bark and rice paper. There were thieves and braggarts in that company and men of great honesty and unmatchable reserve. Some came from families with money and some were so poor they used to sleep at night with their hands on their boots.

In some sense, they were patriotic, yet to call them patriots would be to give this feeling more shape than it had. The country was at war; they heard a call—perhaps an echo of myth or tradition—and for many reasons, some common, some complex, decided to answer it.

Some were on the run when they hit the island, two steps ahead of disappointed parents or a set of failing grades or a girl who called late one night crying that she was pregnant. But in the main, they came to that torrid, sandy place because they were restless and unsatisfied. They wanted something more, something better, something different.

"If I had stayed in Savannah and continued the way I was," said Charles, remembering his days in the streets, "I'd've been some half-assed punk with a nowhere job. The Marine Corps was the best thing that ever happened to me."

It was mid-morning as we neared the main gate of the base. Two sentries manned the guard house on a small traffic island at the north end of the causeway. Charles held his I.D. card out the window. Like other badly wounded men, the Corps had retired him in grade.

"We're just a couple of ex-Marines who've come back for a visit," he told the sentry.

"Welcome back," the corporal said. "Have a good time, sir."

The base was beautiful, green and neat. The grass seemed combed, the streets swept spotless. Even the palmettos were clipped and manicured. No doubt the island was this pristine the night I first came aboard, but I did not notice then. Now, on this Saturday so many years later, I was transfixed by its polished trim and ordered beauty.

"I know you remember that." Charles was pointing to the massive parade deck—the "grinder," we used to call it—where legions of men in heavy black boots have spent endless hours marching to and fro with rifles on their shoulders and drill instructors barking at their heels.

This morning two platoons were out for close-order drill, their DIs on the flanks singing songs of cadence. Yellow guidons in front, the boxlike formations glided slowly across the expanse of gray under the flame-white South Carolina sun.

We stopped by the mess hall to watch the platoons file in for noon chow, then went through the War Memorial Building, shopped at the Post Exchange, and strolled the immaculate sidewalks and back streets.

Much of it was just the same. The old white, rambling two-story barracks of our war years had been replaced by modern concrete and brick quarters, but the men who came pouring out of them and into formation looked familiar to me. The faces were blank, a mask of obedience. At the rifle range, the sharp report of small arms still filled the early mornings and afternoons. Even the decorum of daily life was the same: men still showed one another the respect of a "Good morning, sir" or a "Thank you, Sergeant Major." All the rules seemed in place, all the old orders standing.

And yet this was not the part of the Marine Corps I remembered most. My memory was filled with the obscenity of war, the clouds of bitter yellow dust. The air here was too clean, the vistas too unobscured.

When I first set foot on Parris Island, it struck me as dark and isolated, cut off from the mainland and the laws of civilization, a place where men were driven until they dropped, where they were beaten and bloodied, where, sometimes, they even died. Now, from the far side of the battlefield, this well-groomed academy seemed almost innocent.

"Well, good morning. You sleep okay?" Susan was standing in the pantry, pulling a box of cereal from a shelf. "I told Charles to make sure you had an extra blanket."

"He did his job well." I stepped down the stairs and into the kitchen.

With milk-white skin, she had a somewhat delicate look, but Susan was all order and efficiency, the ramrod of her father's business.

They'd met during Charles's first semester; she was a transfer student; Charles spotted her in a class on western civilization and asked for a date. She told him no, several times; she already had a boyfriend—a National Guardsman who was away for six months' training—a man much in her mother's favor.

Charles was persistent. Finally she consented to an innocent meeting at an intramural basketball game. A few weeks later, on Valentine's Day, they went together to the Sweetheart Dance. Not long after that they were talking about marriage.

Her mother fought hard. She thought the guardsman a perfect match and, as Susan told it, was so opposed to anyone else, she offered her daughter a thousand dollars to cancel the nuptials. (After the wedding, Mary Sharpe, of course, came around. "He was just so quiet," said Charles's mother-in-law, remembering her opposition. "But you know, we've come to really love him.")

Susan went to work in her father's auto-parts business and Charles became a high-school history teacher. Given his innate forbearance, he must have been a natural pedagogue. ("Best damn teacher they ever had," said the owner of a gas station whose daughter had been one of Charles's students.) But much of the effort was in vain. Unsettled by drugs, alcoholism, and violence, Savannah's school system, like urban schools elsewhere in the 1970s, began to founder. Whit felt the bureaucracy was weak and too slow to act and, soon, the students were beyond his reach. In 1978 he decided to leave the chaos behind.

For a while he worked renovating old homes, then joined his father-in-law, Al Sharpe, and took over his battery division, a one-truck operation. Al let him run that corner of the parts business as if it were his own. He delivered the products, generated new sales, serviced the accounts. He liked the autonomy, working alone. It gave him solitude, control.

In the years that followed, Charles and Susan bought the house on Forty-ninth Street. It was a large place with plenty of bedrooms.

"I wanted children," Susan said, "but Charles figured that having a child was one thing you don't *have* to do; you don't *have* to get pregnant. He figured that childbirth was something you could control."

So they stayed a circle of two, keepers of rabbits in the yard and stray cats on the back doorstep.

Sometimes he talked to her of war.

"I didn't understand any of what he told me at first, except as just to say, 'I'm sorry' or 'Uh-huh.' The smell of death, he was telling me about that. He could smell it when people were dead around him. When he tried to kill someone, how bad he felt. That kind of thing, too. I couldn't understand any of that.

"It wasn't until about four years ago, when my grandmother died, that I started to grasp what he was talking about. I don't think death was ever real before that. I just would say, 'Yes, okay, lots of people died.' And it didn't dawn on me he was really talking about the mystery of it, not only the waste of it. I think what he had to work out in his mind was the mortality of man, how frail our lives are, how one circumstance can alter your entire life or end it, so quickly.

"I think the war was where Charles derived a lot of his strength, his values, and character. Honor means a lot to him. When he came home, one of his friends, a best friend, lied to him and he hasn't spoken to the man since.

"As time went on, I avoided hearing his stories. I don't want to hear them anymore. I don't think Charles needs to tell me any more about it and it upsets me."

Charles was tired, but I kept him up, first on the front steps, then, retreating from the cold, back to the dining-room table. It was Sunday night; in the morning I was scheduled to visit the Hagans. I needed to talk.

My comrades had advised against the visit, particularly Charles. He had seen Cora and Jack Hagan several times across the years, the first not long after Bob had been declared missing. Cora Hagan was distraught, he said, filled with that terrible anxiety that comes just before grief. At subsequent visits, little had changed; time had been no healer for the Hagans.

Why, he asked now, would I want to walk into that? What purpose would such a visit serve? Was I going to tell the Hagans how most of the men felt about their son? What did I want to accomplish?

Second Lt. John Robert Hagan reported to Golf Company, Second Battalion, Ninth Marines, in January 1968 on the eve of the enemy's Tet Offensive. The company was assigned to guard the main bridge over the Cam Lo River and took up positions in large reinforced bunkers on either bank.

Cam Lo was an obvious target for the enemy—one night sappers slipped into the river and, before they were gunned down, tried to lash explosives to the legs of the bridge—but we looked forward to duty there. The wooden bunkers were warm and dry; we had a mess tent and regular visits from a PX truck and the kids who were couriers for the local black market.

The lieutenant was six feet, six inches with bright red hair, twenty-two years old, from Wilmington Island in Savannah, an engineering major out of Vanderbilt who had won a commission through the Reserve Officers Training Corps and had volunteered for the Marines.

In front of the ranks, he was stiff and formal, a sharp contrast to Frank Ciappio, the gregarious, loose cannon of an officer he replaced. He rarely listened to his subordinates, even those schooled by long service. At briefings he exhorted the men to "win the war," as if he were a cadre sent by some central committee to harangue us with propaganda and prod us to victory.

In private, however, Bob Hagan was someone else. After Charles was wounded, a lonely lieutenant wrote him a letter.

> *28 June 68*
>
> *Whit,*
>
> *I was sure glad to find out that you are going to be all right.*
>
> *Make sure you go out to my house and find out why all the Hagans are so big.*
>
> *. . . We picked up and went out on the road to Khe Sanh. We have been sitting out here on bridge 26 for the last week or so. . . . Right now we are just waiting [for them to abandon Khe Sanh and blow up the base]. Then we are going to take [Dong Ha] mountain itself (wish I were home). . . .*
>
> *As it turned out Cpl McCarty died of wounds and so did Coats. So together with Grant that made 3KIA's*

[when Whitfield was hit]. Snow went back to the states with a broken knee cap. You two were our worst. Sgt Moore [from Atlanta] had gone home. He was pretty bad off but he recovered in fine form. Norman is back from R&R full of tales. . . . Ski and Troy had left the field to go home.

You asked Lt Ciappio to send you your ID. Well, since that time he was a Medevac with malaria and we haven't heard from him since. I guess that was just his way of saying he wanted out of the field.

Well Whit I must close for now. Write and let me know how your eyes are.

Hagan felt close to Whitfield and revealed to his neighbor a side of himself he showed no one else. When he joined the platoon, he confided to Charles that he felt ill-suited to the infantry and life on the battlefield.

"His first reaction when he became platoon leader was to look for another job," Charles said. "Bob realized just how rough the field was and how dangerous it was and he applied for [the job of aerial observer], thinking that in a few months he'd be out."

When his request was denied, Hagan turned from reluctant warrior to would-be hero and martinet. Some of this, no doubt, was self-defense; at that point Ciappio was challenging him and their rivalry was intense. "Bob and Frank were at each other's throat," Charles said. By putting himself forward again and again, Hagan likely was trying to outmaneuver Frank and win the approval of the company commander.

The more I heard, the more I wanted to know. Hagan was a conundrum: the man who had wanted to cut and run; the man who had tried to shoulder the standard.

Early Monday morning I drove across the Memorial Bridge to Wilmington Island. I had no plan, no idea what to say. I drove slowly, stopping twice at the curb: to check a map I did not need; to read directions I had memorized. At Grosvenor Road, I found the Hagans' house—a one-story red ranch behind a stand of tall pines, shielded from a mid-morning sun—but drove on. Finally, when there was nowhere left to drive but back across the river, I back-tracked to the house, parked at the curb, and crossed the dry grass to the front door.

"Oh, Mike!" said the genial woman who answered the door. "C'mon in, won't you? We've been waitin'."

She was tall with a medium build, gray hair, and a long, open face, but what most marked Cora Hagan was her powerful sense of loss, her mask of mourning.

Her husband, Jack, a retired chemical engineer, was the image of Bob. He had a square face with narrow eyes, high cheekbones, a smile full of teeth, and a jaw that was square and solidly set. He too was tall, a towering man.

The living room was long and narrow. I sat with Cora on an ivory-colored couch against a wall. Jack, with his back to the front window, was in an armchair facing us. It was a comfortable home, eclectically furnished: polished wood and pastel fabric, a modern piece here, neocolonial there.

Cora and Jack had met in Chattanooga, where Jack was working for a chemical company. When it closed in 1966, they moved to Savannah. They had two sons, Bob and Joey; Joey was married now with two children.

Bob was twenty years old and in his third year at Vanderbilt when the family took up residence on Grosvenor Road. He was majoring in engineering, but, quietly, had made up his mind on another career. "He wanted to be a Marine," his mother said.

John Robert Hagan, born August 22, 1945, in Chattanooga, Tennessee, was named for his father, John Luther Hagan, but Cora decided to call him Bob, after his paternal grandfather, Robert.

"I've never seen a more excited man in my whole life about being a grandfather," she remembered. "Why, when he'd come to visit and Bob would go to bed for his nap [Grandfather Hagan would] put his chair outside the door [and sit there] so he could be sure and hear when the baby woke up."

Cora Hagan was struck by the promise she saw in her firstborn. "I guess the day he was handed to me, in my mind there was greatness there." And perhaps because of this conviction, she was determined to make Bob "all around" and "perfect."

He was a dutiful boy. "He obeyed so beautifully. We just knew he was gonna do what he was told." Ordered, for example, to stay in the yard, he planted himself on the grass. "All the kids are riding their bikes in the street, but he'd just sit there."

As a teenager, he was sent to The McCallie School, a preparatory academy in Chattanooga. In class and on the playing field, Cora expected excellence. "I think maybe we put a pressure on him growing up. He was just afraid that we wouldn't be proud of him. He gave it his all in just about anything he did. He gave it his all."

But he was neither a natural athlete nor an intellect. Large and awkward, he could not make the first string in football or baseball until his senior year. And although his grades were respectable enough, he often had to study twice as long as his classmates just to keep apace.

"It didn't come easy for him. He'd come home at night and he'd be down. I'd say, 'Okay, your daddy leaves his problems at the mill; you leave yours at school.' Everything, it seemed like, he worked so hard for. Bob would work himself to death when he wanted something."

By nature, he was attentive, thoughtful, eager to please, and easily wounded. "Our friends used to say he wasn't mean enough," Cora remembered. His favorite place was home. Cora and Jack liked to joke that when Bob came in from school, he would drag a chair to the refrigerator and sit there with the door open watching television. It made his father laugh. "When he'd go to bed, there wouldn't be a damn thing [left]."

He rarely took chances or sought out risk. Once, as a teenager, he set out with a friend to walk a section of the Appalachian Trail, roughly from Mt. Oglethorpe in northern Georgia to Damascus, Virginia, on the border with Tennessee, a steep serpentine route through the Great Smoky Mountains, some 250 thickly wooded miles.

Two days after their departure, Cora Hagan received a telephone call, collect. They'd barely got past their starting point. "He said, 'Mom?' I said, 'Where are you?' He said, 'I'm in Gainesville.' I said, 'How'd you get [back] in Gainesville?' He said, 'I think I came in with the milkman.' They had gotten up there and gone in circles for two nights and it had rained on them."

He was an unusually sober boy, one who gave great weight to even the most trivial matters. At Vanderbilt, during fraternity pledge week, he called home.

"He said, 'I just had to make a final decision [on a fraternity]. I went over to the chapel. I sat over there for about an hour by myself. I thought about everything, the boys I'd been involved with during rush week and all that.' And he said, 'Now I've made my decision and I hope this is the one I'll be accepted by.' And it was, but see, this is how deep he got into everything. He just couldn't treat that light. This used to concern me. He loved his fraternity, but he was not a real party guy. He decided he would bartend and watch everyone else. He was so serious about everything."

Cora made us sandwiches and coffee. We ate lunch in the living room while we talked. Each time I made ready to leave, she seemed to have something else to say, something more to show me. We toured the house—the kitchen where mother and son had spent so much time, the den filled with Marine Corps mementos and Bob's ribbons in a wood-and-glass case hanging on the wall.

I think I lost my anger the moment I set eyes on Cora. Her sadness shamed me.

The house got hot and close—Charles had been right; their grief was almost overwhelming—but I did not leave, for I was sure I'd found a way through the sorrow. I began to listen for the footsteps of a boy. When Cora talked about *her* son, I thought about mine. In the end, that was how I came to know the lieutenant.

*   *   *

Bob Hagan "loved the Marine Corps," his father said. "From the time he was a little boy, military life appealed to him. He was always playing with his little toy soldiers. He did a term paper in high school on Iwo Jima. It was sixteen pages long."

"More than anything else," his mother said, "Bob was a Marine. I used to say, 'Son, why do you have to be a Marine?' He gave me fifteen reasons in ten seconds. The day he got commissioned, I pinned his bars on him. I said, 'Son, I'm going to be the best Marine mother in the world.' "

Cora also became his best friend and counselor. "When he was in high school he used to come into the kitchen and stand there for an hour and tell me about things, his problems and his feelings. He said, 'I've never had a sister. I don't even have a close girl cousin.' He said, 'I went to an all-boys school and I don't know what makes them tick.' He depended on me to open some ideas to him because I guess I was the only girl he [really] knew."

In late 1967, on leave after officer-candidate school at Quantico, Virginia, just before he received orders to go to war, he came home from a day of shopping carrying a book entitled *Heroes of the U.S. Marine Corps, 1861–1955*. He read it several times cover-to-cover. On the flyleaf was a large picture of the Congressional Medal of Honor.

"I think he had a fear of what was gonna happen when he got over there," Cora said. "Maybe it was the unknown or whatever, but he told me he wanted to be buried in Arlington Cemetery if he didn't get back."

His mother wrote him every day overseas, "just some little old something about home and things like that." She sent him packages and clippings from the Sunday comics, particularly his favorite, Snuffy Smith. "I still have a box of clippings I saved for him. Some winter day, I'm gonna build a good fire."

His homecoming was a surprise. "I had picked Joey up at school," said Cora, "and we came out [to the house] and I said, 'I'll bet you we have a letter from Bob today.' And he said, 'Okay, I'll bet we do, too.' So I reach into the mailbox and I pull this letter out and we sit in the car to read it. We don't get out of the car and I'm reading along and all of a sudden I realize what I've read: he's coming home and guess what? It's that night. He's gonna land in Savannah that night. I went in every direction.

"He was home thirty days and we had a grand time. It was unreal. He spent over five hundred dollars for civilian clothes. He rented a car, went up to Virginia to see his little girl, came back through Chattanooga, went to Atlanta. I hated not to have him here [at home all the time], but that was fine with me. I loved seeing him off.

"The first night, as we got ready to go to bed, he put his things up [in his room and spread them out on his bed], then he said, 'I think I'll just sleep in here in Joey's room since I've got stuff all over my bed.' I never have said this before, but I don't think that was the reason. I think he just wanted to sleep in that room with Joey. I believe that it felt good having family.

"He'd get up late and maybe he'd start his day with lunch rather than breakfast. We would sit at that bar in there. I'd put the food out and we'd sit there, the two of us, for four or five straight hours, talking about everything—my ideas about things, his ideas about things, whatever. We wouldn't move, and you know what? I didn't want to move because I just wanted to keep it flowing. I loved it.

"I'll tell you something else he did that is very lasting. He was going over to Beaufort [South Carolina], the [Naval] air station, to buy some boots and he said, 'Mom, would you mind too much if Joey didn't go to school tomorrow? I'd like for him to go to Beaufort with me.' And from that moment on, doggone it if I didn't see a motivation in Joey I had never seen before."

Cora begged her son not to go back to the war. "We could've shot his big toe or something [to keep him home], but he thought he could help the boys. He would've never been fulfilled if he hadn't completed this thing. We never talked about the danger involved in it. We didn't dwell on this. He was just gonna get back."

Bob told a reporter from the *Chattanooga News-Free Press* that he was "looking forward to getting back" and that he had signed up for a second tour because, "I enjoyed my work and liked the challenge of [it] . . . I'm personally sold on our mission. . . . We're doing a wonderful job over there." He went on to describe his new assignment: "I hang out of the window [of the small plane] and look for [enemy] supply points, evidences of recent use of the area. Aerial observers serve as the infantry ground commander's eyes."

"He had seen so many of his buddies killed," his father said. "His idea was, 'I can save an awful lot of lives by going back.' "

In late February 1969 he packed his gear and said his good-byes. "The day he left we took him to the airport and we made pictures just as he was getting on the plane," Cora said. "The last thing he did, he shook hands with Joey.

"Later I got a phone call from him in San Francisco, which was a bonus because I thought he was already gone. He said he had met a girl [a stewardess on the flight]. She was from Tennessee. He called and said, 'Mom, I'm having a wonderful time. I need some money.' They spent time together, forty-eight hours or whatever. They took a cab and drove across the [Golden Gate] bridge. They went down to Chinatown and to an art gallery where he bought a painting. We have it hanging in the den.

"It was terribly, terribly romantic. They just hit it off beautifully together. He was so happy out there. He gave her his address. I called her after he was missing. She came here and spent a week with us. About two years later, she called me and said, 'Mrs. Hagan, this is Mary. I'm getting married and I didn't want to do it without telling you about it.'

"Bob wanted a home and a family, you know."

Two footnotes.

1. In San Francisco, instead of buying his painting outright, Bob Hagan paid on time. Each week from the war zone, he mailed the gallery another check. Later, when he

was declared missing in action, his father settled the debt and had the painting shipped to Savannah. It was hanging in the Hagans' wood-paneled den. "It's my favorite thing in the whole house," Cora said.

It is a large work, perhaps four-by-five feet. In the foreground is the dominant figure of a small boy in a white T-shirt and shorts, six or seven years old. The boy is alone at the seashore, sitting with his right leg tucked beneath him on the hard wet sand at the water's edge. He is staring out beyond the breakwater toward the open sea. In the background, a short way down the beach and just into the water, are three girls at play. The boy does not seem to see these revelers; his gaze is fixed on the horizon. Pictured as he is, slightly from behind, it is impossible to read his face, and yet clearly this is a portrait of longing and loneliness.

2. Bob Hagan received the following citation:

The President of the United States takes great pleasure in presenting the SILVER STAR MEDAL to

SECOND LIEUTENANT JOHN R. HAGAN

For conspicuous gallantry and intrepidity in action while serving as a platoon commander with Company G, Second Battalion, Ninth Marines. . . . On 19 April 1968, Second Lieutenant Hagan's unit was dispatched to a bridge site between Ca Lu and Khe Sanh [Bridge 28]. . . . Earlier in the day a security force and a convoy had been ambushed at the bridge and were pinned down and sustained numerous casualties. Upon arrival at the site, Second Lieutenant Hagan unhesitatingly advanced to the point of heaviest contact and deployed his men to recover casualties from the bridge area. Repeatedly exposing himself to intense enemy fire, he moved from one position to another, aiding the wounded and directing their evacuation to covered positions. On one occasion when he became pinned down by the heavy volume of hostile fire along both sides of the narrow road, he crawled to a tank and directed the movement of the vehicle into the hazardous area, aiding in the evacuation of the casualties from the fire-swept battle area. During the night, Second Lieutenant Hagan disregarded the dangers of numerous booby traps and mines as he maneuvered through the difficult, mountainous terrain to ensure that all casualties had been recovered and evacuated to the relative safety of the company perimeter. The following day and night, he refused to return to the command post and remained in the area to direct mortar fire against the enemy positions and assist a reinforcing company which was pursuing the fleeing enemy. . . . By his extraordinary courage, indomitable fighting spirit and selfless devotion to duty, Second Lieutenant Hagan upheld the highest traditions of the Marine Corps and of the United States Naval Service.

So what was it? Gamecock or Fainting Goat? Had I given a decent man the cast of a coward? Or had the Corps concocted a cruel fiction?

Maybe that morning on the road Bob Hagan had done his best after all. Perhaps, with a friend's cry for help ringing in my ears, I had made a case of gross diffidence out of a few seconds prudently spent checking a map. And maybe that night in the hills, maneuvering through the difficult, mountainous terrain, the lieutenant had not turned to stone at all, but had been numbed or knocked senseless by the same grenade that had blown me off my feet. He was—thinking back—only an arm's length away.

And yet, now, turning all this over in my mind, my business still seemed so unfinished.

Cora had said that her son went off to war carrying the weight of great expectations. And Whit had said that when Hagan got there, he did not want to fight. He inherited an experienced platoon that had been led by a popular platoon commander. He was raw and untutored in the ways of the field. The lessons learned at officers' school in Quantico counted for little in the bush. And he did not have the kind of hard childhood and adolescence that sometimes prepares a man for the isolation of command and the brutality of combat.

So he postured—what else could he do?—became a simulacrum of a leader because he could not be a real one. He played a tin drum and gave speeches about winning the war. And to men who had been bloodied, such a pose was not only preposterous, it was dangerous as well. He took his cues from the book, and in that steamy, muddy venue, the book was as useless, as patently absurd, as brass polish and shoe wax.

He never asked for help. Perhaps he thought that to ask was a sign of weakness or failure, a violation of what he had been told in the spit-shined ranks at officers' school.

But even if he had, would we have responded? We could have won him over, but no one approached him, offered to help. We did not show him the same kinship we showed one another. Instead, we made him our foil. He was stiff and unyielding and to us represented the faceless generals and politicians who kept sending Golf Company into the slaughter. With the lines drawn thus, he was alone.

Cut off from the camp fires of his comrades, from their comfort and good advice, he fell back on old instincts. His mother had taught him, and urged him, to put himself out front, set the example. So he set out to prove himself, volunteered again and again. Patrols, ambushes, rescue missions—all dangerous, all building for him a deep well of enmity with the men. Did he know this? Likely not. He was busy fighting failure. Playing the stalwart was probably the only role he knew, the only clear way out of his quandary.

I gave Cora and Jack Hagan the broad outlines of this story.

"You're talking about a twenty-two-year-old man who had never been involved in anything like war," Cora said. "There was no violence of any kind at all in his life. All of a sudden he was thrown into this, so perhaps he felt the veneer had to be there. I don't believe that child ever had an enemy in his whole life. I know his capacity to love and to care about people. I know this. There wouldn't be any doubt in my mind that any one of the men that he worked with, if they had the opportunity to know him as a person, would have liked him. Everybody adored Bob. He was very strong and he was knowledgeable and he had a fate bigger than anything in this world."

CASUALTY MESSAGE

9 MAY 1969

MR&MRS JOHN L HAGAN

I DEEPLY REGRET TO CONFIRM THAT YOUR SON FIRST LIEUTENANT JOHN R. HAGAN USMC HAS BEEN REPORTED MISSING IN ACTION. HE WAS THE AERIAL OBSERVER ABOARD AN OBSERVATION AIRCRAFT ON A VISUAL RECONNAISSANCE MISSION WHICH FAILED TO RETURN TO QUANG TRI AIR BASE AT. . . 4:30 P.M. 6 MAY 1969. THERE WAS HEAVY THUNDERSTORM ACTIVITY IN THE AREA AT THE TIME. SEARCH EFFORTS ARE IN PROGRESS BUT NO INFORMATION OR EVIDENCE HAS BEEN OBTAINED TO DETERMINE THE FATE OF YOUR SON . . . SINCE THE POSSIBILITY EXISTS THAT YOUR SON IS BEING HELD CAPTIVE, IT IS SUGGESTED THAT YOU REFRAIN FROM FURNISHING ANY PERSONS OUTSIDE OF YOUR IMMEDIATE FAMILY WITH ANY BACKGROUND INFORMATION . . . SUCH DATA COULD ADVERSELY EFFECT HIS WELFARE SINCE IT MAY BE USED FOR COERCION AND PROPAGANDA PURPOSES.

"It's been my contention from the beginning that if Bob was conscious when his plane hit, they wouldn't have taken him alive," Jack Hagan said. "As long as there was a breath in him, he'd have continued fighting."

2 Jul 1969

Dear Mr. and Mrs. Hagan,

A report of the circumstances surrounding the missing in action state of your son . . . has been received at this Headquarters. . . .

At approximately 3:20 P.., a severe thunderstorm developed in the western portion of Quang-Tri province, the area in which your son's aircraft was flying. It was enormous in size and developed very fast. According to weather observers it contained electrical and heavy turbulent activity. It was not until 6 P.M. . . . that the storm subsided enough to permit search and rescue operations. Aerial search was conducted. . . . They searched the entire western portion of Quang-Tri province east to the Laotian border, north to the Demilitarized Zone and west to the ocean with negative results. . . .

The chances for survival under the attending circumstances are uppermost in your mind, I know. There is no sure answer that may be given; however, let me discuss with you the possibilities as I understand them, based on all available information. First that the aircraft became uncontrollable due to the thunderstorm and crashed with no survivors. The fact that there were no received trasmissions over either the aircraft's radio indicating difficulty or over the survival radios, of which there were two, tends to support this probability. Second, that the aircraft crash-landed and the crew survived. In the event this did happen the chances for survival are good. The terrain in the area of their operation is mountainous and heavily vegetated which would have made evasion slow and difficult at best, and coupled with the knowledge that the enemy is known to be operating in that general area, capture would be a strong presumption. There is no definite way of ascertaining the fate of your son and the probabilities discussed above are presumption not based on fact . . .

Your son's personal belongings have been inventoried and will be shipped to . . . Camp Pendleton . . . for storage. If you desire that his personal belongings be sent to you please advise this headquarters.

All the pay and allowances to which your son was entitled at the time he became missing will remain in effect. . . . These funds and the interest accrued will be paid to your son upon his return to the United States control, or, in the sad event of his death, to his designated beneficiary. . . .

My sincere sympathy is with you during these uncertain times. . . .

> *Daniel R. Evans*
> Colonel
> Personal Affairs Branch

"I've always tried to be patient about the things my government was doing," Cora Hagan said. "I've tried to believe in them. They've been at it for a long time. So I just hope against hope."

Dear Mr. and Mrs. Hagan,

Regrettably I have no news for you concerning your loved one. I'm sure, though, that he shares with me the prayer that you will find the strength to persevere as I share with you the prayer for his well-being and early return to those who are deserving of his love.

. . . I realize that without families such as you, who even under these most trying circumstances are willing to stand behind your Marine and his convictions, neither the spirit, our Corps nor the Nation could long prevail. On behalf of every Marine everywhere, I salute You!

Sincerely,
Leonard F. Chapman, Jr.
Commandant of the Marine Corps

"More than anything else," Cora Hagan said, "Bob was a Marine. I think that probably he was a Marine when he was a little bitty boy."

From: Commandant of the Marine Corps
To: Commanding general, Marine Corps Recruit Depot, Parris Island, South Carolina
Subj: Casualty Assistance Program for the next of kin of missing or captured Marines.

1. It is the opinion of this headquarters that it will be in the best interest of the individual Marine, his family and the Marine Corps if a representative of the Marine Corps were to periodically call on the next of kin of those Marines who are listed as missing or captured. . . . The primary purpose of the visit should be to determine if any difficulties are being encountered in which the Marine Corps can appropriately be of assistance. If no other purpose is served, it will be an indication that the Marine Corps is concerned

about the welfare of these families and that efforts are continuing in behalf of the Marine involved.

2. Your command is assigned the Casualty Assistance Call responsibility in the case of First Lieutenant John R. Hagan.

3. A full report of each visit [to take place four times a year] is to be forwarded to this headquarters.

(The Marine Corps showed Cora and Jack Hagan photographs taken of men in captivity. Once, Cora thought she spotted Bob, but the man was only a look-alike.) "I was searching, searching, searching," Cora said. "You've got to watch your imagination. You've got to watch it. Then, I don't know, just all of a sudden, it's a long time."

[Casualty Assistance Call,
2 September 1971]

. . . Mr. and Mrs. Hagan were visited in their home in Savannah Thursday at 1800. Present also was their son "Joey." . . . During the visit, a copy of the CMC ltr [commandant's letter] proclaiming March 21–27 as National Week of Concern for Prisoners of War and Those Missing in Action . . . was delivered for their records. The CACO [casualty assistance call officer] furnished and placed devices [stars] on ribbons which had been mounted. [A] letter to be written by parents to be delivered upon release of POW's was discussed. . . . The family indicated they would not attend the National League of Families of American Prisoners and Missing Annual Convention. . . . Mr. and Mrs. Hagan were invited to the Marine Corps Ball on 12 November 1971 as guests of Major Altman; however, Mrs. Hagan indicated she wanted to wait to attend at some later date with her son, when and if he is one of the released POW's. The only family concern at present, is for Mrs. Hagan's sister who resides in Florida and has terminal leukemia. The Hagan family is in good health and has no problems.

J.L. Altman Jr., Maj, USMC (Assigned CACO)

"Nineteen sixty-nine was a horrible year for us," Cora Hagan said. "We discovered my sister-in-law had cancer. In May Bob was lost. In June my mother's brother died. I'll tell you something. I thought, 'Don't touch me. Don't touch me 'cause I'm bad luck all the way.' "

[Casualty Assistance Call,
22 December 1971]

On Wednesday Mr. and Mrs. Hagan were visited in their home in Savannah. . . . During the call, Christmas Flowers, a live poinsettia plant, and message were delivered in accordance with CMC Msg [commandant's message #] 152138Z Dec 1971. Both were well received. The family has not received any mail from Captain Hagan nor have they participated in pleas by mail for release of POW's [organized efforts by the league of families and other groups angry with Washington's lack of action]. [The Hagans] feel the government is doing all that is possible for POW release. Mrs. Hagan's sister, who resided in Florida, did succumb from leukemia. Mrs. Hagan asked if she could talk with one of the released POW's to determine if he had seen her son. I explained that each POW that was released went through an extensive debrief and any confirmed information on her son would be made known to her. She was satisfied. The family had received no information on their son from unofficial sources and had no special requests other than as mentioned. My observations are that the family is in good health and has no problems.

J.L. Altman Jr., LTCOL USMC (Assigned CACO)

"I spent two years in this house without going out at all because I knew I was gonna get that phone call and I wasn't gonna be away from here," Cora Hagan said. "I tried to make a happy home, I tried to for Jack and Joey. Joey was still in high school. He used to say, 'Mom, if you and Daddy want to go out, I will not go anywhere tonight. I will stay here for the phone.' I asked him to let me handle it my way."

[Casualty Assistance Call,
20 December 1972]

Mr. and Mrs. Hagan were visited in their home. A poinsettia plant and message as authorized by CMC msg 011941Z Dec 1972 was delivered and well-received. . . . They were disappointed in the peace talks, but concurred wholeheartedly with the stepped up bombing. A family Americans can be well proud of. . . .

Their son, "Joey," was home from college for the holidays and wanted to get married in June to a previous "Miss Savannah" who is graduating at the same time with a degree in education. Their cat "Budha," a member of the household for many years, was found dead on their lawn after apparently being struck by an automobile.

They were all apparently in good health and had no special requests. The visit was terminated at 19:15.

J.L. Altman Jr., LTCOL, USMC (Assigned CACO)

"If we could have known something, or [had] a declaration truly proving to me Bob was dead, then I think I could have handled it maybe a little better," Cora Hagan said. "Joey kept saying, 'Mom, at least you have something to hang on to.' But you don't know where he is; you don't know where he is not. It hasn't been the easiest thing."

[Casualty Assistance Call, 28 January 1973]

Received telcon at 27 Jan 73 at my home in Beaufort, S.C. from SGT C.M. Smith, HQMC [Marine headquarters in Washington]. The following message was received and was to be passed on to Mrs. Hagan:

"I regret to inform you that your son, Captain John R. Hagan's name was not on the list recently released to our Government on prisoners held in Southeast Asia. There will be no action taken to change his status from missing until we have had an opportunity to analyze all information provided our Government and obtained from the returning prisoners. You will be kept informed of any further developments."

. . . I personally contacted Mr. and Mrs. Hagan by a visit to their home in Savannah, Georgia at 28 Jan 73, and delivered the message.

J.L. Altman Jr., LTCOL, USMC (Assigned CACO)

(Cora Hagan hung on. She wondered if her son was cold and hungry, surviving on rice and rotten fish, filthy, perhaps hurt, perhaps being hurt. A cousin who claimed to be a psychic had a vision of Bob Hagan "confined and in the rain." "I think he's fine; I think he's all right," the cousin said. Cora wanted to believe this. She went to her priest and told him what the psychic had said. The priest thought about the matter. God, he told her, might be like a telephone wire between two minds. Anything was possible.)

"I'm just worried that Bob is living somewhere worrying about us, that we're not doing well," Cora Hagan said. "He wanted us to be happy. Anything he ever did, he did to make us happy."

[Casualty Assistance Call,
27 September 1974]

. . . Mrs. Hagan expressed concern about the possibility that the Government would soon review her son's case and change his status from MIA to KIA [killed in action]. She stated that she would contest such a change in status. She firmly believes in the possibility that her son may still be a POW.

I subsequently checked with the Casualty Section at HQMC and was advised by Major Dietrick that current policy was to review and affect changes in status only when requested by the next-of-kin. This information was provided to Mrs. Hagan by telcon on 1 Oct 1974.

J.F. Vaillancourt, MAJOR, USMC (Assigned CACO)

(In 1978 the government reviewed the cases and changed the status of the more than 2,500 Americans then listed as missing in action. Maj. John Robert Hagan and the others who had been consumed by ten years of warfare were finally presumed to be dead and listed simply as "unaccounted for." On May 8th of that year, a gravestone bearing Bob Hagan's name was placed, as he had requested, in Arlington National Cemetery. A Marine band played funerary music and an honor guard fired a twenty-one-gun salute. Standing there on that hallowed national ground, Cora Hagan was sure her son was with her.)

"I don't know, you just felt like he might be looking over our shoulder somewhere," Cora Hagan said. "I can't understand why he did not make it back. I think he had too much to give to this world to be snatched away like that. I'm still looking for that answer why Bob didn't come back. I'm still looking for that answer. I haven't found it, but maybe someday it'll be there. I have to be patient. I can't go after it too hard. I can't give up, I can't give up. I do have my life in some kind of order now because I'm willing to wait for whatever time it takes.

"You see, I just keep thinking, someday he might walk in our door."

(6)

Joshua Dempsey Norman, the firstborn of our two sons, presented himself just after dawn on a sun-drenched day in the early fall of 1978.

His father acted like a fool when he arrived. He became, there is no getting by it, philosophical; the boy, he thought, had taken his earthly space, his foothold in the cosmos.

Fortunately, through those first foggy days, I kept this nonsense to myself. I rushed through work, then made for the hospital. By midweek Beth had been assigned a new roommate, a woman in her twenties who had just given birth to her fourth child. She was a welfare patient; when she went into labor she packed her kit, walked to the corner, and caught a bus to the delivery room. Her husband had bolted, which was just as well, she said; the man had beaten her.

There were no flowers on her side of the room. She received no visitors. In time she felt the need to talk, so we listened. Soon the room grew too small and we took to pulling the curtain between the beds.

At week's end, her doctor arrived with bad news. Her

baby was not well, he said. It needed a specialist and must be moved at once. A medical team was on its way for the pickup.

The doctor left. The room filled with silence. In short order, a second physician appeared. He spoke in a hush, but we could hear through the curtain.

The baby, he said, was small, underweight, suffering from a blockage to the stomach. It was dangerously dehydrated and urgently needed surgery. And there was more. The child had "a chromosome problem," a birth defect.

The room grew quiet again. On our side of the curtain, Beth eased back on her pillow and stared at the ceiling. Joshua was next to her on the bed. I reached over and scooped him up, never more clear-eyed or sure-footed.

SEVEN

NO PEER FOR
A BRAVE MAN

I left Savannah on a Wednesday; rose early, packed, then called Cora Hagan to say good-bye. She would try to keep in touch, she said, "but I can't promise anything. You understand, Michael, the last forty-eight hours have been a lot and I've got to get some distance. It's getting too close."

My flight was not scheduled to leave until later that morning, so Charles and I were able to spend a few more hours together. I went along in his battery truck on a service call at a used-car lot. "This is my friend, Mike Norman from New Jersey," he told the owner. "We were in the Marines together. He was standing right next to me when I was shot."

We finished early and decided to return to the house and fetch my rental car. "Let's go for a walk," Charles said, alighting from the truck. "You have time. C'mon."

The morning was dry and sun-drenched, but it was cold for early fall in the South. We walked in silence at first, then, at the corner, Charles stopped and turned. "I . . . I've really looked forward to your coming," he said. "I wanted to spend as much time with you as possible. I don't have the kind of friendships we all once had."

We had walked a ways; it was getting late; I turned back to the house where the car was parked.

"Wait!" Charles was standing in the middle of the sidewalk, his hands hanging loosely at his sides. "Wait, you've still got ten minutes."

With the trip to Savannah, Bob Hagan's story was almost complete. Just one last detail now: How did the lieutenant get back down that hill? Only one man knew for sure what had happened that night—Mike Caron, the corporal who had helped lead the patrol and had somehow effected Hagan's rescue.

Mike and I had talked briefly on the phone before my trip to Savannah; when I returned, we arranged to meet for dinner.

In every war there are a handful of men like Michael Arthur Caron, rational in every respect except one—they simply have no fear. Without exception, Mike Caron was the bravest man I'd ever met.

On the third day of the battle for Bridge 28, he crawled down a narrow trench on a hillside to retrieve some of the wounded and dead. The trench was pitched downward, exposed to gook positions on the next razorback, and the enemy was raking it with fire. Yet Mike kept going. Everyone else on the hill wore a look of terror, but Mike crept forward with a benign smile on his face. I've never forgotten that scene. He had an arm hooked around the chest of a man who had been shot between the eyes. The dead man appeared startled, but his deliverer looked strangely content.

Mike was "gung ho." He loved the Corps; believed in its standards of order, its zeal for discipline, its reputation of valor and daring. After six months of battle, most men were bitter, filled with an insidious acrimony. Not Mike. He went about the work of war cheerfully. Another patrol? "Hey, no problem," he'd say. "Let's do it." Another day without water? "Hey, we still got chow, don't we? What are you complainin' about?"

He had no love for letting blood—he was a religious man, a Roman Catholic who cherished the sacraments and held fast to the mystery of faith; for many years, in fact, he had even thought of becoming a priest—but he thrived on contest. "I know how to play this game," he would tell himself, "how to deploy my men, where they have to be, know that I have to be on the high ground, have to stay off the trail. Oh, I hope I can catch Charlie not thinking right today. He's gonna be mine."

He was raised in Rhode Island and Connecticut, the oldest of four sons of a construction engineer who believed in teaching his boys to, as Mike remembered, "stand on our own two feet and pick ourselves up if we were knocked down."

An athlete—baseball, football, track—he applied to Central Connecticut State College in the spring of 1965 and was accepted for the fall term. "I really didn't want to go to college," he said, "but I thought, what the heck, I can play maybe another couple of years of football. But I never made it.

"During that summer one of my teammates called me up and asked me for a ride to the post office in Bridgeport. He said he wanted to go down and see the Navy recruiter. 'Yeah,' I said, 'okay.' [Sitting in the Navy office were] a couple of old-lady chiefs [petty officers]—beer-gut coffee-cup look, just kind of sloppy looking. Thought as long as I was there I'd ask them about a ROTC program. 'Naw, we don't have a program like that,' they said. I started walking down the hall, right past the Marine Corps recruiter, a staff sergeant sitting there in modified Dress Blues, straight as a whistle at his desk, short haircut, razor-sharp creases in his shirt, stripes around his arm, medals on his chest, posters on the wall—tanks, jets, infantry—esprit de corps, teamwork, gung ho, the whole bit. I go in there and say, 'Hey, you got anything like ROTC?' 'Nope,' he says. 'Well, what about a regular enlistment?' 'Yep,' he says, 'we got that.' 'Well, how does that work?' 'Go take your physical. If you pass, you sign up. Then you go to boot camp. Then you're a Marine.'

" 'Well,' I said, 'I'll be damned.' "

When I caught up with Mike, he was working for a large national tire company, training in one of their retail stores to become a sales manager. He lived in West Haven, Connecticut, near the store. We arranged to meet after work.

Rush-hour traffic was heavy and I was delayed. When I finally pulled up, the front door of the tire store was locked. I cupped my hands against the plate-glass window and peered inside. There was Mike, in back, standing just behind the counter. His face had changed little: a large, round jaw, bulbous cheeks, big dots for eyes, still a friendly face, just older. There were pouches under the eyes now. The hair was still short, close-cropped, military style, but it was laced with gray.

I knocked on the window. He looked up, smiled. Then he stepped around from behind the counter. If I had not been harried from the traffic, his limp might not have unsettled me so and left my jaw hanging.

Mike, hit? I couldn't remember. I was sure he had walked away whole. How had it happened? How could I have forgotten?

He had the key in the dead bolt now and was beginning to turn it. I tried to remember . . . tried to remember . . .

"Hey, how's it goin', buddy. Good to see ya." His handshake was firm, deliberate. Except for the heavy limp, he was fit and lean.

I fumbled for words, but could focus on nothing save his leg. He caught me staring, pulled up short, and grinned. "Heh, heh, heh. Not so young anymore. I was playing basketball and the knee gave way. Had the brace on all day and just took it off. Sure is stiff now."

The restaurant, a stone's throw from Long Island Sound, was noisy and crowded. He had steak for dinner; I ate flounder. We talked through one sitting and halfway into the next.

Mike had tried to make the Corps his career. For a while, after the war, he worked at Portsmouth Naval Prison as a sergeant of the guard, then applied for a transfer to Parris Island to become a drill instructor, or "Hat," as those spit-shined stewards with the wide-brimmed, brown-felt Stetsons called themselves.

"I just wanted to be your typical, gung ho, esprit de corps, poster-type Marine." He laughed, took another bite of meat. "I figured, hey, the best of the best."

Marine Corps boot camp training has always been tough, but it was not until World War II that it turned savage. With global war and mobilization, there was a shortage of qualified instructors, and by 1942 the Corps had begun to take young Marines fresh from boot camp graduation and put them back on the drill field as DIs. Without the experience, these instructors tried to bully their way through the training cycle. Protected by the authority of their office, they established their dominance with their fists.

Soon the hazing and degradation became part of the system, the infamous "shock treatment" of Marine Corps boot camp. For years the Hats ruled the island, relying more on their own idiosyncratic training methods than on those prescribed by the book. Men were made to shave without water or soap while running in place. They were shut in wall lockers, scrubbed raw with Parris Island sand, forced to dig holes and then buried with their own dirt. Noses were broken and jaws shattered.

Then came "Ribbon Creek." In 1956 Staff Sgt. Matthew McKeon, the junior drill instructor of Platoon 71, thirty-two years old, a veteran of World War II and Korea, decided to teach his seventy-four derelict recruits a special lesson and marched them out behind the rifle range into the salt marsh and a tidal stream called Ribbon Creek. It was a black night with a high tide. There were screams and sounds of thrashing in the darkness.

Six men drowned at Ribbon Creek. McKeon was court-martialed, reduced in rank, briefly jailed. The book was rewritten, reforms put in place, but little changed, really.

The brutality just went underground. Many DIs still thought there was only one way to toughen a recruit, one way to guarantee the blind obedience that combat demanded. A man who balked in boot camp would not, later when it counted, willingly move forward to take a fortified hill or capture a fire-swept bridge. So the Hats continued to practice their calculated chaos. And the officers whose job it was to supervise them and enforce official policy usually looked the other way, particularly during the war years of the 1960s when drill instructors, most of whom had seen combat, were readying their charges for the battlefield. The unseen thumping and bashing, the screaming and debasement, the calisthenics that ended in collapse, even the butt of a rifle brought to bear against the kidneys or in the small of the back, must have seemed tame next to the bloodshed most DIs had known.

If the war had gone well, it is likely that all of this might have gone unchallenged, but by 1969, when Mike Caron reported to Drill Instructors School at the Recruit Training Depot on Parris Island, the home front was beginning to question the "victories" overseas. As the cost mounted, opposition grew. Soon society was taking a hard look at the military, not only on the battlefield, but at stateside training centers too. At Parris Island, regimental monitors—"spies," the Hats called them—were assigned to roam the base and report on what they witnessed. Headquarters wanted its drill instructors to be tough, but with an antiwar electorate now sensitive to any form of abuse, it could not tolerate violence.

One day the spies turned in one of Mike's fellow Hats. The man, a fifteen-year veteran with a tour of combat, had slapped a recruit on the shoulder to get him moving and had been charged with maltreatment. The Corps busted him from Staff Sergeant, E-6 on the pay scale, to Private, E-1. A short time later the monitors got Mike.

He, too, they said, had mishandled a dawdler, grabbing him by the arm and shoving him along. "At that point," Caron remembered, "we couldn't even yell at them in the mess hall because it might give them indigestion."

The infraction drew a warning, but Caron had had enough. "I thought, 'Wow! Wait a minute. I worked awfully hard for these stripes and I'd just as soon not lose them.' So I looked for a way out. I said to myself, 'I gotta get off the drill field 'cause they're watching me and if I stay I'm gonna get shafted.' "

He had signed on for a three-year tour; reassignment was all but impossible.

"The older DIs told me, 'Go down and see the regimental shrink. Have him get you off the drill field. It's probably the only way you're gonna get off with all your stripes.' So I did, I played the game. The shrink said, 'What seems to be the problem, Sergeant?' I said, 'I have no problem, sir. I just like to beat recruits.' 'Oh my gosh,' he goes. 'How's your sex life?' 'Real fine, sir.' Then he says, 'When you were in high school and you got frustrated, what did you do to relieve tension?' 'I worked out harder, sweated harder.' 'Well, how do you get rid of tensions now?' 'I beat recruits, sir.' 'Sergeant, I'm gonna recommend that you be relieved of your duties.' 'Aye, aye, sir, but do I get to keep my stripes?' 'Yes, you do, but you're off the drill field.' 'Aye, aye, sir.' "

After that he joined an air wing at New River, North Carolina, as a maintenance chief. He was married by then, to Pat, a girl from upstate New York he had met on leave. They had a baby, Melissa, their first. Soon the bills began to mount. He pushed for a promotion and raise, but when he appeared before his commanding officer, he was told that rank had been frozen. Then came the clincher. He received transfer orders to Okinawa—without his family— and the hard-core, career-type, gung ho, spit-and-polish U.S. Marine resigned.

He came home, back to Connecticut, to a string of jobs across a string of years: a line worker in a helicopter factory, the manager of a gas station franchise, a superintendent in an apartment complex, a man-Friday for a land developer, a sales supervisor for a garage door company, and, finally, a salesman, then manager-trainee, for the tire company.

In each situation he made the same small speech to his boss: "If at any time you feel that I am not the individual that you need for the job, don't ever be embarrassed. Just tell me and I'll make room for somebody else. And if at any time I feel I'm uncomfortable, I'll give you plenty of time to find somebody."

The changes—brought on by layoffs, closings, corruption, irreconcilable differences—often worried his wife, Pat, but Mike, as always, was unafraid: "She would say, 'We have a baby. We have a baby.' So I'd come back,'What's the problem?' 'What are we gonna do?' she'd say. 'I'm gonna go out and get work,' I'd answer. 'Well,' she'd go, 'what are you gonna work?' 'I don't know, but I know that I can do anything.' "

The waitress brought us coffee. Mike fished a cigarette from his breast pocket. He said he rarely thought about the war, had put it behind him, but he remembered Bob Hagan, all right, especially at Bridge 28.

"Oh, yeah, that night on the hill. Sure. He was just . . . just sitting there. He really didn't want to play anymore."

So, I'd been right. But what about leaving him? How did Hagan get back?

He took a sip of coffee and thought for a moment.

After the enemy sprang the ambush, Mike said, he led a group of stragglers down a path to a point where the hill became a straight drop, perhaps twenty or thirty feet, to the road below. He ordered two men to make their way to the road below and set up as a rear guard. Then he helped the stragglers negotiate the precipice and sheer grade. All at once it occurred to him that someone had been left behind and just then, one of the men, he was not sure who, emerged from the shadows above him.

The man said that the lieutenant was "frozen" back up the path and that help would be needed to move him. Caron ambled up the hill—"really without thinking, just like I was going out for a pack of cigarettes"—and found Hagan.

"Seems to me there was somebody with the lieutenant.

The best I can remember was just kind of grabbing the lieutenant by the arm—'C'mon, let's go, we gotta go,' I said—and more or less just kind of giving him a tug and helping him back down the hill.''

Who was the man who'd come out of the shadows and who was the one who had stayed with Hagan? Caron couldn't remember. I told him it was important. I wanted to know if I'd left a man to die.

"I think you'd have a hard time convincing me of that," he said. "If it was a case where you had decided, 'I've had enough of this, you're on your own,' you would have come down the hill to the road and gone [silently] back to the perimeter. Look, there were things happening: boom, boom, boom. When you sit down and think about it later, I'm sure you could probably rationalize it any way you wanted, write the ending that you want to write.''

(7)

The boy's name has long since left me, but he was among the first of my comrades—I'm sure of that—for he was a fisherman.

One day the two of us stumbled on a spot near an old mill that had long since gone to seed. A part of the foundation, a flat slab of concrete, had settled at the water's edge and we perched there to loll and fish. It was a perfect spot: the stream eddied into a pool; a grove of maples and oaks and thick understory screened us from sight. We caught brown trout and painted turtles. Day after day, we went back, from sunup till the light turned the water blue, fishing and filling the woods with our wild chatter.

My first stepfather said he fished, but only in the deep water, nowhere else. One Saturday before dawn he took me out on one of the ocean charters that sailed from Brooklyn's Sheepshead Bay. He was an ironhanded man. Perhaps that is why I disliked his style of fishing as well. It always reeked of chum buckets, diesel oil, and scotch whiskey. I found no fraternity there. One summer he took flight from my mother and their five children. After that I never again went after red porgies or saltwater blues.

Not long after Beth and I were married, I met my most faithful fishing partner, "the Mick," as his daughter called him. Every summer we fished the waters of the north country: Point Salubrious, the Black River, Chaumont Bay.

Out we went twice a day looking for that perfect southwest wind to carry us across the ridges and deep-water pools where the small-mouth bass like to gather. We'd take along soft drinks, crackers, and cheese and drift from breakfast till dark.

The promise of such days always brought me back. It did not matter whether the fish were biting or not. I went north to be with the Mick. We never missed a summer together on those green bays off Lake Ontario, probably never will. Our history is whole; there are no breaks in the long line of friendship.

I met the Mick my first day at Guffin Bay, the place where my in-laws had their summer cottage. I was sunning myself on the lawn next to the porch when he wandered into the yard, a tall man with a crewcut. He was slightly stooped and, with long legs and long arms, a bit ungainly. He shoved his hands deep into his back pockets and faced the water for a moment. The wind was blowing gently from the southwest.

"Hear you're a fisherman," he said. "Wanna go out?"

I put my book down on the grass. "Okay."

"Well, c'mon then—get your pole." Just like that. No warmups, no preliminaries.

We got on, right from the start.

The Mick was fifty years old in that, the summer of 1972. He owned a small liquor store and a bowling alley in Watertown, a self-made man well-established among his neighbors. I was twenty-four at the time, a newspaper man just getting started.

He had grown up poor, one of seven children of the town junk man. After high school he was drafted into the Army and fought in France in World War II. He came home to a clerk's job at the local air-brake company and to Helen, his wife. Helen's father, a businessman, offered to help the Mick take over a failing liquor store that was up for sale. The Mick rebuilt the business, then, the year we met, acquired the bowling alley, which was also faltering, and dug in all over again.

He had a talent for fixing things: broken-down engines, badly run businesses, younger men who had gotten off track.

I don't think that Mick ever meant to be my father; he had two sons of his own: huge, strapping athletes. But across the years, I sometimes used him as a model. He was a natural shepherd and counselor. We built a dock together, installed a water heater, fixed a pump and winch. I thought I knew a thing or two about carpentry until I met the Mick. He even changed the way I held a hammer. Like other men, he added to the figure I made of myself, the shape whose form was constantly being refashioned.

The Mick never dissembled. I always knew where he stood, could always approach him. We talked of losses and gains: troubles with kin, troubles over money, troubles from the past. For the most part, we just shared the silence, two men out on the water waiting for the bass to strike.

One year at our favorite spot near Henderson Harbor— "the silos," we called it—the Mick began to talk about his war. It was our fourth or fifth summer together. I did not know, until then, that he was a veteran, shot in the head during the Allies' push through France in the summer of 1944. I cannot say why he revealed that to me. I think he knew I, too, had heard the guns and smelled the smoke, but back then I never spoke of such things.

At all events, one day, drifting by the silos, he came out with it—the wound, the recuperation, the homecoming—then retreated back into the silence and never spoke of war again. I think I'd always known the Mick was different. There was something ineffable that set him apart from the other fishermen on our shore. I finally understood why, from the moment he first wandered into my yard, he seemed so familiar.

EIGHT

"YOU CAN'T MAKE
AN OMELET WITHOUT
BREAKING SOME EGGS"

A few weeks after Bridge 28, as we rested at an observation post outside Ca Lu, Golf Company acquired a new commander, David Nelson Buckner, Captain of Marines.

The Skipper was twenty-six years old, a "Soldier of the Sea," as career officers often called themselves. From the late spring to the early fall of 1968, I was his radioman. Most of that time we were tethered together, sometimes night and day, by the three feet of black cord that stretched from his handset to the transmitter on my back.

At first it was all business between us, an E-4 doing the bidding of an O-3. Then one day I heard him reciting "The Screw Guns" and I came back with "Gunga Din." After that we grew close, unusually so for a corporal and a captain.

We played cribbage and back-alley bridge, traded stories, talked late into the night. We worked well together. On the trail, after a long march, I dug our hole and put up our rations while he checked the perimeter and set the defense. We became partners; we became friends.

And yet, though he was a comrade, he was the commander, too. On his word we withdrew or pressed a fight. On his order some men went home and some to their grave. As close as we became, I never forgot that.

Dave Buckner took control of Golf Company at Observation Post Texas, two bald, dusty knolls off Route 9, a few miles east of Bridge 28. We were gun-shy, still reeling from the bridge, when he came aboard, but he brooked no slack. We were his first combat command and this young captain with the gimlet eye and the long black handlebar mustache desperately wanted to prove himself.

He got off, however, to an unhappy start. One especially hot, dry day, a few weeks after he arrived, the company ran short of water. (Unlike the Army, which always seemed well-supplied, the Marines, a much smaller service attached to the Navy, usually got short shrift—never enough ammo, food, or water. Our only surfeit, we used to joke, was the enemy. God knows there were enough gooks.) Toward the end of the day, the sole source of water for more than a hundred men was a small Lister bag outside the Skipper's bunker. And he refused to let the men line up. He likely was husbanding that water, lest resupply fail a second day, but the men believed he was holding it back to demonstrate his authority. In either case, his order made him a marked man.

Then came the fight for Hill 174. One morning in early summer, Golf received orders to ascend a hill—174 on the map—near the Demilitarized Zone, a dangerous strip of land by the Ben Hai River just south of the 17th parallel. The DMZ was supposed to be a neutral no-man's land, but its neutrality was regularly violated by both sides, especially by the enemy, who massed there in regimental strength.

Hill 174, often called "The Three Sisters" for its three ascending ridges, was the highest point that close to the river and the DMZ; from the crest of the hill, we could see north to the enemy's staging points, and from the same spot, the enemy could see south to our main bases and patrol routes, a field of view some 270 degrees wide.

American bombers regularly pounded the hill, but the enemy had constructed a series of sheltered footpaths on its slopes, trails set down into the ground about three to four feet and covered with a canopy of brush. It was on one of these trails that Golf Company made its ascent that morning.

The climb was hard and hot, but Buckner kept pushing the lead squad. He had no reason to expect contact—there had been nothing ominous in the intelligence reports that morning—but he was eager nonetheless. And then, suddenly, the point called back that it had come upon a bomb crater with a tunnel dug into its side. Beside a path leading to the crater, the men had spotted fresh feces. And now, exploring the mouth of the tunnel, they found a pot of rice cooking over a fire. Someone had left his breakfast, in a hurry. Buckner sprinted forward with me in tow.

As he explored the tunnel, which was too low and narrow for me to enter with a radio strapped to my back, I surveyed the crater, a yawning conical hole some twenty-five yards across and perhaps twelve to fifteen feet deep at its lowest point. I climbed the incline to a point on the lip facing west along one of the three ridges. I was alone for the moment. The men in the lead squad along with the Skipper and the artillery officer had disappeared into the tunnel. It was a clear day with little wind, almost peaceful when the shooting began.

The men from the north fought fiercely and it was not long before the bomb crater, which became Golf's command post, began to fill with the wounded. A man we called "Limey," a college student from England who had enlisted, was killed in the first volley. His friend, Tom Brown, a scout and interpreter, was wounded trying to talk one of the enemy into surrender. The artillery officer—we called him Snuffy Smith, my partner in a running game of chess—took some shrapnel in the arm. Into the bomb crater came a wounded Marine from the Third Platoon and another from the First. Corpsmen dragged the worst cases to the bottom

of the crater. "Oh, Mama!" one of the men yelled. "Mama
. . . Mama . . . I'm gonna die." And a minute later he did.

Buckner called for air support and the jets came screaming in; an F-100 made a napalm run so low and close to the
crater, the air around us filled with fire. Now spotter planes
were overhead, looking for the enemy. One of them passed
to the north side of the Three Sisters, the side closest to the
Ben Hai River.

"Goddamn!" the pilot shouted into his radio. "There's a
battalion of gooks coming right out of the DMZ."

Buckner was grinning. Here, facing him, was a rare opportunity, an infantry officer's great dream. He held the peak
and military crest of a hill and, below him, his enemy was
massing for an attack. The helicopters that had come in to
take out the wounded had resupplied him with water and
ammunition. One had even dropped barbed wire. Yes, it
was getting dark; yes, he had come to the hill undermanned;
yes, he was taking casualties.

"But I'm in what I know is a damn good position," he
told himself. "I've got a resupply of ammo. I'm in range of
every friendly artillery battery in northern I-Corps. I can
get flare ships up all night. Those little peckerheads are
going to come for us. Let them come. I can literally stack
them up like cordwood. You're not going to get many
opportunities like this, the crème de la crème of land warfare: make them do all the work, you just mow 'em down.
To be in the Goddamn driver's seat at last—what a golden
opportunity."

He said all of this on the radio to the battalion commander, a plump pink colonel. The colonel was holed up
safely with the rest of the battalion on the south side of the
Three Sisters. He was, by some accounts, a timid man who
planned to spend only enough months at war to "get his
ticket punched," advance his career. I knew the man's
radio operators and they used to complain that he made
them carry a canvas and aluminum field stool so he could
rest his tired feet and mop his fleshy forehead with a towel.

Buckner's proposal made the pink colonel nervous: Golf
would be outnumbered six to one, perhaps more; the battle

would be fought in the dark; one attempt to reinforce the company had already failed in the difficult terrain; and the company commander was untested in battle. This "golden opportunity" could easily turn into a bloody misadventure. Body counts cut both ways and the battalion commander did not want the wrong kind on his record.

"But, sir . . . But, sir . . ." Buckner was begging now and he did not care who heard him. He was, as he later put it, "absolutely ripshit that the colonel couldn't see the golden opportunity being presented him." The Corps' mission, after all—indeed, the grand strategy of the entire war—was not to capture ground or pacify hostile provinces; it was to kill as many of the enemy as possible, run up the body count, make them pay a price far dearer than the one they exacted from us. And here was a chance to "stack them up like cordwood," for surely the soldiers from the north, hoping to overwhelm a smaller force, would come rushing up the Three Sisters in the dark and would keep coming until they had won or could no longer fight.

There were several survivors of Bridge 28 in that crater on top of that hill and they did not see the pending engagement as serendipitous. It may have been a chance to execute a textbook maneuver, but as the French had learned, this was a place that made a mockery of the manual of war. The men who had been lucky enough to walk away from Bridge 28 wanted no part of what the new company commander was now proposing. To us, he was a madman with a suicidal plan.

The colonel stood firm: the company was to withdraw, immediately. Buckner, cursing and growling, ordered his platoon commanders to disengage, and after several hours of trading lead, down the Three Sisters we went.

So I was wary of the Skipper. He was a professional, the Corps was his career. I was a civilian, temporarily in uniform. He hankered for a fight. I'd already been blooded.

For him, the war was a job, an assignment, and he looked on the consequences of doing that job—the sure knowledge that he was sending some of his men to their deaths and others to a life of disability and pain—with a certain fatalism: war simply had its cost. My position was equally direct: I didn't want my name on a government telegram.

Thus we coexisted, tethered by three feet of wire cord. We slept under the same poncho, ate from the same cans, ducked incoming shells chest to chest in the same small hole. Leashed like that, one man quickly comes to know another.

He was a bantam, not more than five feet, ten inches, perhaps 140 pounds. His dark hair was brush cut, three-quarters of an inch on top, skintight on the sides. His dark eyes were slits; he peered at a man as if he were trying to penetrate his woolly thoughts. The face was egg-shaped, with a chin that jutted out and curved up, a belligerent promontory. Most of all, there was his mustache, thick and black with rolled, waxed handles that circled neatly up his cheeks. It was an ideal ornament for a captain of Marines, sinister and malevolent.

He was stubborn and he was fit. He could out-hike any man in the outfit and often, to his radioman's dismay, tried to prove it. His weapon of choice was the single-barrel shotgun loaded with double-ought buckshot; this instead of the common-issue M-16A1, which was lighter, but less effective at close range. And from all appearances, that was where he wanted to be. In the beginning he often patrolled on point. For a company commander, this was a reckless and foolish show of bravado, but it kept the men off balance and thus gave him an edge.

He was not, however, without a sense of humor. He called the enemy "those little gooners" or "peckerheads" as if they were a comic annoyance instead of a deadly nemesis. And he enjoyed practical jokes: when one of his lieutenants neglected to clean a latrine, the Skipper took a torch to it; when one of the men caught a lizard, the Skipper had it for lunch.

On the march, he knew his business: tactics, technology, above all, leadership. One day in the late summer of 1968 we again ran short of water. This time resupply was critical, for we were pursuing the enemy, not holed up in cool bunkers. As the last of the water gave out, the Skipper stopped the company in a circle of trees and brush around a clearing. Soon, under the equinoctial sun, the men began to wilt. One by one, the victims of heatstroke and heat exhaustion were tagged and carried into the clearing to be medevaced. Buckner roamed the lines; it would be dark soon, he said, cooler then. "Men can go without water a long time. Three days—isn't that right? C'mon now."

Thirst, however, can be as enervating as fear. Buckner spotted a young lieutenant new to the bush. The man was crossing the clearing and was headed toward one of the helicopters. On his flak jacket was a medevac tag. Buckner rushed after him.

"Where are you going, Lieutenant?"

"Can't make it, sir," the man said. "Can't."

"What's the problem?"

"Sir . . . I—"

"You're thirsty? Right?"

"Yes, sir," said the brown bar.

The Skipper's stare cut the man deep. "Get back to your platoon, you peckerhead." Then he shoved him to the ground.

After that, the wait for the water went easier.

By the end of the summer, we'd become friends. I helped him write love letters to his wife; he taught me how to direct artillery fire. Just before Labor Day he called me aside. He was sending me out of the country for thirty days to a training school in Okinawa. The course was nonsense—I knew how to read a map and deploy a squad of men—but Okinawa was an island of hot showers, thick steaks, and cold beer. It was the Skipper's way of saying "Thank you," and, for a while at least, taking me out of harm's way.

A week after I hit Okinawa, I came down with malaria—which had been incubating in my system for weeks—and landed in a hospital with high fever and convulsions. The cure took fifty-three days, then a doctor with apologetic eyes stamped my file "FFFD," fit for full duty, and seventy-two hours later I was right back at war.

When I got to Ca Lu, the jumping-off point for the bush, Golf Company had a new commander, Dan Hitzelberger. Dave Buckner was now the battalion's supply and logistics officer. He was holed up in a moldy hooch of plywood and canvas right there at the base.

I was surprised to find him at a job in the rear. He was a warrior, a Captain of Marines, not a timorous office pogue. And then I heard about a battle near a place called the Rock Pile, in September, where eighteen men from Golf Company had been killed and a large number wounded—Squeaky Williamson among them. The men told me that something had happened there between the Skipper and a superior officer. I could not get the details, but I knew it would have taken more than a disagreement over tactics to make Dave Buckner give up his command.

Three months passed before I saw him again. It was mid-December, just a few weeks before my tour was scheduled to end. I was still the company radioman. The new Skipper was a decent and able commander, but I did not serve him well. I had been at war more than a year, and the closer I got to my rotation date, the more tentative and distracted I became. Finally, Hitzelberger had had enough. As the company was getting ready to jump off from the rear on a rescue mission, he asked his other radioman to summon Buckner to the airstrip. Soon the Skipper appeared.

"Listen, Buck," Hitzelberger said, "my company radioman isn't worth a shit anymore. You want 'im?"

"Yeah," Buckner said, grinning at me. "I'll take 'im. I need a garbageman."

And just like that, my part in the fighting was over. I spent my last twenty days in country hauling barrels of brown, viscous slop. On my second Christmas Day in the war, I played cards with Dave Buckner. The enemy twice rocketed the airstrip that month, but I kept close to the slit trenches and green sandbag shelters. Then one morning after chow, during the first week of January 1969, the Skipper called me to his hooch.

"What's up?"

"Pack your gear," he said. "You're going home."

The Chelsea section of London, S.W.3, runs north from the River Thames and, as a point of reference, has as its fulcrum the Albert Bridge. Here, hard by the gray river, lived some of the city's best-known artists and literati—D. G. Rossetti, Whistler, Swift, George Eliot, Oscar Wilde, Henry James, and that celebrator of the spirit and searcher of heroes, Thomas Carlyle. In 1834 Carlyle and his wife, the former Jane Baillie Welsh, moved into a modest, three-story brick row house at 24 Cheyne Row, roughly half a block from the Thames. No one can say why they selected Cheyne Row. It was then, as it is now, one of the smallest and most modest streets in the borough. Perhaps the relative isolation and quiet suited them. Carlyle is known to have liked the odor of ships and tar that came off the river.

When Dave Buckner was posted to London in 1983 as a Marine logistics officer at Naval headquarters, he moved to Cheyne Row, to a tiny but hospitable basement flat in the house next to the one preserved as Carlyle's. The Skipper inherited the flat from the man he had replaced; the landlady was happy to have another Marine officer; they were so neat and so quiet, "nice boys," she said. And David was happy to be living on Cheyne Row, with its flagstone sidewalks, black wrought-iron fences, and window boxes with pansies spilling over the sides.

The flat was down a flight of steps from the street. It had two main rooms: a bedroom in back, not much bigger than an officer's quarters aboard ship, and a sitting room in front, half again as big, with white walls, two beige couches, a coffee table, a fireplace. Attached to the bedroom was a small loo with a bathtub. Off the sitting room was a kitchenette.

In this trim space, David assembled his favorite collectibles, a trove gathered from forays through the city's antique shops and auction houses: huge copper pots, antique wooden tools, prints and lithographs from the early nineteenth century set in rosewood or cherry-wood frames. On the floor of the front room was a thick black-and-white Greek shepherd's rug, which, during one especially sunny week in the early fall of 1984 served as my bunk.

The sinister mustache was gone now and with it the air of belligerence. The hair was longer, parted on the left and just beginning to gray; he had even allowed a small forelock to grow. Age had softened the cheekbones and that pugnacious chin. The eyes were not nearly so penetrating as I remembered. He wore glasses, wire-rims, even looked a little scholarly. When he fetched me at Heathrow Airport, he had on faded blue jeans, a blue windbreaker, and hiking boots. But new look or no, he was still a Marine, a lieutenant colonel now, forty-two years old, nine years from mandatory retirement, a father of three and three weeks' divorced.

We spent five days and nights together. We sat in his flat and talked for long hours over a cup of tea or a bottle of vintage port. Each morning we made a sortie into a different quarter of the city, exploring his favorite shops and haunts. On one such outing, we walked some ten miles side by side. All that was missing was the tether of a radio cord. Now, at the end of the day, instead of coffee brewed in tin cans, we shared two pints of bitter and a wedge from a wheel of Stilton cheese served up at the King's Head and Eight Bells, a warm pub at the end of Cheyne Row.

"I'm glad you came," he said. "I'm glad you made it."

When he returned from war in the spring of 1969, David Buckner was assigned as a leadership instructor at the Marine Corps' Basic School, the preparatory academy for newly commissioned officers at Quantico, Virginia. Quantico, as it was called, was the cradle of the officer corps, the place where young lieutenants learned loyalty, obedience, proficiency—in short, all the ways of a military life. (It should here be noted that although Dave Buckner went through Quantico as well, he had long before been exposed to its lessons. His father was a Marine, Col. Jean Buckner, a polite and modest man, when I met him, who had retired from the Corps in 1962 after twenty-seven years of service.

The colonel had fought in two wars and served in half a dozen posts, but never, in all those years, as Dave remembers it, did he come home with vainglory in his wake. In fact, if he wanted his son to follow him, he never said so. He had his stories, of course; what Marine doesn't? But only once, as his son was about to embark for the battlefield, did he sit down with David and talk about his lethal business and the fine line between bravery and fear. "Number one, don't try to be a hero," he said. "And number two, keep a tight asshole.")

Leadership at Quantico was taught by example, sometimes from the lights of old campaigns—such dauntless luminaries as Lewis B. "Chesty" Puller, the winner of five Navy Crosses—sometimes from the conflict at hand. The protagonists of our war had the advantage of being fresh from the field. Theirs were not the dusty lessons of history. They still had mud on their boots, still carried the moldy smell of the bush. Their testimony animated the abstractions of the textbooks, made real the weight of command, the awful responsibility of sending men to do battle.

"You're gonna get people killed; you're gonna get people wounded. It's an absolute surety," Dave Buckner lectured the subalterns.

Casualties were part of the profession of arms, the consequence of unsheathing a sword or aiming a gun. They could not expect to take ground, he told them, or hold it without spilling blood.

"To be quite crude about it," he said, "you can't make an omelet without breaking some eggs."

We were up early my second day in London, down to King's Road, then up to the Underground station at Sloane Square. King's Road, a narrow two-lane street some twelve to fifteen feet across, is Chelsea's thoroughfare. In the 1960s and 1970s, when the borough was a haunt for the smart set, King's Road became a boulevard of pop culture. Some of the oaken pubs were transformed into swinging watering holes. Boutiques appeared; basements became wine shops. And ever since, in one form or another, trendsetters have made their way there.

"Hey, mate, wanna take a picture with me? Fifty pence." He had a pimpled face, runny nose, and chartreuse hair that had been fashioned into a stiff cockscomb. "The flora and fauna of King's Road," the Skipper called the bizarre dandies, the punk-rock panhandlers, who staked out the street.

Each weekday, on the walk to work and home again, he had to run their gauntlet and it disgusted him. He had spent half his life training young men for serious work.

"There . . ." He eyed their rainbow ranks. "There goes the flower of British youth."

We rode the Underground to Charing Cross, then changed to the Northern line. Before long we were in Camden Town, a neighborhood in the city's northern quarters famous for its open-air markets. Not far from the Regent Canal, in what was once a railroad staging area, peddlers and craftsmen had established a great city of a flea market. Hundreds of stalls, covered overhead with tarpaulins, sheets, and blankets, stood side by side, back to back, row upon row. The perimeter of this city was on slightly higher ground than its center; one descended into it as if entering a sunken labyrinth. The passageways ran in many different directions and it was easy to become quickly lost. Even the Skipper, who usually knew his ground, stopped often to take a bearing.

It was late afternoon when we returned to the flat on Cheyne Row and went around to the King's Head and Eight Bells for a supper of meat pie and bitter. Afterward, we settled down in his front room across the Greek shepherd's rug. The Skipper poured two glasses of port, then lit himself a cigar.

All commanders, at all levels, are in large measure removed from the men in their charge. Even those in the trenches, who share the danger, who face the bullets, bayonets, and shells, never really come to "know" the men who fall around them. The professional cannot afford such intimacy. He must be detached, democratic in the choice of those he sends to die. I have often wondered whether casualties were real to men like Xenophon, Wellington, "Black Jack" Pershing. One historian says that commanders of the modern era felt the stress of battle and loss so keenly, they sometimes broke down—suffered nervous stomachs, heart failure, blackouts. But I wondered. Could a professional really connect? Feel a part of the circle? It was not his billet that isolated him, it was his business, so deliberate, so grim. "You can't make an omelet without breaking some eggs."

And yet. And yet.

In the early fall of 1968, while I was in the hospital with malaria, Golf Company was ordered to ascend a small summit 15 kilometers northwest of Route 9, near a place called the Rock Pile. The assault began at mid-morning. More than 130 men climbed up that hill. Some fourteen hours later, less than eighty retreated in the dark. Eighteen men were killed, twenty-two, Squeaky among them, wounded.

The battle near the Rock Pile sounded as savage as the battle at the bridge. The Skipper thought it his greatest failure and, at Quantico after the war, said as much to his leadership class.

"I told those young lieutenants—it was a particularly painful memory for me—that I kept punching up against that hill and against it and against it and I kept losing people. It was getting dark and I knew we would never take the hill at night, no matter how hard we punched it. It was time to stop, to regroup and give it a shot the next day. That was the first time as a Marine officer I failed to do something I set out to do. But it would have been sinful pride to continue that battle and get more and more people killed."

That, however, was only half the story.

His advance stalled, his men exhausted, the Skipper ordered a withdrawal. With one of his senior sergeants at his side, he guarded the company's rear as his men made their way down a razorback. At the bottom he reported to a senior officer at the battalion command post.

The officer who took his report was a careerist, more politician than Marine, filled with ambition and caution.

"What happened?" the careerist demanded.

"Sir, we punched it as hard as we could, but we've had a lot of men hit and, with darkness, I couldn't see taking more casualties."

"But you didn't *take* the hill. You didn't take it! How the hell am I going to explain *that* to regiment?"

It is likely that the death of eighteen men would have been explanation enough, but the careerist was bent on covering himself. And it was at this moment that David Nelson Buckner seemed to step out of character.

Many kinds of men spend their lives in uniform: brave and craven, wise and empty-headed, careerists and cold-blooded killers. Marines are taught to ignore these shades, especially in combat. A professional follows his orders not because he holds those who issue them in high regard; he steps smartly because obedience is part of the code. Like them or not, he gives his betters their legal due.

What is more, all officers at war know they must live with loss: "You can't make an omelet . . ." They are trained to kill—killing is the aim of all that target practice, all those hours of drill and lectures on leadership. But sometimes, when the killing begins and the bodies on both sides begin to stack up like cordwood, something happens even to the most disciplined of men. At moments like this, when the dead are many and the weight of loss is great, even a professional is staggered by the cost. His humanity wells up, comes pouring out of him, and he begins to reel. Such a man is not out of character; he is simply acting the way all reasonable men should act in the face of such slaughter and brutality, such obscenity on the soul.

Dave Buckner swung the barrel of his shotgun forward and pointed it at the careerist's stomach. He had been angry at the man since morning. When the assault was first mounted, he had asked this superior for artillery fire and air power to support the attack, but the careerist, not wanting to risk the disapproval of his betters, refused. *He* was going to demonstrate his toughness, take the hill the hard way, from the bottom up, with riflemen, just Marines. Now, not only had that policy failed, it had been profligate. A platoon of good men had been lost. And suddenly regiment was asking what had happened, who was responsible.

"Well, Captain, what am I gonna tell 'em?"

Dave Buckner put his finger on the trigger—the careerist turned ashen—but he did not send the hammer home and spill the sycophant's blood. His position, however, was clear: the Skipper stood with us, a comrade, as full of fury and grief as any other man. He could not have sung the dead a better song of mourning or given the living a more eloquent apostrophe of loyalty and love.

In November 1972 David Buckner went back to war. The fighting was almost over by then. Most Americans had been pulled out of the war zone; the rest would follow in the spring. The Skipper was assigned as an adviser to the local forces. *Dai-wi-rao,* they called him, "Captain Mustache."

By February 1973 he had been reassigned to an infantry company at Camp Hansen, Zukeran, Okinawa. Here, on a U.S. military base, surrounded by his professional kin, he fought a different kind of war against an enemy more insidious than any he had ever known.

The discontent that had fractured society at home—the feeling of ideals betrayed and systems gone corrupt that had sent great mobs crashing against the gates of government—had dislocated the military as well. During the last years of the war, in several army units in particular, men openly challenged authority, refused orders, even assaulted their officers.

Young black men in uniform, inflamed by the racism and bigotry they encountered in their comrades, and encouraged by civil rights protests back home, began to band together. This self-segregation threatened to expose as false the foundations of camaraderie and brotherhood on which the Corps was built. Combat, of course, mitigated some of this. Black or white, when a bullet or a piece of shrapnel ripped them open, men bled the same color. But in the rear areas, where they did not need to rely on one another as they did in battle, there was little esprit de corps. Blacks went one way, whites another. (In January 1969 on my way out of country, I spent a night at the company office and headquarters in the rear at Quang Tri. The racial oaths and slander in the transient tent bristled with such menace, I slept with a loaded handgun at my side, something I had never done in the field. Later, back home at bases like Camp Lejeune, the hostility played itself out in lynch-like mobs.)

Some of this likely was the excess animus, the violence and bitterness, left from the war, but much of the trouble came from those men who had never been near a battlefield.

By the time the war ended, the face of the Corps had changed. The barracks were filled with young misfits—criminals and dropouts who, in the face of military manpower shortages, had found a welcome in the ranks.

"I think every company commander in garrison on Okinawa right after the war, if he was lucky, was one step ahead of a riot every day," the Skipper said. "If he was unlucky, he was right in the middle of one."

The Skipper commanded Alpha Company, First Battalion, Fourth Marines, roughly 140 men. Most were new enlistees who had not seen combat, but were belligerents nonetheless. "These young Marines had grown up watching on television as college kids waved enemy flags and Jane Fonda visited the enemy's homeland posing behind antiaircraft guns," the Skipper said. "They joined the Marine Corps telling authority to shove it up its ass." Worse, "many of the troops in my command had signed their enlistment contracts reaching through the bars of city jails."

By the Skipper's reckoning, 30 percent of Alpha Company was black. In that number there were many good and loyal Marines, but among them was also a loose group of twenty renegades. These men were not, as the Skipper saw them, social reformers outraged by bigotry. They were thugs ready to exploit racial unrest and determined to undermine Dave Buckner's authority.

This conspiracy, this underground, organized itself along familiar lines; it, too, had a skipper, a gunnery sergeant, and platoon commanders, "a black infrastructure," David called it, that mirrored the official chain of command, the mostly white hierarchy it was trying to usurp. Their strategy, as far as anyone could tell, was to create chaos in the ranks with extortion, threats, and beatings.

"There was a tremendous amount of racial tension in the barracks," David said. "Whites were sleeping with entrenching tools in their hands; they were terrified. Everyone slept in four-man cubicles; a person only really owed his loyalty to himself or at the very most to the people who lived in his cubicle. So there was really a socially unacceptable, militarily unacceptable, situation.

"It was a breakdown in authority and discipline. The NCOs [sergeants and corporals] were afraid of the black troublemakers, so afraid of them they weren't enforcing discipline and respect. We didn't know the troublemakers' ringleader. We code-named this little peckerhead the Spider King, and quite frankly, I set out to destroy him."

The Skipper pushed his NCOs to act, and soon the Spider King's men were being demoted and heavily fined. "All of his soldiers started asking the Spider King why he wasn't doing his bit, why was he just laying around on his bunk and not taking the heat like them," the Skipper said. "Well, I guess the criticism got to be too much for him. One night he and his lieutenants got all drunked up and beat up a white Marine nigh unto death and left him lying in a drainage ditch."

At the hospital, the Skipper interviewed the victim, then returned to the barracks with a list of names and summoned the Spider King's troops. "I told them they were in a heap of trouble and it would behoove them to cooperate with my investigation." And one by one they cracked until only their leader was left. "He immediately wanted a lawyer. I told him he couldn't have one. He said he wasn't going to talk. I told him I wasn't going to ask him any questions. I just wanted to watch him twist."

In the end, twelve men were jailed, the Spider King among them. "Civil rights activists don't beat people with entrenching tools or extort money. Those are the actions of criminals. When I was commissioned an officer, I took an oath to preserve and to protect the Constitution against all enemies, foreign and domestic. To me, they were domestic enemies and I destroyed them.''

As it happened, the Spider King held an important job, a position of trust in the company. He carried secret codes, knew the weekly schedules, helped with the daily flow of men and materiel. He was among those closest to the Skipper; David must have felt especially betrayed when he finally unmasked the man.

"That young stud, the Spider King, he turned out to be my company radio operator—just like you, Michael.''

In January 1974 the Skipper was transferred to Camp Lejeune, North Carolina, as deputy operations officer for the Second Marine Division. In the summer of 1975 he was assigned as a logistics officer to an amphibious squadron attached to the Sixth Fleet and he deployed to the USS *Shreveport*, the flagship of the squadron, for a six-month Mediterranean cruise. Then, in the middle of 1977, headquarters sent him new orders.

Assignments were made on the basis of need—the Corps' need, not the individual's. Sometimes a man was given a choice, often not. This was the way of the professional. During the course of a thirty-year career, an officer was likely to change jobs a dozen times. Postings came from "monitors" in the Corps' Officer Assignment Branch. If a billet needed to be filled, a computer cranked out a list of names. A monitor making an assignment was supposed to keep in mind that his brother officers were trying to build a career. As the guidebook said:

You must have a balanced career [combat experience, staff experience and so on]. . . . It is one of the important functions of Marine Corps Headquarters to see that . . . every officer gets assignments designed to develop his potentialities, to give him equal opportunity for advancement, and to qualify him for command. . . .

It is hard to say what particular potentiality the monitors had in mind when they assigned Dave Buckner to a desk in a backwater called the History and Museums Division. The billet, he was told, called for combat experience and writing ability; he had a war record and a degree in journalism from American University.

Rare was the officer who made his reputation behind a desk, especially one cluttered with musty archives. The Corps prized its history, its traditions, but it did not make generals of those it sent to guard the flame.

For four years David Buckner filled the pages of a quarterly historical magazine and wrote a 131-page monograph entitled *A Brief History of the 10th Marines*. Much of the tract was dense, a recitation of names, dates, and places— "The first elements of an all-Latin, five-nation Inter-American Peace Force began to arrive on 25 May. The 6th MEU began reembarkation the next day; Battery E went on board the USS *Wood Country . . ."* and so on—but his sentences were clean and his metaphors unbroken: "The cast of characters had changed in the Dominican Republic since Captains Wise and Fortson had gone ashore from the old *Prairie* some 50 years prior, but the plot had remained the same." Never mind that he, an infantryman, a grunt, the aristocracy of the Corps, was writing about malodorous pack mules, the artillery.

He missed the ports of call and the excitement of landings and maneuvers, but he found a certain challenge in the writing and a kind of contentment in a commonplace life. He and his wife, Jackie, bought a house in Woodbridge, Virginia, and each workday he commuted to his office at the Navy Yard in Washington, D.C. Soon he had befriended several of his new shipmates and before long had settled in for a desk-bound cruise.

In 1980 he again became eligible for promotion, this time to lieutenant colonel.

Promotion never comes automatically. . . . Determination of who is best fitted for promotion is accomplished by boards of senior officers, known as "selection boards". . . . Officers who are best fitted are selected for advancement, while those least fitted are passed over and must ultimately retire.

The Skipper seemed well qualified to wear the silver oak-leaf clusters of a light colonel: he had two tours in a war zone and two at sea; he had commanded in the field and had worked in logistics and administration; he had served in Asia, in Europe, and at home; he was thirty-five years old, in good shape, an officer of many talents who carried himself well.

To determine if a man was "fitted for promotion," his promotion board looked at his "fitness reports." These reports, a log of a man's performance, were drafted by his various commanders during his various tours, usually at six-month intervals or at the tour's end.

Fitness reports present a composite judgment of your military character and relative merits compared with other officers of the same rank. . . . The suitability of an officer for future assignments, selection, or retention is based in large degree on the evaluations made by his reporting seniors.

Since these files carry such weight, since they, in fact, can make or break a man's career, the senior officers who compose them are warned to

Guard particularly against the attitude of the moment. . . . Remember that you evaluate sustained performance, not odd, uncharacteristic events that deviate from the trends you have consistently observed.

All of which, of course, recalls that day in September 1968 when a certain young captain, brooding over his losses, ran up against an indifferent careerist bent on covering his behind. In filling out his fitness reports on David Buckner, the careerist made no mention of the shotgun or the captain's baneful intent. He knew the guidelines; guarded against the "attitude of the moment." But he knew how to raise a red flag, too.

Under "Remarks," he wrote, "Captain Buckner is overcoming a tendency to be inflexible when faced with decisions of higher authority not to his liking."

It was a deft stab. In so many words, he had accused the Skipper of disobedience, but by couching it in the ameliorating phrase "is overcoming a tendency," the criticism, officially, could not be considered a derogatory comment and thus the Skipper did not have the right to rebut the report with headquarters.

The effect of all this was devastating: "To say I was overcoming this tendency, that's kind of like saying the guy's trying to stop being a cocksucker."

The report did not affect his promotion to major in 1974 because a great number of billets were open and men were needed to fill them. But the hierarchy of the Corps, like that of most organizations, resembled a pyramid. The higher the rank, the smaller the number of spaces and, therefore, the more selective and inquisitive the promotion board became. Now it read way back in a man's record.

It was roughly mid-morning in the spring of 1980 when the news came down from headquarters. The Skipper was at his desk at the Historical Division. The wife of a colleague worked at headquarters and had agreed to call her husband when the list of new lieutenant colonels was posted. The list went up around 10 A.M. The telephone rang on the colleague's desk. The man listened for a few moments, then looked at the Skipper and rolled his fist over with his thumb to the ground.

David Nelson Buckner was a "passover."

The Skipper said nothing. He left his desk, made his way downstairs to his locker, and changed from his uniform into running clothes. The weather had been fair that week; the cherry blossoms were in bloom. From the Navy yard he ran northeast, parallel to the Anacostia River, first along Water Street, then into Anacostia Park and past Robert F. Kennedy Memorial Stadium, then into the park again and by the National Arboretum, north now along the shore. Running . . . running . . . running. . . . To where he could not say; the river's source, perhaps.

I cannot account for all the events of my second night in London. We set out, by the Skipper's plan, to drink a pint of bitter in every pub in the borough. Three hundred? Five hundred? I stopped counting at six.

"London is so civilized—" David stopped, smiled, finished off another draft. "The map is littered with watering holes."

We began at the Man in the Moon, then went to the Water Rat on Millmans Street.

"How's everything in the White Rat?" the Skipper asked the publican.

"We're starving comfortably, thank you, sir."

In front of the Cadogan Arms, a dozen or so roisterers in two columns made their way down the street. "You can always tell civilians." The Skipper laughed. "They're out of step." And in we went for another pint.

The next morning, Monday, seemed to come especially early. The Skipper, likely dissembling, showed no wear from our wanders. He bounced out of bed, insisted I use the tub first, and, while I bathed, fixed us coffee and toast with marmalade. Then off we went to his office to check his messages and mail.

The walk was roughly three miles, first northeast along King's Road through Belgravia to Eaton Square, two long rows of columned, white-stucco terraces flanking two parkways of green. North of these posh flats and townhouses, past gray cobblestone mews, was Hyde Park Corner with its white-marble memorials to the Royal Artillery and Machine Gun Corps and to the Duke of Wellington. Then north again up South Audley Street to Grosvenor Square, the heart of London's "Little America." On the west side of the square is the American Embassy, a modern, overpowering monolith with a gold eagle looming on top. "I love it," said the Skipper, looking up. "It's not a sitting eagle, it's a screaming eagle." On the north side, in a six-story, block-long, red-brick and Georgian terrace, was U.S. Naval Headquarters, Europe, the building that served Gen. Dwight David Eisenhower in World War II and now housed the bureaucracy in which David worked as a plans and logistics officer.

Marine guards in dress uniforms manned the front door

and lobby. They looked young, much younger than I remembered the comrades of my youth. While the Skipper saw to his chores, I strolled around the corner to Grosvenor Park and Gardens and waited by the statue of Franklin Delano Roosevelt. The memorial faced south, roughly in the direction of Buckingham Palace. Beneath it, at the base of the pedestal near a bed of yellow roses, sat an old man in a tweed cap, feeding the pigeons. Nearby, a nanny with a white wraparound collar pushed a perambulator across the park. It was autumn, but the trees had not yet begun to turn and the boughs of deep green brushing against the Georgian brick on a warm, sunny day gave the city a look of luxury.

When the Skipper was done, we went shopping, first at Burberry's on Haymarket for a green trench coat for me, then to Harrods on Knightsbridge for a box of sweet biscuits to take home. We took the long route back, circling the Mayfair district, first through the bustle and traffic of Oxford Circus, then down Regent Street toward Piccadilly past display windows rich with crystal and silver and porcelain, finally west again through Berkeley Square with its thick sycamores—plane-trees, the Brits call them.

That night, after a dinner of smoked mackerel and Stilton cheese, we walked southeast along the dark gray Thames three-quarters of a mile to an auction house at 71 Lots Road. It was at these sales that the Skipper bought old prints and antique frames. His plan was to hoard this loot for shipment back to the States, where, upon retirement, he would open a store in North Carolina and sell framed prints along with handmade furniture from his own workshop. Future enterprise aside, I suspected that he made those regular trips to Lots Road simply because he enjoyed the contest—hunting the bargain, pressing the bid, carting home the prize.

"Twenty to the gentleman in the blue jumper," said the auctioneer, and the Skipper went to the cashier to claim his trophy, a folder of nineteenth-century prints and lithographs.

Back at Cheyne Row, we spent the rest of the evening on the shepherd's rug sorting through the stack, laughing at the

Victorian ditties on the prints, and lowering, by an honorable measure, the level in a bottle of Napoleon brandy.

He was a passover. There was no hiding it. The list had been posted at headquarters; the news would go out on the wires, the regular message traffic, to all the posts of the Corps. His failure would be public, there for his brother officers to see.

Every morning for two weeks during that spring in 1980, his first thought was, "Goddamn! I got passed over!" He was ashamed of "being judged by a jury of my betters and found not to be equal to my peers. It was hurt. It was shame. It was an absolute kick in the balls."

His father shared the ache: "Don't let it get you down," he told his son.

"I used to want to hide," the Skipper said.

But shame was not the worst of it; he would soon have to leave the Corps. Each rank carried a date for mandatory retirement, a practice that insured a regular renewal of leadership. In theory, the higher a man was promoted, the more able he was and thus the more valuable. One-star generals were allowed to serve thirty years, lieutenant colonels twenty-eight, majors twenty, and so on. Now, in five years' time, the Skipper would be forced to retire. And this, just as the Corps was enjoying a renaissance.

The thugs and thieves that had fouled the ranks in the early 1970s had been flushed from the system. Recruiting standards had been raised; enlisted men were better educated, easier to train, much more loyal. The Marines had new weapons and new tactics. It was, at last, close to the service it was always meant to be: an elite, mobile force able to strike quickly anywhere in the world. The country seemed poised for a move to the right; Ronald Reagan, a flag-waving conservative, had won some important victories in the Presidential primaries and appeared headed for the White House; the defense budget would grow, military shortages would disappear.

"It was a very exciting, vibrant time and I saw myself cheated of it. I wasn't gonna be able to be a Marine anymore. Five years and I'd be out. Once I got past the personal and emotional hurt, it really struck me: Goddamn, I can't be a Marine anymore after 1985. That really pissed me off. I wasn't worried about making a living as a civilian. It was just contemplating the fact that I was gonna have to get out of the Marine Corps. The Marine Corps had been my life since I was seventeen years old. I love the Corps. I love Marines.''

In truth, his first love had been the sea. Twice his family had sailed from the West Coast to Hawaii, where his father had been stationed, and with each passage, he was swept up in the mystique of a seafaring life. He read stories of sail and steam and saw himself ''riding the seven seas with a girl in every port.'' He attended a military high school, St. John's in Washington, D.C., where he grew up, but early on he had made up his mind to go to King's Point, the Merchant Marine Academy.

In 1959, acting on the advice of a family friend who said an enlistment in a reserve unit might help him win an appointment to the Academy, he signed up with the Marine Corps Reserve. The next year, he won a spot at the Point and off he went to its campus near Great Neck, Long Island.

Six months later he had resigned. ''Some three hundred merchant masters were out of work, sitting on the beach in New York City,'' he said. ''I realized that the bottom had just rusted completely out of the Merchant Marines.''

Back home in Washington, a letter arrived from the Marine Corps: as a reservist, he owed the Corps six months' active duty, an obligation that had been deferred by his appointment to a federal academy. He was to report immediately for basic training at Parris Island.

Paying the debt turned out to be a privilege. He was so taken with the Corps that, the next fall, he enrolled in the Marines leadership program at his college, American University. Four years later he was commissioned a second lieutenant.

After infantry assignments at Camp Lejeune and cold-weather training in Norway, he was ordered to report to the Marine detachment aboard the USS *Wasp*, a small aircraft carrier fitted for antisubmarine warfare. In October 1967 he married a twenty-year-old computer keypunch operator from Otis Air Force Base, Jacqueline Homsher, whom he'd met at a social club at nearby Camp Edwards. Then, early in January, with his bride four months' pregnant, he got great news: he was ordered into combat. On May 15 he made his way to the 9th Marines' forward combat base in the valley at Ca Lu and assumed command of Golf Company. He was twenty-six years old, a young professional who had been trained at the best posts in the Corps, a fighting man with courage, common sense, and a talent for leadership. He had arrived in the right place at the right moment; the enemy had never been so strong or so close. A company of infantry waited on his orders. A career was his to make.

He emerged from the spring of 1980, the season of his passover, shamed and disappointed, but not bitter.

"I guess no life is complete without failure," he told himself. "Every experience that you have, good or bad, has some utility in it."

A year later he was passed over again.

The following year he became a three-time passover.

The utility of the experience was getting thin. It appeared certain he would stay a major and, within forty-eight months, be forced out of the Corps.

He was back at Camp Lejeune now, after a tour in Beirut commanding a field support unit. He had worked hard at the assignment, caring for the infantry that had been sent to Beirut to keep the peace. Word of his proficiency with equipment and materiel filtered up to Gen. Al Gray, commander of the division. The Skipper took great pride in this; he had done his duty; passover or no, he was a professional.

One Friday in late March 1983, he left early from his office at Camp Lejeune. When he arrived home, "two of my kids ran up yelling and screaming, laughing and giggling and hugging me. They said they had gotten a call from my command while I was en route. The caller said, 'Tell your daddy he's a lieutenant colonel now.' ''

"Nobody," he told himself, "nobody gets passed over three times and makes it on the fourth time," but a few telephone calls and a little guesswork told him what had happened. The general he had impressed the year before in Beirut, an officer who would go on to become the Commandant of the Corps, was an inquisitive man and wanted to know why an able major was a three-time passover. So he made some inquiries, "orchestrated a few things," and "lo and behold, lightning struck."

"You know what I felt most," the Skipper said, "relief—relief that I didn't have to leave the Marine Corps."

On the Monday after lightning struck, he called headquarters and asked to speak with a monitor. His promotion opened up new venues: Chicago, Albuquerque, sunny Puerto Rico or London, as an amphibious plans officer at U.S. Naval Headquarters in the heart of the city, a sweet plum of a job.

He was sure Jackie would welcome the news—"What woman in her right mind wouldn't want to go to London?" —but on hearing it, her face turned dark. She wasn't going, she said. She wanted a divorce.

They had argued, as most marrieds do, but he had seen no signs of disaffection, the loss of love she now said she had suffered for so long.

She told him that she had planned to ask for a separation when he came back from Beirut, but, thinking they would soon be civilians, dropped the idea. Then came the promotion and now this. No, she was not going to London.

He pleaded: the city would be beautiful, a wonderful opportunity for their children, two girls and a boy. There would be no long absences there, no cruises or deployments away from home; they would be together; they would be happy.

Finally she gave in and off to Britain they went.

A month and a half later, he was living alone in a basement flat on Cheyne Row.

*   *   *

"She said she was not in love with me anymore, if she ever had been—her words, not mine. I said we owed the children the congenial, if not loving, environment of a home. She said, 'No.' She just couldn't do it. She wanted a divorce.

"She was twenty years old when we got married. She immediately got pregnant. She never had the life of the young, the footloose and fancy-free. She later went back to school and became a nurse, a very good one, an excellent Goddamn nurse. She went to work in an orthopedic hospital and did a lot of operating-room work. That's a very demanding thing. So she developed a very meaningful career herself.

"I felt her career became more important to her than I did or the family did and that was the source of some contention on my part. Also, after I got passed over three times and it looked like I was gonna be getting out in 'eighty-five, she began to adjust herself to the prospect of being the breadwinner for a while. Then, lo and behold, I get promoted. That was the straw that broke the camel's back because now I can serve up to twenty-eight years of commissioned service, not just five more years, and she said, 'I've had enough.'

"When we were married, I told her that I loved the Marine Corps, but if push ever came to shove, where it was the Marine Corps or the marriage, then I would give up the Marine Corps. I told her that from the get-go and I meant it. If she ever said to me, 'Give up the Marine Corps and we'll stay married,' I would have given up the Marine Corps. The family, that should be the choice. But that wasn't our trouble; it wasn't the moves. She wanted something that I couldn't give her. I told her I hoped to hell she finds it.

"I really missed the children. This was a time of deep reflection for me. I buried myself in my job, got a flat, walked to work every day. Then, in October, I met Anne."

Anne Victoria Riffey was from Virginia, five feet, six inches, thirty-four years old, with raven hair cut above the neck. She had graduated from American University, signed on with the government, and, most recently, been posted as a manager in the personnel office at Naval Headquarters. By David's description, she was smart, efficient, and able. I met her my fourth night in London.

Off duty, she was charming, "a classy lady," the Skipper had said, and he was right. She had fair skin and dark eyes and an aspect that was never distant or stiff. David had been seeing her for nearly a year, lots of walks and dinners and weekend trips to Spain, Portugal, and France. He was eager to have me meet her; wanted to show her off.

By all outward measure, theirs was an unlikely coupling: she was a liberal Democrat, he a conservative Republican; she was drawn to literature and music, he to his collectibles and antique tools; she was sensible but not tight with money—he could make a penny squeak.

Both possessed strong wills and both liked to spar. They debated politics, religion, the price of a meal.

He could not posture with her. Each time he tried to haul out one of his soldierly apothegms, some macho slogan or heroic bromide, she would simply smile and say, "Here comes one of David's famous Marine-isms."

She had sized him up quickly and, with a few exceptions, the picture she offered of him—in a letter to me—was a fairly accurate one.

I expected someone very attuned to a hierarchy (one's place in the pecking order, rank-wise), devoted to the Marines, and very military. This from what I was told to expect about Marines. Also (from all those John Wayne movies) a patriotic type, someone fairly nationalistic; and someone whose idea of a good afternoon's sport is to storm a beach pulling grenade pins out with his teeth as he goes. I expected someone who is reticent about discussing feelings or showing affection. I expected someone with a fairly simple range of tastes. What I got is all of the above except as to the element of bellicosity, which if it exists (as I think it does; he speaks of the adrenalin charge of killing the enemy) is tempered by a very gentle side. . . . He is a simple soldier with the soldierly virtues, a variation of the old code of chivalry. As a result I think he views most problems and issues simplistically and tends to give short shrift to the complexities. . . . He is a lot more sensitive than the cigar store Indian stereotype (it took me a while to catch on to that). . . . He is very patient. I almost never see him down and I almost never see him mad. He doesn't discuss feelings, he intellectualizes, but he does express affection and appreciation without any evident embarrassment. He is either the most sincere person I've ever met or the world's most gifted actor—I believe the former.

While it might have amused him to let others think otherwise, he did not look on war as Sunday sport.

"Every good Marine ought to have one war and if he survives it, that's great, but to wish for another war is immoral. I don't see how anybody could love war. I really don't. Wars would be great if it's only the other guy's people that get killed, wounded, maimed, but there's never a one-way war. Both sides have got to pay the price."

Although he tried to give the impression that the fighting had left him unaffected—"I don't have nightmares about the war; I don't think about it, brood about it, think of the waste of it, curse my government for not thrusting home a victory; basically, it was a job"—although he claimed this, he had indeed thought deeply about the waste; I was sure of that.

"I went through three distinct phases. The first was when someone got killed. I cried; this was someone's son, somebody's brother. The second was a reaction to this. I made an attempt to be terribly, terribly proficient, 'cause if I screwed up, somebody got killed. The third phase was during the heavy fighting. I found myself losing a man in the morning and not being able to remember his name in the afternoon. That was about the time I got out of the field because I really worried that I would get to the fourth phase: the point where human life didn't mean anything to me, where I didn't care if I lost people."

* * *

I left London on Wednesday evening. The day before, my birthday, we had finished our daily ramble early and returned to his flat to dress for dinner. Just before 7 P.M. we climbed into his tiny 1963 green Morris Minor for the drive to Wimpole Street and Anne's place, a two-floor apartment, which, by London standards, was spacious.

It had rained a little in the afternoon, but by dark the weather had cleared and we went without topcoats. David, with a blue blazer over a white turtleneck and gray wool trousers, looked rather stylish for the "Old Soldier of the Sea" he fancied himself.

At La Petite Montmart in Marylebone, the three of us ate a quiet but elegant meal of escargot and salmon. Then it was back to Wimpole Street for cappuccino and Bailey's Irish Creme. We were late saying good night and getting to bed.

I left the next day at dusk. We walked down Cheyne Row past Carlyle's house and the King's Head and Eight Bells. At the foot of the Albert Bridge, I looked for a taxi to Heathrow Airport. The lights from the bridge reflected off the Thames.

We waited at the curb, watching the flow of traffic, and as we waited, something David had said earlier came back to me.

"Men don't talk about love very well as far as men loving other men. But when it comes down to it, I've loved more men than women. I love Marines. When they triumph, I just love it. That's the essential difference between Marines and everybody else. They really care about one another. It's the thing that makes us different. It's the thing that makes you different, Michael."

(8)

I rarely see my mother now. She calls occasionally, as do I, but years go by between visits.

We do not speak of the trouble between us; I doubt she'd acknowledge it was there. She turned toward God a few years back and I could not follow. Our disaffection goes deeper than that, but faith is always the dividing line: she believes; I do not. The mortar was set seasons ago. We are intractable.

My mother was married three times. She divorced my father when I was five. They were ill-matched and knew it. He was gregarious, a collector of friends, but small-town, tied to family. She was ambitious; had plans.

She could draw, she could model; she was talented and beautiful. At first she found work in West Virginia, defining fashion for a large department store. I was left in the care of a black governess, a hill woman who killed her own chickens and baked her own bread.

"It won't be long," my mother said. "Effie will take care of you."

We moved to Florida. She was working in a new business; television, they called it. After school I sat with sitters. In the evening, by arrangement with the owner, I took my meals at a small table in the kitchen of an Italian restaurant around the corner.

The job went well for my mother. New York noticed and summoned her. She would be "very busy" now, she said, so I was sent to my grandmother in Ohio.

"You'll like living with Nana. . . ."

A year later, in New York, she remarried. After the reception, after the honeymoon, after the new apartment and the unpacking, she sat me down. At my stepfather's suggestion, she said, she was sending me to boarding school.

"Only for a year. . . ."

I was in high school when she married again. Her third husband was a decent and generous man; he took her with six children in tow. The family moved to Montclair, to a thirteen-room house around the corner from a small park with a skating pond and a pair of swans. I went off to college in Philadelphia. One day, a year later, I came home and joined the Corps. The morning I left for war, my mother got up to cook breakfast. My stepfather drove me to the airport.

"You'll write?" she said as I climbed into the car.

"I'll write," I answered.

"See you in a year, Michael."

"Yes, you will. . . ."

NINE

THE WOUND DRESSER

The spasms began the day after Bridge 28. By week's end, one knifelike convulsion followed another. I could not eat or sleep. Hour after hour, I lay on my side, knees drawn up to my chest, hands clutching my gut. Each attack came suddenly, cut deep. The pain left me senseless. I imagined I'd been shot.

Every night Doc DeWeese was at my side. It seems to me now that he was silent most of the time, a shadow sitting in the dark at the end of my cot in our cool wooden bunker at Ca Lu.

Hobbled like that, I was useless.

"Get him outta here, Doc," Hagan said finally "Medevac him. Now!"

"No sir!" said the Doc, looking up from his vigil. "Not yet."

The Doc could be difficult, but his decision to hold me in the field had nothing to do with his temperament or military prerogatives. Scuttlebutt had it that the Navy psychiatrists in the rear treated battle fatigue with electric shock and psychotropic drugs, cures that could turn a mind to mush.

And true or not, Doc was taking no chances with one of his own. Eventually, he thought, I'd come around. All he had to do was keep me with my comrades. He knew what was wrong; he'd been at the bridge.

So he fed me tranquilizers and sat at my side. In ten days I could take a little cocoa and a tin of bread. In a fortnight I could stand a night watch on the radio. And by the end of the month I was on patrol again, ready to fight.

I owed that corpsman and never forgot.

Once, in good fun, the Skipper tried to give Doc a nickname. "You tell that redheaded pecker checker to get the hell down here," he said over the radio. But, crimson mop and freckles aside, the moniker did not stick. Corpsmen were always "Doc." Nothing suited them better.

His round-rimmed glasses gave Doc DeWeese a gentle, almost literary look. (Later it seemed to surprise no one when he announced he was a divinity student.) His skin was so fair, the tropical sun left him freckled and pink, like a pomegranate. He was a short, slight man, the near side of five feet, five inches. And quiet, too. No bluster, not even an occasional gust. But he had a farm boy's stamina and he matched the sturdiest Marine step for step.

Like all Navy corpsmen assigned to the Corps, he had been trained to shoot a Colt .45 caliber automatic, which he carried in a holster. But he abhorred that weapon—all weapons, in fact—and refused to have anything to do with it. He would not take target practice, check his sights, strip his piece and clean it. After four months of neglect, the slide was frozen fast with rust to the trigger housing. This corruption of a lethal tool gave Doc a great deal of pleasure. "Good ole 'Trusty Rusty,' " he'd say, patting the corroded and useless hunk of metal that hung on his hip.

The war sickened him. Riflemen fought and moved on; corpsmen were left with the cleanup. We did not see the wounded as he saw them, piled up, pleading for help, a chorus of final sighs and dying declarations. He knew the sum total of our fatal business—its rueful aggregate, its

appalling inventory. "Corpsman up! Corpsman up!" someone was always yelling. The Doc saw terrible things.

A week after Bridge 28, he sent his pastor a letter.

*We had 19 KIA and somewhere close to 30 WIA
(some of these stayed and fought even after being
wounded). We had two tanks with us and they were
pinned down too. Whenever we moved we had men
killed and wounded. More than once I could see no
way out for any of us, but God kept assuring me that
some of us would make it.*

*God honored both our efforts and prayers. I saw kids
become men in minutes. I saw unswerving determination in the face of <u>certain death.</u> I saw men pray who
had not prayed in a long time. I saw miracles and
God's grace in action.*

*My most anxious moments were always for . . . my
patients. I had nine severely wounded and couldn't get
them medevaced for 12 hours. . . . Two of my corpsmen were wounded. . . . Each time I helped load a
dead Marine aboard a truck or chopper a little part of
me went with him.*

Corpsmen were sailors, hospitalmen in the Navy. If they
volunteered, or were unlucky, they were assigned to the
Marines. We taunted them, called them "swabbies" or
"deck apes" or "squid," but we revered those plucky
medics. Their job was to keep pace with us, no matter how
withering the fire, and then, without regard for their own
safety, rush to the side of the wounded. A Marine's mission
was easy: point the weapon, pull the trigger. A corpsman's
was impossible, pure self-sacrifice.

Doc DeWeese never faltered. Once, at Cua Viet, he tried
to run out in the middle of an artillery barrage to some
wounded who were screaming for help just beyond a paddy
dike. I grabbed the neck of his flak jacket and jerked him
back down. "Not yet, Doc."

"Let me go," he snapped. And I did.

At Observation Post Texas, when we ran out of water on

the hill, it was Doc DeWeese who confronted the Skipper. "You get these men water," he said, "or I'm going to medevac the whole company." It was a beautiful bluff; even the Skipper was impressed.

He was older, twenty-six; most of us were between eighteen and twenty. And perhaps because he had two years of college and seemed to know something of the world, perhaps because he nursed us, tended us, took care of us, many of the men approached him as they would an older brother or a father. They could talk to the Doc and he would listen. He was always at hand; patient, tender—comfort that was hard to find on the field of battle.

He came to Golf Company at the beginning of Tet, early in 1968. At first he traveled with the company command group, but after Bridge 28 he decided to park his kit with the First Platoon: "You guys always seemed so tight—I liked that—and you seemed to get hit hardest at the bridge. I figured that was where I was needed the most."

In the fall, he was transferred to the battalion hospital at Quang Tri, which was where I saw him last. I was on my way back to the field from the hospital in Okinawa. My malaria was gone, but I had been ordered to check in with the battalion surgeon before catching a chopper to the bush. After the exam, I found Doc.

He was living in a dry tent with wooden floorboards. His uniform was pressed, his red hair cut and combed, his skin now tile white. He offered me a cold Coke and a seat on his bunk. We talked for a long time.

He said he would be home by Christmas and planned to return to his Nazarene college and become an ordained minister.

"How about you?" he asked. "You thought about going home?"

I had not. I was headed back to the war, fixed on what was waiting for me. The Doc was reassuring, as always. The unit had been in reserve at Ca Lu, he said. Lately, casualties had been light, and there was no word of anything big coming up.

He said he'd been thinking about the old circle. "Who's left from the First Platoon?"

"I'm not sure, Doc—Squeaky, Louie, Mike Caron, maybe. I've been in Okinawa for fifty-two days."

We exchanged particulars; I wrote his address and number on the frontispiece of a red prayer book I carried in my hip pocket. Then we embraced.

"You be careful," he said.

"Don't worry, Doc."

I left him standing there beneath the tent flap, a doleful look on his face, almost as if he wished he, too, were headed north, with me, back to the fighting.

When I found him again sixteen years later, the Doc was so excited that he started to spin. "When we gonna get together?" he said during a telephone call. "How are the others? Tell me about yourself."

In the months that followed, he wrote or called me from Seattle every week. "You'll be the first one, the first one from the old days I have seen," he said one night.

On a Monday in late January 1985, four days before my flight west, I checked with him one last time.

"Even if I just have to walk off my job, I'll be at the airport," he said.

"Calm down, Doc."

"Are there any foods you don't eat?"

"No, don't make any special preparations."

"Your voice sounds so . . . so . . . just so much like it always used to," he said.

"I haven't changed all that much."

"You still have curly blond hair?"

"Same hair, Doc."

"Okay, Michael, I can't wait. I can't wait."

"You better take it easy, Doc; you'll be bouncing off the walls by the time I get there."

Now, at the end of the Jetway, he was standing quietly by a check-in counter. His hair, once bright amber, had turned burnt orange. His face and neck had thickened some;

he looked slightly stout but fit. He wore a dark-blue three-piece suit that gave him the aspect of an undertaker, maybe a Mormon missionary. He did not move, though it was clear as I approached that he recognized me.

"Doc," I said, "it's good to see you," and reached out to hug him, but all he did was offer his hand, a stiff and formal address.

We made small talk as we waited to claim my baggage, but I think he would have preferred silence. He was on edge, wound tight. There was no picking up with the past, as there had been with the others, no easy crossing between then and now.

In the parking garage, he forgot where he'd left his car and he panicked, dashing frantically up and down the lanes. Finally, collecting himself, he remembered, but by then was so frazzled he could barely get the key into the ignition.

Outside we got caught in the morning rush. It had snowed overnight, a rare event in sodden Seattle, and although there was barely an inch or two on the ground—just dark slush at that—traffic crawled cautiously, as if a blizzard had struck.

"I guess this kind of weather is a big deal out here."

The Doc stared straight ahead. "Yes . . . it is."

Finally I'd had enough.

"All right, Doc, what the hell's goin' on? Why so quiet? On the telephone I couldn't shut you up."

We were stopped at a light; he turned in his seat.

"Seeing you," he said, "it's like somebody coming back from the dead."

There is no getting warm in Seattle. In the winter, day-long rains wash across the city. The sidewalks and streets are always wet and a mist hangs in the air soaking everything that passes through it. The sky is gray, charcoal overhead and ash along the horizon. Great banks of nimbostratus clouds roll in from Puget Sound or off Lake Washington. The water along either shore has a slight chop and is sometimes deep purple, sometimes dark blue. When the sun shines, Seattle is probably a beautiful place, a city of gentle lakes and seven hills covered with evergreens, but in the winter, when the sky is cast iron and the air is a cold spray on the face, Seattle sets the bones to rattling.

From the airport in Tacoma, we drove north to his apartment in West Seattle, a large peninsula of land, between an inland waterway and Puget Sound, forming a separate district of the city. The apartment was on the third floor of a three-story, motel-like building set on a hill; its long living-room window looked west down the hill across the sound to Bremerton and, in the distance, the Olympic Mountains.

The apartment had one bedroom, occupied by Doc's roommate, Tom, a gangling young man, dark-haired and, at moments, delicate. Doc slept on a single bed in a corner of the living room behind an alcove fashioned from an antique chest of drawers and a bookcase, roughly twenty-five square feet of jerry-built cell.

On a wall near a counter hung the enameled wooden plaque that was given to the survivors of Golf Company, an emblem with the battalion motto, "Hell in a Helmet," engraved on it. On top of the chest of drawers sat snapshots of two men in uniform, one a shipmate of Doc's from his days at corpsman's school, the other a native interpreter Doc had befriended. Next to these lay the insignia he had worn on his field uniform, a medical caduceus: herald's staff with two snakes entwined around it, the symbol of healing that nonbelligerents have carried across the ages.

Doc said he had given up the bedroom for a lesser share of the rent and that, at all events, space was not important to him. Tom kept to his room most of the time, entertaining friends. Doc felt like he had the place to himself.

He worked five days a week, twelve hours a day, as a nurse/chauffeur/attendant and legal assistant to a young Seattle lawyer left a quadriplegic from a swimming accident. The Doc had been with the man for five years—had helped him pass the bar, find his first job, even establish a firm. But theirs was not a happy partnership. The lawyer paid pitiable wages and, from Doc's description of him, was a curt, almost uncommunicative man.

The rest of the Doc's life was occupied by friends, two in particular: Dennis, who was tall, handsome, bearded, in his early twenties, living well on earnings from property, and Gene, who had been Doc's roommate in college and now worked as a stereo salesman, a man of medium height, dark hair, nervous and voluble.

From all this—the apartment, the roommate, the friends— from the many telephone calls over many months, I began to see someone different from the comrade I had known, or rather, *imagined* I knew.

Was this the same gutsy corpsman who had rushed out under fire, the hand with the anodyne touch that had held me from the edge? Old offices and honors notwithstanding, I thought not. And knew the others, encountering him all these years later, would see the same thing.

The Doc had changed. He was no longer an easy fit.

He had been raised a pious boy set early on the straight-and-narrow, a catechumen of the bedrock Church of the Nazarene. Like other holiness Christians, Nazarenes believed in the Bible's literal truth. In the main they tried to be simple and chaste—did not smoke, drink, or dance, did not idly watch television or read corrupt magazines—and if all of this left them somewhat circumscribed, cut off from the society and culture in which they worshiped, then what they missed was well worth what they hoped to gain, the great and glorious blessing of everlasting life.

In 1945 a group of holiness Christians in Castle Rock, Washington, a tiny lumber and farm town on the Cowlitz River, forty miles from what was then the inactive volcano of Mount St. Helens, formed a local Church of the Nazarene. At first they held meetings in a building owned by the Castle Rock Women's Club; then, in 1953, they built a small sanctuary on Studebaker Avenue about a half-mile from the center of town. The building was one-story, made of cinder block and painted yellow, with a white steeple on top. Inside was an arched roof with laminated beams, a worship platform, and a simple wooden cross eight feet high. Sunday worship took place at noon and again in the evening at six; during the week there was Bible study; on Saturday a teen group gathered; and once a month the elders met. In 1946, a year after the church was founded, Rita Perry DeWeese, a strong-willed woman who had been raised a Nazarene in the apple country around Yakima, joined the church at Castle Rock.

Every Sunday at the family farm, she loaded her children—who came to number seven—into a black 1939 Plymouth sedan and drove to services. The church, the Sunday school, the youth group, the tenets of the faith became part of the family's life. They followed its proscriptions, adhered to its doctrines in their daily occasions. Two of her children, Dan, born third, and Keith Eugene—just Gene, as he was called—the oldest, seemed to embrace this religious life.

By the time he was a teenager, Gene had become a certified Lay Minister. He helped conduct the worship service and assisted in the rite of communion. He had already made up his mind to go to Northwest Nazarene College in Nampa, Idaho, to earn a degree in theology, then attend the Nazarene seminary in Kansas City, where he would be ordained.

His father, Eldon DeWeese, did not attend church. Work was his religion. By day he was a manager down at the lumber mill. Early mornings and evenings he worked his farm, baling hay and raising hogs and a herd of beef cattle. He taught his oldest son all he knew about livestock. Before long the boy was winning awards with the Future Farmers of America.

The farm was the family's haven, some forty acres of rolling land two and a half miles from the center of town. They had started from scratch, blowing out stumps, cutting and clearing thickets of scotch broom, leveling the topsoil with a big D-8 Cat, then setting down seed. In a few years, they had good pasture for the cattle. A two-story, frontier-style white Victorian house sat on the land. The frame was Douglas fir, hauled in years before by horse and wagon from mills close by. The studs had been set in place at the turn of the century.

Rita DeWeese spent most of her time in the kitchen, Eldon in the fields or barn. On Saturday he would take the boys downtown for haircuts to Lester Green's barber shop in the National Bank building. Lester put bathtubs in the back of his shop. Saturday mornings the loggers would wander in from the woods, strip off their cork-sole boots and long black woolen underwear, and begin their weekend romp with a good hot scrub and a shave.

Doc kept busy. In high school he was president of the student council, a member of the honor society, a public speaker and parliamentarian. With all this and his duties on the farm, however, he had time for little else. There were no athletics, no girls, no Saturday nights on the strip, Route 99, the old two-lane highway between Portland and Seattle that cut through the middle of town.

His recreation was the church. He played the accordion and sang at the worship service; he ran youth groups and taught Sunday school. He believed he had been summoned.

The call came in a dream, "a dream of people being lost and calling out for help and a strong presence, in the form of a life, calmly coming to me and assuring me that some-day I could help those people."

The meaning of the dream was made clear by a piece of Scripture, offered by the Strong Presence, from Isaiah, Chapter 42, Verse 6:

> I am the Lord, I have called you
>   in righteousness,
> I have taken you by the hand and
>   kept you;
> I have given you as a covenant to
>   the people,
> a light to the nations.

He declared his calling publicly one Sunday, in front of the whole congregation, then avowed his belief in the Nazarene articles of faith: that all men were born depraved, full of original sin, that repentance is demanded from all sinners, that atonement of sin was the only grounds for salvation, and, finally, that the impenitent "shall suffer eternally in hell."

His father shook his head. He had tried to talk him out of it. His mother was proud. She had prayed that one of her sons would hear the call; it had been her dream.

The family could not afford to send him to college, so he worked for several years in a local auto-parts store and put his salary in the bank. In the fall of 1964, at the age of twenty-two, he enrolled in Northwest Nazarene Bible College in Nampa, Idaho, some twenty miles west of Boise. He took classes in the basics, studied the Scriptures. On weekends, he would team with a trio or a quartet and drive to small rural parishes in the brown flatlands and iron-gray mountains of Idaho, Washington, and Oregon, singing and preaching the Gospel.

Two years later, well on his way to a degree and still committed to serve as a covenant to the people, a letter arrived from his draft board.

By the end of 1965, 200,000 American ground troops had been committed to battle. In 1966 the call went out for 200,000 more. Draft boards, combing their list of registrants to fill the new quotas, became less and less liberal in their deferment policies and less sympathetic to those who made appeals.

At first, as a lay preacher, Doc carried a ministerial deferment, but later, because he was not ordained, the draft board reclassified him. "Let me at least finish the semester," he pleaded. But the board stood firm.

His professors urged an appeal. "The Nazarene Church needs ministers more than the military needs cannon fodder," one of them said. But Doc decided not to resist. This letter was like a call, he told himself, a kind of destiny.

"At first, when I got the letter, I was devastated," he said. "I'd been on the dean's list and was part of the campus ministry, was planning to go to the theological center in Kansas City two years down the road, probably planning to marry. I wondered why this was allowed to enter my life. Then I said, 'It was God who allowed it and so this must be the direction He wants me to go.' "

Rather than be taken, he enlisted in the Navy, to him "the least combative, the most humane of all the services." The Navy assigned him to corpsman's school, then sent him to war.

Before he shipped out, he went home to Castle Rock for one last leave and, of course, attended church. It was, he recalled, a beautiful service. The sanctuary that late November night glowed with candlelight, more enfolding than he had ever known. Pearl Dixon, the minister and his religious mentor, invited him to play the accordion while his brother David sang the hymn "Beautiful Hands," an apt song given the job that was waiting. Doc delivered a sermon entitled "Spiritual Inventory," took his communion, then made a silent vow.

From his training, he knew that he would see terrible things, but he was determined not to lose his composure and let his comrades down. "I'll wait till I get home," he told himself, "then I can cry buckets."

Doc's friend Dennis was at the door—sandy hair, thin face, long legs. "He's going to be our chauffeur," Doc said. "I want to show you Seattle."

The rain had stopped, but the day was gray and cheerless. Downtown, a few blocks from the waterfront, the morning wind off Elliot Bay swirled around the buildings and through the parks and squares. It was a raw wind and people walked quickly along the pavement with their hands shoved deep into their pockets and their chins upon their chests.

We parked by Pioneer Square, site of the city's first settlement, now restored with chic restaurants and shops with a turn-of-the-century cast: red-brick buildings with rough-stone entranceways, high arched windows and ornamental brackets. The square was cobblestone; in the middle was a huge black cast-iron arbor with a curved roof of smoked glass and beneath it wooden park benches.

We lingered for a while.

"I'm hungry," said Doc finally. "How 'bout you? . . . Yes? . . . Okay. Hey, Dennis, let's go to the cafe now."

The cafe was a small one-room brunch bar on a side street up a hill at the edge of a residential district. It was crowded when we arrived, so we had to stand for a moment scanning the booths and tables to find a place to sit.

It did not take long to notice that all but two of the patrons were men, white men, prosperous-looking men sitting close to one another on benches or holding hands across the white tablecloths.

"That was our first signal to you," the Doc said two days later. "Did you pick it up?"

The meaning was hard to miss, but the intimates of the cafe only told me what I already knew—or at least had sensed. His semaphore aside, the Doc, by design or not, had been sending out signals since our initial telephone conversation many months before. But I had said nothing.

Ça ne fait rien, I had told myself. Between old comrades, such things should not matter. I had been on the edge once and this man had kept me from going over. He might not seem like the comrade I once knew, but what he did now between the sheets was his business. It might color the past, but it could not change it.

When he came home from combat, the Doc was assigned to the Naval Hospital on Whidbey Island in the mouth of Puget Sound. It is likely there were a score of jobs there he could have done well. He had treated gunshot and shrapnel wounds, broken bones, fractured skulls, shattered jaws, snakebites, heatstroke, dehydration and dysentery, neurosis and psychosis. He was an expert in first aid and trauma, a good candidate for the emergency room or the operating suite.

Instead, with the smell of the field still on him and the echo of gunfire fresh in his ears, he was sent to an obstetrics and gynecology ward and put to work scrubbing down bloody delivery rooms.

In April 1970, his hitch done, he left the Navy, but did

not return to his tiny Nazarene college in Idaho. He went home, back to the shelter of Castle Rock and a quiet job selling auto parts. When family and friends asked him about the ministry, he told them, "I'm not ready," and let it go at that.

He said nothing of his guilt, of how one day at the battle on the Three Sisters when a friend was killed, he had asked heaven for something dark and unholy, the death of his enemies. He also said nothing of his utter loss of faith. After seeing so much suffering and waste, it was hard to believe in anything at all.

So he went back to the auto-parts store, back home behind the safe fences of his youth. For a while he tried to return to church as well; he wanted to be wrong about himself.

"I was hoping the old feelings, the old fervor, would come back, but it didn't. It began to feel more and more like just a sham. They'd sing songs like 'The Old Rugged Cross' and I'd start to cry. People would look at me and say, 'What's wrong with him? What's he crying about? We're just singing "The Old Rugged Cross.' '' But, you see, that song brought back the memories of the Marines who never made it back. I could really recall names, faces, even medevac numbers. I never cried in the war, but I did lots of crying then in church, where I thought it would be understood. Sometimes I would even go forward to the altar and try to pray and try to come close to what I felt when I was close to God. You should be able to have your feelings in your church, whatever they are, and you should be able to express them quietly. But people would kind of say, 'He must be feeling guilty about something. Did you do something in the war you're ashamed of?' And I would be furious inside.''

So he resigned, cut himself off from his Nazarene roots. Now, without the anchor of the church, he began to wander. He quit his job at the auto-parts store and went to work on the family farm baling hay. Then he hired on at a warehouse, then took courses at Lower Columbia College and Western Washington University. He had no track, no thread to pick up and follow.

In February 1975 his father died of a heart attack. "Dad and me were close. His death had a profound impact on me; it was the second biggest thing in my life next to the war. It took me two years to get through the pain of that."

Eldon DeWeese, a large man with a heart left weak from rheumatic fever, had finally pushed too hard. "In 1957 the doctors told him, 'Eldon, either the lumber company or the farm, but not both,' " Doc said. "He wouldn't listen." He had heart surgery to replace a mitral valve, but the surrogate caused blood clots and in 1974 these led to a massive stroke. Another followed early the next year. "The strokes left him incapacitated," Doc went on, "but he lingered—he was a strong man—and he fought hard, just like he always had. Sometimes I would say to him, 'Dad, just relax.' "

"You should have seen us when I got back from overseas. Often we'd just work together. I remember when we painted the new house. The whole weekend, not a lot was said; we just worked side by side. He understood my fears, my weak points. He used to say, 'You're real high-strung, Gene; you got to learn to control yourself.' He knew how, at the right moment, to give me encouragement, especially after the war. I think I earned a lot of his respect when I made a go of the military.

"He was very much against me being a minister. I don't think my mother ever understood why I didn't fulfill my original calling, that life and circumstance and situations change. And that's okay. My father knew."

That fall Doc transferred to a small liberal-arts school in Olympia, Evergreen State College, an "alternative" school, as they were then called. Instead of a formal course of study, undergraduates attended a series of round-tables and seminars. Instead of grades, their teachers offered appraisals of their character and intellectual growth.

The Doc was planning a career as a counselor or psychotherapist. His loss of faith aside, he still believed he had a mission. "I said, 'I can no longer preach at people, but there's other ways to minister without preaching.' " He signed up for a somewhat amorphous course of study called "Human Ways and Helping Relationship Skills." For him, Evergreen was like Castle Rock: small, intimate, safe. He bore down on the course work, rarely missed a class. But his grades, his reviews as a scholar, were mixed.

"Gene took an active part in stimulating discussions, asking questions, and submitting his own feelings," one professor wrote on his end-of-term evaluation. Another thought the Doc too abstract: "In moving away from writing academic and analytical material, he becomes superficial in his responses to the complexities and depths of the issues. They don't ring of action in reality, only of ideas of the mind." He failed to "engage assertively" in class, said one professor. He was "very quiet," wrote a fourth. In him there was "much left unexplained and unexpressed."

In one course he was required to undergo therapy. Since formal analysis was expensive, to satisfy the requirement the Doc and a classmate, Jim Burke, organized a weekly encounter group for men.

Burke, a large man, six feet, four inches, 230 pounds, was a Roman Catholic from a gritty, working-class neighborhood in Chicago. A former soldier in the Army's Special Forces, or Green Berets, he had been to war as well.

"Gene and I just sort of fell in together," Burke said. "Evergreen was just a radical place. Lots of time, I felt isolated from the other people just because our experience was so different. Doc and I had a natural affinity without even realizing why, though we never talked about the war. By the end of the group, we were really strong friends. I felt a real closeness to him. He had a real quiet strength."

The men's group talked about men's roles: what it meant to be called a son, a brother, a father, a friend. The group had a leader, but in Burke's view it operated for the most part "spontaneously and intuitively." And because at least a third of their number were homosexuals, it was not long before the discussion turned to identity and attitude.

"After we started talking about how a number of the guys were gay, there was a suggestion: 'Let's have one meeting at the men's sauna at Evergreen.' And I said, 'Absolutely not,' " remembered Burke. " 'I'm not going into a sauna with a bunch of gay men. There's no way. You can call me homophobic, but there's no way.' "

Sometime after this, the Doc went to his new friend, his fellow veteran, and confided that he was a homosexual. Burke went off to think: "I explored my whole feeling and came to the conclusion it was just a choice. I've always been able to differentiate between sex and love. To me it's always been real clear. It doesn't bother me for men to show affection for men. Gene was just real solid. I got to the point where I loved him as a friend."

"I guess you know Gene's gay?"

Burke was sitting with his wife, April Gerlock. They were looking hard at me, waiting for an answer. It was easy to understand why Doc was drawn to him, why he considered this huge man with the thick dark beard and unfettered mind the most enduring of his friends. Burke was loyal, a rock.

We were at a dinner party across Lake Washington in the suburb of Bellevue. Doc had staged the affair in my honor, and two of his friends, Dennis and Gene, had agreed to help. Gene and Doc had been roommates at Evergreen. Dennis, a much younger man, was, as I gathered, a compatriot from Seattle, more of a chum than anything else.

At all events, as we gathered in Gene's apartment across the lake, the first thoughts of our party of eight were of food. All week Doc had been trumpeting Gene's talent as a gastronome. The Doc was right; the man could cook.

The appetizer was a rich brie en brioche, the soup, cream of leek with red potato. Then came cold salmon in a Chardonnay aspic, a salad of julienne of beets and walnuts covered with a raspberry vinaigrette on winter kale, then a lemon sorbet before the entrée—medallions of pork covered with sauce Calvados and puree of parsnip. We washed

down this feast with six bottles of wine and followed dinner
with cognac.

The Doc was beaming, proud of the expensive spread. I
knew the limits of his salary, how dearly the hospitality had
cost him.

Afterward Doc walked out to the parking lot to bid one of
his guests good-bye. Gene, with Dennis assisting, retired to
the kitchen to clean up. Burke settled on the couch next to
April. I sat on the floor facing them.

"I guess you know Gene's gay," Burke said in a voice
too low for the others to hear. "How are you going to
handle it?"

From early in 1863 to the middle of 1865, Walt Whitman,
the good gray poet, set out to learn something of war. On a
self-appointed and self-financed mission in Washington, D.C.,
he roamed the fetid hospitals and makeshift infirmaries of
the Union Army and nursed the troops. In letters to friends
and family and in his notebooks and newspaper reports, he
made a record of these ritual visits—by his estimate, some
600 trips to aid between 80,000 and 100,000 of the sick and
wounded. The Civil War was the first modern war, the first
industrialized war, and its new weapons, forged in America's foundries, tore at men in ways then beyond all imagining.

. . . O the sad, sad things I see, the noble young men with legs
and arms taken off—the deaths—the sick weakness, sicker than
death, that some endure after amputations.

As he worked his way from cot to cot, Whitman came
upon "scores, hundreds, of the noblest young men on earth,
uncomplaining" who . . .

. . . lie helpless, mangled, faint, alone and so bleed to death, or
die from exhaustion, either actually untouched at all, or with merely
the laying of them down and leaving them. . . .

"My boys," was how the poet thought of them as he
went among them, day after day, writing their letters, mop-

ping their sweat, changing their bloody dressings. "So I go round—Some of my boys die, some get well."

He loved them and he wanted them to love him.

I spent three to four hours yesterday in the Armory hospital— one of my particular boys there was dying, pneumonia—he wanted me to stop with him awhile—he could not articulate—but the look of his eyes, and the holding of his hand, was deeply affecting.

What kind of love, what kind of longing was this? There is no doubt that much of Whitman's passion was carnal.

I was at Armory last evening, saw Lewy Brown. . . . Lew is so good, so affectionate—when I came away he reached up his face, I put my arm around him, and we gave each other a long kiss, half a minute long.

But the attachment was more than temporary. As the tall, gray, bearded poet worked his way among the rows of cots—the "butcher sights," the "sad cases . . . silent, sick heavy hearted"—as he ministered to his "comrades"—so he called them—he discovered the fierce feeling that grows between men at war. Here was a yearning that ran deep, "a new world . . . of the soul."

I have never before had my feelings so thoroughly and (so far) permanently absorbed, to the very roots. . . . I feel so engrossed. . . .

"One of my instructors at Evergreen once said something that I can relate back to my job as a corpsman in the war. He said, 'You know, some of my best times in life have been with women, but underlying all of that is the fact that my deepest passions lie with men.' And I thought, 'Yeah, that's what I felt in the war, a deep passion for my comrades in arms, a passion that went beyond the sexual, and I think it's still with me today.'

"The war is what got me in touch with that deep passion. Otherwise, it might've stayed under the surface and never come up or out. At church I would always cover it over with something theological.

"I suppose the essence of passion was the thing that caused me to go out under fire and bring men back. I can't define it. I think to try to define it takes something away from it. I know that it changed me."

After the war he gave appetite and desire free reign, "started really living with a vengeance."

Among his haunts in those "crazy" years were Seattle's steam baths, meeting places for the amorous. The sexual liberation, or awakening, of homosexual men that had begun in other cities had not yet taken hold in Seattle in the late 1960s. The so-called "gay community" was still a small circle of "old queens," as Doc knew them, middle-aged men drinking together and keeping one another company. In the baths with the old queens, a young redheaded corpsman just back from the war was a welcome interloper.

He wanted sex, of course—he was just back from a year of hardship—but he wanted something else as well.

"When I first got back to Castle Rock, I wanted to talk about what I'd been through, but no one wanted to hear. At the hospital at Whidbey, other military people who had never been there said, 'Oh, it's just another war story. We've heard all those fucking war stories. The people that have really faced anything tough don't talk about it, they just keep it to themselves.' When I tried to talk to my parents, they said, 'You're back, you're alive, that's all we care about. Don't tell us about anything that happened there.'

"But those old Seattle gays listened. They wanted to hear because it was an experience that most homosexual men had never had. They couldn't go to war—they couldn't even get in the military at that time—and they wanted to hear. They held me while I sobbed and cried and talked about all those kids that died. I could remember names; I could name events. I was letting it all out. I cried buckets to those gay men. And they supported me, helped me. That may seem like kind of a strange group of people to turn to, but I wonder how many veterans of our war had anybody like that?''

Through the years that followed, he jumped from one job to another, looking for . . . what? A career? A calling? He could not say.

In June 1977, after graduation, he signed on with the state bureau of disabilities, then switched to an outreach center for senior citizens, then moved east to Salt Lake to a Veterans Administration hospital, working on an orthopedic ward. Two years later, homesick, he was back in Seattle at another VA hospital, scrubbing walls and engraving signs. After that he filled out forms for a heath-care company.

One day, along the way, a censorious bureaucrat sat him down to talk. "You've really bounced around," the man said, sniffing at Doc's résumé. "You were real stable in the military, but you haven't held a job for more than a year since. What's wrong with you?''

"He was right," Doc said. "My father always told me, 'You start something, you finish it.' I decided I'd better settle down."

A short time later, scanning the want ads, a tiny item caught his eye.

Handicapped law student, Seattle area, seeks attendant.

The man, in his early twenties, had been injured several years before diving into shallow water. A quadriplegic now, he had gone through several attendants. Some had left, some had been told to leave.

On the face of it, there was nothing to recommend such a position. The work was wearing, the day long, and the pay miserly—$7,800 a year (lunch included, packed by the man's mother in a brown paper bag). But Doc took the job.

From the first, they were fire and ice: the lawyer was cool, distant, flat; the Doc was mercurial, a cheery kibitzer one day, an angry sulker the next. And yet these two men, so antipodal, stayed together for seven years, through college, law school, a first job, a partnership, a new firm.

It would be wrong to suggest that Doc was moved by a spirit of selflessness, though clearly the seed of such was there. And it would be making too much of the past to say that there was a lot of the Nazarene left in him, though the summons to serve—to be an agent of one kind of redemption or another—was still strong.

Doc says he just wanted to stop his drift. He saw the lawyer, whose need was abiding and unequivocal, as an anchor. "I thought, 'This is what I'll do for the rest of my life; I can hitch my wagon to his dream; eventually I'll get my rewards.' "

But the Doc also saw in the lawyer's situation a chance to satisfy an old account. When he looked back on the battlefield, he felt his work unfinished. Who, now, he wondered, was caring for the worst of his wounded—the blind, disfigured, lame men he had loaded onto helicopters, then had all but forgotten? He had helped get them home, but had no part in the really hard work, the fight to recover what had been lost.

Question: How does the day begin?

I usually start the van to warm it up because he doesn't have much circulation and he gets cold easily. Then I take the briefcase out to the vehicle, then go back into the house and transfer him from the bed to the wheelchair. When we arrive at the office, we usually pick up any phone messages and see if there's anything urgent.

Q: If there are calls to make, do you dial the phone for him?

Yes, and then I stand and hold the phone to his right ear. After that I usually tie his tie on me, then put it on him. I get him tea; he drinks lots of hot tea. And we just begin the day's work of either seeing clients or starting to work on cases.

Q: Let's say you start to work on a case.

He'll ask for the file, then spend a little time reviewing it. I'm right close usually—I don't have a desk yet; that's something I've been asking for for two and a half years. It took me a year and a half to get a chair with wheels on it; before that I was sitting on one of his family's folding chairs from the basement of their house—I usually sit at the edge of his desk, wheel back and forth between the filing cabinet and his desk. I'm up and down.

Q: You sign his papers?

I sign his name to everything. My handwriting is his signature. I signed the papers to form his law firm. Someday I'm gonna forget and sign it to one of my own checks; once or twice I've started to.

Q: What happens when you see a client?

I meet the client in the conference room and I usually have them take a seat. I ask them if they'd like some coffee or tea. Then I get my man ready to go meet the client.

Q: Get him ready?

I make sure that his tie is straight. By this time I probably have also drained his leg bag of urine at least once or twice. He wears a catheter that comes into the bag that he wears on his calf. He just moves out from the desk so I've got room to kneel down and get down to his leg. Most of the time he just keeps working while I do it.

Q: Is there much exchange between the two of you?

He tries to speak as little as possible; it's just him. It's usually short, clipped answers to questions. He does a lot of gesturing, points when he wants tea or to get the information and material that he needs.

Q: So now you're with the client.

I have to take all of his notes for him. We've worked together long enough now that he doesn't even have to tell me what to write; I just know. I love it when we see clients. That's some of our best times because that's when some of my personality can come through. If the client is terribly upset, then I go to work to help calm them down a little bit.

Q: Let's say it's midday now.

I usually have to ask for a lunch break. He only eats one meal, his big meal in the evening. He doesn't get hungry during the day, he says.

Q: What's the routine in court?

On a jury trial I take all of his notes. I help him with jury selection. A few times he's asked for my opinion on a juror.

Q: And when he makes his summation, you turn the pages for him?

Uh-huh. We have a trial notebook that's all side-tabbed and labeled, so it's easy.

Q: Will he introduce you to the court?

Most of the judges now know that I'm just part of the package.

Q: What's your salary?

I started out five years ago at $7,800 a year; now it's $15,600.

Q: Fringe benefits?

Well, I didn't get any medical coverage for the first two years. I had to talk him into it. I get around a $500 bonus at Christmas, two weeks' vacation, no pension fund. I'm not sick very often. If I don't go to work, he doesn't go either unless he gets somebody from his family to take him. Right now, with a new firm, he's working real hard to prove himself.

I met the lawyer the day before I left Seattle. Doc drove us over to the house early that afternoon. The sun, at last, had appeared, and though only fifty degrees, the day, set against a week of rain, seemed almost balmy.

The lawyer was in his wheelchair, waiting in the kitchen. He was polite, quick-witted, articulate, not at all taciturn, as his aide had reported him.

Perhaps he saw the Doc as nothing more than an employee, perhaps read into his gentleness a lack of strength and will. Who could say?

Whenever I was able, I turned our conversation to Doc, particularly to the war. I had brought with me a photo album of Golf Company; set it down in front of the lawyer and opened to a page with pictures of Doc sitting on top of a sandbagged bunker. There was no mistaking the message of that milieu. (A few days later, after I was back in New Jersey, the Doc called to say that the lawyer now seemed to be looking at him with newfound respect.)

That night, my last in town, we ate supper at a small Chinese place off Pioneer Square. The rain returned; the city again was sodden and cold.

"Maybe I've stayed at this job too long," Doc said. "I always told him to tell me if it was time for me to leave, and maybe he's trying to tell me in the only way he can. I'd made a commitment to work for him until my retirement age. I don't take my commitments lightly; I didn't in the war. I got a lot of satisfaction when he got his diploma at law school, and I got a lot of satisfaction handwriting the state bar for him, and I got a lot of satisfaction when we started our own firm."

The restaurant was drafty. We ordered another pot of tea. When it arrived, I pulled the kettle in front of me and wrapped my hands around the bottom while it steeped.

"I guess I hang on because of those good moments," Doc went on. "I don't know—maybe it's just time for a change, for more respect and a better salary and some security. If I leave him, I'll be able to look back and say I helped him accomplish something. I don't want to go around leaving a lot of unfinished business."

We drove back through the rain to Doc's hilltop apartment. A heavy mist hung in the valley. The sky was black as onyx.

"You know, every man that I medevaced, a little piece of me went with him." The Doc was standing by the stove, boiling water for more tea. "Every man I zipped in one of those horrible green body bags, a little bit of me died. Maybe working for the lawyer, I was trying to complete some of that 'cause I couldn't go with those guys: I couldn't see them through triage, through their surgery, through the intensive-care unit, through whatever ward they were placed on, then through the rehabilitation process and getting started in life. Maybe I was trying through my work to complete that. Maybe I've just about completed it, too."

The next morning, we were up before dawn and out to the airport. The Doc looked heavy-eyed. He had insisted that I take his bed and had spent the night on the high-backed couch across the room. But he was in good spirits, a far cry from the tense, taciturn man who had first greeted me.

I checked in at the ticket counter, then we walked to the gate to wait.

"Well, Doc, the other guys are pushing for a reunion this year, so start saving your pennies."

"Don't worry," he said. "I'll be there."

Finally the call came to board.

I put my hand on his shoulder. "Gimme a hug." He smiled. We embraced. "You take it easy, Doc." Then I turned toward the Jetway.

"Michael!" Doc stepped forward; looked like he'd forgotten something.

"What is it, Doc?"

"I love you," he said.

(9)

Michael Goodman, my maternal grandfather, was born in Ayer, Massachusetts, November 13, 1893. He is said to have had fair skin and light eyes, like his mother, Rose, like his namesake, me. Beyond this, from those who are his kin, not much of him is known. He left behind no letters or diaries. His wife, Sarah, my grandmother, is dead. She loved and revered him and to almost every question of character or mood would answer only, "Your grandfather was a good man." He died March 18, 1930. He was thirty-seven years old.

My mother, Hadassah, was a child at the time. A few days after her fifth birthday, my grandfather was admitted to a Boston hospital for an operation to relieve an intestinal obstruction. According to official city records, the cause of death was a pulmonary embolism that presented itself during the operation. Seizing on this connection with his lungs, my grandmother, and mother after her, both insisted it was the war, the Great War, that killed him.

He was a victim of the gas, they said. My grandmother reported that not long after he came home from France in

255

1919, strange sores began to appear on his body, the kind suffered by men in the trenches, and that from then until his death he never had a day that was free from suffering. She insisted that the agent of his undoing was mustard gas, an insidious vapor—carbon, hydrogen, sulfur, and chlorine— that burns the skin and assaults the respiratory tract. She took his pulmonary embolism as proof that he was killed by this "lung gas," and carried this belief till her death, even though there were no medical records or recollections of other relatives to support her.

Now, whenever the question is asked, my mother echoes her mother's refrain: Michael Goodman was a casualty of war, just as surely as if he'd been shot.

This much is known of him: he was trained as a pharmacist and likely served as one in Army Mobile Hospital 9, later redesignated Camp Hospital 119, which was organized in Belgium in September 1918, shortly thereafter moved to France, and, following the armistice, was demobilized at Camp Devans, Massachusetts, in July 1919. The "mobile hospitals" of World War I followed closely behind the fighting and treated those who were too seriously wounded to be moved. In effect, they were the first M.A.S.H. units, tent and hard-back surgical wards that operated close to the trenches.

Of life in these units, little has been written. Responding to a government questionnaire, Joseph T. Abrahamson, a laboratory technician in Mobile Hospital 8, said: "We were within walking distance behind the front lines at Exermont on a bald hill marked with a large white cloth cross. We were only 85 men out of [an authorized strength of] 125. We put in double duty. I acted as a cook in addition to medical and nursing help. There was a field hospital on wheels that brought in bed patients. Our canvas tent hospital could be taken down in 6 hours and moved and put up in another 6 hours."

Walking distance behind the front lines . . . double duty . . . Perhaps my grandfather volunteered to carry litters from the trenches and perhaps one day found himself in a trench filled with gas. Who can say?

Little is left from his war days: a blue cloth-covered prayer book, *La Tefila du Soldat,* written in French and Hebrew, sent to his sister, my great aunt, Edna, and inscribed, ". . . forever her brother somewhere in France, Oct. 7, 1918"; a postcard to his mother assuring her "there is nothing of importance to write just now"; finally, two formal black-and-white portraits—the first, likely taken in 1917 when he entered the service, shows a young man, short and fair, with a clean, empty face and wire-rimmed spectacles, the second, a double-image taken, one guesses, less than two years later, adds a mustache and a look that is considerably older and now full of thought.

As a boy I was told simply that my grandfather had died from an illness he caught in the trenches of the great war. He was a hero, they said, and I should remember him so.

TEN

JUST PLAIN LOUIE

Every outfit has its clown, sometimes the savvy jester, sometimes just a buffoon. Ours was Pier Luigi Tartaro, medevac number TPL 1611—to us, just plain Louie.

Louie turned out to be a hero, of course. Such is the way of war: it makes mountains of the most unlikely of men. But all that came later—at the bridge. In December 1967, when he arrived in country with me, Louie was a disaster, a certified "shitbird."

He had a round face and black curly hair, bulbous eyes, and a brick-toothed grin. At five feet, nine inches, and 180 pounds, he was stout and extremely strong, but seemed unaware of his power, had little endurance and almost no cheek. He was, in short, a man-child, juvenescence in jungle green.

But he was smart, street-smart. His parents had emigrated from Florence, Italy, to Queens, New York, when he was a child. In the way of the immigrant, he had learned the value of friends and the art of making alliances. He had found a way to survive.

With us, his way was to play the fool. "Yeah, I was the company clown," he said. He mugged for our cameras, pinched our cheeks, hung on our shoulders. He was preposterous, sometimes idiotic, but no one derided Louie, for he had a way of leveling the man who tried to patronize him or put on airs at his expense.

"Norman, I love you, Norman. You're all right, kid," he used to say—which, of course, meant I was anything but.

None of this was malicious, so we suffered Louie, most of the time gladly. Then one night, at Cam Lo, just before the onset of Tet in January 1968, Louie and I had a falling-out.

We had been assigned to a listening post, an exposed two-man position set out at night 75 meters ahead of the front lines to warn of an impending attack. One man would sleep, one would watch, usually in four-hour shifts.

"Be careful with that shitbird," Belknap had warned me.

Louie insisted on the first watch. I was in a foul mood; it was my fifth night out in the rain.

"Okay," I snapped, "whatever you want. Just don't fall asleep."

He was indignant. "Fuck you! I ain't gonna fall asleep."

I pulled my poncho over my head to ward off the rain and quickly drifted off.

It is the dream, and what was waiting for me when I came out of it, that makes that night come back to me. I dreamed that a gook with a long knife in his teeth was crawling toward us through the paddies. He was a small gook and, masked by the rain, he slithered noiselessly across the dikes. Onward he came, yard after silent yard, until he was nearly at the edge of the hole. In my dream I could not understand why Louie did not see him, and then I realized my watchmate had fallen asleep. Suddenly the gook was in the hole, first on Louie, then on me, driving his knife through my poncho, again and again and again.

I woke with a jolt. When I threw off my cover, there was my guardian, head resting comfortably on his arm, reposing sweetly in the arms of Morpheus.

I stuck my rifle in his face; he woke with a start.

I was furious. "Motherfucker! You fell asleep!"

He blinked several times. "What the hell you talking about? Get the fuck away from me."

We finished the night together, both on watch. And I never again went on an LP with Louie.

He clowned his way through the months that followed. I have pictures of him hamming it up in a tank and at a Buddhist shrine. In each photograph he has that same wide smile, that "shit-eating grin," we used to call it. He was the company character, all right, the only guy who managed to get leeches attached on each of his personals and his rear end at the same time.

After a while I got over the incident on the LP. As long as we stayed out of trouble, Louie seemed harmless enough. I even came to appreciate his comic relief. Who else among us could have made a burlesque of war?

Then came Bridge 28.

His part in the battle, a part no one could have foreseen, is best described by a memo written afterward by W. S. Mack, Jr., the company commander.

Subj: Meritorious promotion to Lance Corporal, case of Private First Pier L. Tartaro.

Throughout his tour, PFC Tartaro has demonstrated a highly spirited disposition and strong sense of initiative which have made him an indispensable part of his platoon and company. On 19 April 1968, these qualities were shown to be particularly outstanding. PFC Tartaro was dispatched with his squad to recover casualties from a highly dangerous killing zone on a bridge on Route 9 between Ca Lu and Khe Sanh. The bridge was laden with dead and wounded and one functional 6X6 truck with a dead driver. After losing three quarters of his squad to enemy fire, PFC Tartaro joined up with one other Marine and braved the heavy enemy fire to retrieve the serviceable truck and one casualty and drive it through 150 meters of killing zone to pick up more casualties and drive them to safety. PFC Tartaro then took the initiative to drive the casualties all the way to Ca Lu over the dangerous Route 9 and bring back badly needed supplies. PFC Tartaro and the other Marine made over seven trips over that deadly stretch of road, running friendly roadblocks and braving enemy sniper and mortar fire to aid their comrades.

And that was not the only time the shitbird of Golf Company rose to the occasion. In September, near the Rock Pile, he pulled one of Dave Buckner's lieutenant's to safety after the man lost his wits and ran headlong into enemy fire. As a reward, the Skipper plucked Louie out of the field before his tour was done and put him in the battalion mess hall at Ca Lu. A few weeks later, near the end of my tour, I joined him there. He cooked. I hauled slop.

In the end, after a year of combat, it was just Louie and me. The others from the old First Platoon and Charlie Squad had either been killed, wounded, or rotated home. We, alone, were the circle now.

Each morning, after a garbage run, I'd stop by the mess tent to visit. And every morning he'd have an extra ration of breakfast—two thick slices of fresh-baked bread topped with grape jelly—waiting for me. We made our peace in those last days at Ca Lu. I came to see that there was little difference between us: I, too, was unsure and afraid; I, too, wanted badly to live.

When Louie shipped out overseas, his father refused to speak with him. At fifteen, he had dropped out of high school, worked odd jobs, "hanged around," mostly. Two years later, a year short of legal majority, he tried to enlist, but his parents disapproved and would not sign the papers. "You'll get killed," he remembered his mother saying. When he finally went, his father, silent with fear, would not go to the airport and see his son off to war.

A year later, when Louie came home, a certified hero, the whole family was there, applauding him as he stepped from the plane.

For a while he floated from one job to another: a bouncer

at the Cloud Nine discotheque, a truck driver, a landscape worker. Nothing fit his plan, his great vision. "I wasn't gonna get my hands dirty no more. I had made up my mind to be a big wheel."

He told this to an employment counselor at the Veterans Administration. The man handed him a slip of paper and told him to report to a brokerage firm on Lexington Avenue in Manhattan. Here was his chance.

Louie launched himself in style. "I went out and bought two thousand dollars' worth of clothes—suits, leather coats, a sealskin jacket, everything. My two sisters chipped in and bought me a Samsonite briefcase. I looked like a big wheel."

The firm, of course, had not hired a high-school dropout to manage its accounts. It wanted a clerk, someone to endure the tedium of recording daily transactions in the long columns of huge ledgers. "By the end of the day, your hand was numb," he said. After two weeks of this, he approached his supervisor. "I said, 'Look, nothin' personal, but how long you been working here?' He says, 'Fifteen years.' I say, 'How much you make a year?' He says, 'Twenty-one grand.' I say, 'I ain't gonna work here twenty years to make no twenty-one thousand dollars.' "

Louie had a dream. When he turned thirteen, it came to him that he wanted to be a "big shot." As it was first conceived, this ambition took the form of a long black Cadillac with gleaming chrome fenders and tail fins slicing the wind. Later, after the war, the dream included a house. No house, he thought, no wife. "I needed the house 'cause married people like to yell and I didn't want no landlord knocking on the pipes saying, 'Hey, you're making too much noise.' Know what I mean?"

Finally he decided he just wanted to be a millionaire.

He got the black Caddy, with LPT 1 plates, and he got the house, too, a trim split-level on Long Island's south shore, with two fireplaces, a finished basement, and a two-car garage.

He found a wife, Joanne, a quiet yet exceedingly friendly woman who worked as a legal secretary. (I could not imagine her yelling at anyone.) And, when I first went to see him again in the fall of 1984, they had a nine-year-old daughter, Jennifer, who seemed to take after her mother.

He did not appear close to his first million, but he was, indeed, a big shot. He was a union man.

Twelve years before, he had taken work as a bus driver for a large transportation company on Long Island. The year he came aboard, two unions were vying for recognition in his shop and Louie threw his lot with the one that came out the winner.

Now he was a senior shop steward and delegate with his own office in the garage and his own men. "What do I do all day? Answer problems, settle grievances, give dental forms, doctor's forms, take care of the members' health plan, the contract, make sure none of the members' rights is violated. I'm their messiah. Know what I mean? Eh, Norman?" Then he laughed.

He had made enough friends and built enough alliances to stay in office through several elections. And he had managed along the way to learn enough finesse to juggle the competing interests of the company, the union, and the men.

It was hard to think of him in a position that required tact and diplomacy. To be sure, he was full of bonhomie; I had never met a more voluble glad-hander. And he could be tough, too. He'd proved that. But a union ramrod needs more than a big mouth and a large foot. He must have perspicacity, an ability to judge character.

Louie kept it simple. He reached back and applied some old lessons.

"I learned from experience on the job that the guy who comes to you only when he's in trouble, that guy's gonna stab you in the back and not support you in an election. Know what I mean? It's the guy who comes in every day just to do his job, who does the regular routine checking in with the union, that's gonna be one of your soldiers.

"The best way to win an election is to go right to the members, to their faces, grab 'em in a room, or grab 'em outside, and tell 'em—I tell 'em all—'If I ever screwed you before or injured you in any way, don't vote for me. But if I have been true to you and taken care of you and always been with you, then I deserve your vote.'

"You don't have to be no scholar, no genius. If you take care of your people, they will take care of you. Simple as that. The main thing is being true to them. If you're faithful, they'll be faithful to you. Know what I mean, Norman?"

(10)

On a birthday a few years back, I asked my father for a special gift: his war, in his own hand. He agreed and, across a month or so, writing nights and weekends in a string-bound composition book, set down what he remembered of that time in his life.

He begins in August 1940. The newspapers of the day were full of the fighting in Europe.

It seemed like I was just marking time for something to happen. So Paul Berstein, a close personal friend from High School days, and I decided that rather than wait to be drafted and wind up God knows where, we would enlist together in the Delaware National Guard.

My father, Bernard J. Goldman, was twenty-four years old, a lean, handsome college man from Wilmington, Delaware, with a degree in textiles, the oldest of two children of Meyer Goldman, a garment worker, and his wife, Fanny.

My Dad seemed to understand why I was taking this course of action but Mom was hard to convince.

In the fall of 1941, his unit, a regiment of antiaircraft guns, headed north to train in New England.

During this time all sorts of rumors were going around. Because of the German invasion of Poland things began to look pretty bleak and the general feeling around camp was that we would go to war.

He seemed eager to serve, at that point unafraid.

I got a pass to come home 2 or 3 times on the weekends and you really felt proud to show off your uniform to your friends who were still at home.

On leave at Thanksgiving 1941, he "picked up a terrible cold." When he got back to camp, he was sent to the hospital with the flu.

I was pretty sick with fever, couldn't eat and just felt lousy. All of that changed pretty quickly on the morning of Dec. 7th. . . . When the news came over [the radio] there was much excitement on the ward. . . . The chief of staff of the hospital came through requesting each man to return to his unit, fever or no fever.

A few weeks later, in January, the men of the 198th Coast Artillery Regiment, Delaware National Guard, got a new mailing address: A.P.O., San Francisco; they were headed west, to the war in the Pacific. Now "the thought of fighting the Japs was really frightening."

Their port of embarkation was Savannah, and to reach it, the troop train, carrying the men from Delaware, passed through the station at Wilmington.

Meyer and Fanny were waiting on the platform in the

crowd. The train was not scheduled to stop, but it slowed to give the boys from Delaware a last look at home. My grandparents did not see my father, but he spotted them. "Once the train was on its way," he said, "most of us felt pretty sad."

A month later, in mid-February, the men from Delaware landed on Bora Bora, one of the Society Islands of French Polynesia, 2,700 miles south of Hawaii. The 198th was part of a task force sent to the Pacific to establish safe anchorages and refueling depots between America's West Coast and Australia.

At first the threat of attack was real—the Japanese began the war with a bigger, better-gunned Navy, and at their attack on Pearl Harbor they destroyed or disabled much of America's Pacific force—but after the sea battle at Midway, where the enemy was badly stung, the war, in the words of an officer from the 198th, "passed right on by" Bora Bora.

Now the duty was "extremely boring." Dad opened a canteen in the mess hall and sold beer, candy, and cookies for the regimental slush fund. They ate C rations at first, and bought coconuts, bananas, and pineapples from the locals. Soon they had a refrigerator, cold beer, and "a little native girl" who did their laundry.

And so it went—no action on the combat front on the island— never did see a Jap plane.

He made sergeant that year and early the next was accepted for officers' school. After a leave, he reported to Camp Deavans near Ayer, Massachusetts—the same camp where my grandfather, Michael Goodman, had been demobilized—and in May 1943 was commissioned a Second Lieutenant. He was assigned to the 398th antiaircraft regiment at Camp Edwards, not far from Boston.

On the weekends, the officers of the 398th would take a train to Boston and gather in the Statler Hotel. One Saturday a friend arranged a blind date for my father. She was a beauty, nineteen years old, large brown eyes, dark shoulder-length hair. Her name was Hadassah, my mother.

I don't know whether it was the uniform or the times, but we fell in love, I think, at first sight and from then on it was into Boston each weekend. If I remember, I think she came out to Edwards one weekend with some of the girls and of course I was in heaven. We saw each other as often as possible and were married in the spring of 1944. The ceremony was in Brooklyn since most of her relatives were from New York. I could only get a weekend pass for the honeymoon and we rented a hotel room in Buzzard's Bay, Mass. Very romantic.

Fourteen days after D-Day, the invasion of Normandy, the 398th sailed for Europe.

The sinking feeling I had in my stomach that [June] day is indescribable. I had married a few months before and who knows when and if I would ever return.

On the morning of July 28, 1944, he boarded a ship at Southampton, England, crossed the English Channel, and went into battle.

We landed on Utah beach in the late afternoon . . . the noise was almost unbearable. The half-track I was riding in was being driven by the 1st Sgt. and we pulled into a grove of trees to get some cover. We had just stopped when the Sgt. reached around to get his Thompson machine gun. The gun fired, somehow hit the Sgt. and he was gone almost immediately. Words cannot describe how I felt.

His unit was assigned to Patton's Third Army and began to sweep through the hedgerows across France. At night the German bombers came over.

I would always shiver lying in the foxhole no matter how much clothing I had on.

He crossed the Seine and "saw plenty of action on our way to Paris." Along the way, he won a Croix de guerre.

That fall and winter, Patton pushed through the Alsace and into the ice and snow of the Vosges Mountains. By February they had reached the Rhine. "Our spearheads were cutting up the German Army pretty good."

Crossed the Danube on April 29th, liberated some more Prisoner of War camps, our guys. My God—the feeling was unbelievable. The sights and conditions were horrible. The poor guys must have suffered pretty badly. You should have seen them when we threw them C & K rations. They almost went wild.

At last it was over. V-E day left him giddy.

Words cannot describe how I felt—to think I came out of the war without a scratch. My prayers were answered.

Looking back, he remembered three things. The men he had commanded:

Almost all of them were good G.I.'s, did their duty and were dependable.

The discipline he learned:

It still has a strong influence on my daily life.

And the sacrifice:

Whether it was worth all the lives that were lost, well, who's to say? I truly felt the patriotism that all of us had in those days; my country needed me and we knew why we were fighting.

I was five years old when my parents divorced. My mother rarely spoke of my father—I saw him once in twenty-five years—but in the top drawer of her dresser, under some scarfs, she kept his picture, a small black-and-white snapshot. I have always suspected that she left it there for me to find, left it year after year through one move after the other. She said the photo was taken somewhere in France during the war; my father was sitting bare-chested on a camp stool in a field of high grass, one of his half-tracks, with its antiaircraft guns, behind him.

With each year that passed, another piece of him was lost—I could not remember his touch, his voice, his step on the stairs—until at length, the only image of a father was in that field in France, a soldier at war.

In the early spring of 1980, I decided to find my father. I was thirty-two years old and had not seen him for twenty-one years. My mother set me on the search. One night, quite late, she called from Colorado, insisting that I locate him. Something—misplaced guilt, born-again fire—something had seized her. She was adamant; he needed me, she said, and I needed him.

I was tired; resented the call. I lied; said I'd find him.

A few weeks later my maternal grandmother fell ill and I caught a flight to Illinois to be with her. One day, alone at her bedside, I spoke of my mother's strange call. "Sure, why not find him," Nana said. "I bet his people are still in Wilmington."

She was right. I found a thoughtful man with white hair who looked remarkably like me.

He was not the man I'd expected: the stalwart, the special success. Instead, he was a salesman for a car-leasing company who liked his work and was good at it. His wife, a bookkeeper in a sporting goods store, had given him two daughters, "nice girls," as he described them. He played golf on weekends, read mystery novels, called home from the road every night.

We began slowly, but before long drew close. My father felt the weight of the missing years much more than I. I had not forgotten the past—Dad said he'd searched but could not find me and my peripatetic mother; I think, perhaps, with a new family, he did not search that hard—but I kept no ledger, had no desire to call anyone to account. For me, the past was simply a starting point. My son had his grandfather now; the line could look back. I was content.

Once or twice in the years that followed, I would watch my father across a room, looking for the man in the snapshot, the army captain sitting by his guns in France. But there was little of the soldier left in him.

One day hence, I suspect, it will be that way with me.

ELEVEN

REUNION

April 21, 1985

Gentlemen,

It is official. The date of our reunion is Friday, August 9 here in Montclair. We'll begin with an all-day, all-night party at my home on Friday. I figure Saturday would be a good day to take the out-of-towners into New York City. . . . Perhaps on Sunday, we can make a day trip.

If everyone comes, there will be 18 people: The Skipper, Ciappios, Belknaps, DeWeese, Troys, Williamsons, Carons, Whitfields, Hefrights, Tartaros and Normans.

The long sweep of lawn in back of the house was thick and green that summer. We put tables beneath the pin oaks and strung party lights overhead. The tables were set with bouquets of carnations in red, white, and blue. Across the front of the house, between the first and second stories and facing the street, we hung a fifteen-foot tricolored banner inscribed with letters a foot and a half high: WELCOME 1ST PLT. GOLF 2/9 USMC. Along the easements on either side, flying from small wooden sticks, were two dozen American flags.

For that first night, Beth had planned a feast: trays of hot and cold hors d'oeuvres, whopping mounds of paella, bowls of tossed salad, loaves of French bread, and a long white sheet cake with red-and-gold icing that formed an eagle, globe, and anchor surrounded by the names of all the men.

Kitchen help had been hired and was in place. Bottles of liquor had been positioned on the tables and great loads of beer and soda put on ice.

Finally, on the afternoon of Friday, August 9, the survivors of the First Platoon of Golf Company began to assemble in the backyard beneath the canopy of oaks.

Craig and Jean Belknap had arrived from Mesquite the day before. Now, from Connecticut, came Mike Caron and his wife, Pat; from Northern New Jersey, Dave and Sheryle Troy and Frank and Karen Ciappio; from Seattle, Doc DeWeese; from Lick Ridge in central Pennsylvania, Doc Hefright; and from Georgia, Charles Whitfield. Ciappio had also invited Newton Moore, a platoon sergeant from Atlanta who had spent much of his time in the command group. Newt had been Frank's sidekick for several months in 1968 and the two of them, and their wives, paired up for the weekend. The Skipper had been unable to leave London—his children were on hand for the summer—but he sent a note in his stead.

Friends,

Can it really be 17 years since we did all those things you are privileged to recount to one another? To me, some things seem like yesterday and others that they happened to someone else in another lifetime. But 17 years is a reality and one wonders where the time went. I think it's marvelous that you all have gotten together and wish I could join you. . . . Have a grand time.

We had no agenda other than what the Skipper had wished for us. The men were eager, but somewhat wary, too. No one wanted a maudlin affair; we'd had our share of melodrama. Frank, in particular, guarded against the past. The sorrow that was submerged in most men was often just beneath the surface in him. What, I wondered, was running through the rest of them?

It started slowly. Here was a broad smile and handshake, there a light touch on the shoulder or a long embrace.

". . . How ya doin'? . . . You remember Tex? . . . This is my wife, Sheryle . . . What's goin' on down there in Savannah? . . . It's been a long time—what, sixteen? No, seventeen years. . . ."

They moved from one to the other, clusters of old intimates reacquainting themselves. Sometimes two men would slip off to a corner of the yard to sort out some old business or mine an ancient memory.

Now and then, in the middle of all this, a howl would fill the treetop canopy and I'd look up for Belknap. The men seemed to pay him particular respect, seeking him out, greeting him warmly, taking him aside for a private moment. Occasionally someone would steal a second look at his claw, or track him stone-faced as he limped across the yard. Watching the others watch him, the man among us most marked by war, I remembered the first time I saw him in Dallas. Were the others, too, now feeling the deep ache of his wounds?

It was a strange scene unfolding there beneath the tall trees, strange, at least, to see these men in button-down shirts and steam-pressed pants; this, the same gritty, malodorous crew that had fought its way through the yellow dust one hot April morning so long ago.

Some showed the years more than others. Mike Caron was going gray and Dave Troy was discomfited by middle-age spread.

Squeaky had the longest hair—shoulder-length it was—and suffered more ribbing than he deserved. He was, of course, a willing foil and it did not take much to get him to tell again the story of how steroids had turned him into a duck. "I hated going to sleep because it was just tireless flying and all you could see was the ass of the Goddamn duck in front of you. . . ." How he made us howl.

Charles Whitfield charmed all with his Southern manners. Tall, soft-spoken, completely at ease, he was ever the chevalier.

Doc DeWeese, on the other hand, seemed at odds with himself. He was stiff, taciturn, at moments remote. None among us had changed as radically across the years. The Doc had moved a long way from center, perhaps, in his mind, beyond anyone's reach. His friends in Seattle, sending him off, had urged him to relax, but he was clearly worried and wound tight.

Doc Hefright, too, had some disquieting moments. On Friday when he arrived, some of the others spotted the big bear sitting alone in the back of the yard, his chin on his chest, sobbing. Belknap went to his side, talked to him gently. Later Craig told me the Doc had drifted back to the battlefield for a while.

"What did you say to help him?" I asked.

"I just thanked him for saving my life," Craig said.

Louie was the last to arrive. By the time he made his grand entrance into the backyard, everyone had told a story about him. Belknap, Ciappio, and I had gone to Long Island earlier in the year to see Louie and, a few hours before he arrived for the reunion, we had tried to warn the others that he had changed, substantially. But our reports did not do justice to what now ambled into view—295 pounds on a five-foot, nine-inch frame.

He was more than a hundred pounds heavier than his Marine weight, in white Bermuda shorts and sandals, a polo shirt and sunglasses. He was round; he was massive. Some of the men gasped.

Squeaky slid up beside him and smiled, an obelisk flanking a spheroid. "Whaddya say, Louie?" And pumped his hand. Most of the others, dumbstruck, just stood in a semicircle and stared.

"Hey!" Louie broke the spell. "Hey! Where's the beer? . . . What's-a-matter-witcha? . . . Norman, I love ya. Norman, you're all right, kid. . . . Hey, Chuck? Hey, Doc! What's-a-matter? No chairs? Hey, Norman, where do I sit? . . . Hey, Caron. You see my man Squeaky here? . . . Hey, Cappy! . . . Belknap! Hey, man. Hey. All right."

We passed the afternoon trading vitae, telling stories—Dave Troy, finally in his element—and leafing through albums filled with pictures from the war: here was a young Belknap squatting in front of barbed wire, a cigarette dangling insolently from his lips; and Louie, grinning, emerging from the hatch of a tank; finally, Squeaky on a hot day stripped to the waist, a heap of ribs and shoulder blades stacked on a pair of big feet.

Here, too, were Tommy Gonzales, Bob Hagan, Jim Payne.

Squeaky was the first to speak of the empty chairs at the table. "You know, the reunion and all is great, Mike, don't get me wrong. But I gotta say, I really miss Tommy." Then, in the middle of the evening meal, Frank stood up at his place and held out his glass. "I think," he said, his voice beginning to crack, "I think we should offer a toast . . . to our comrades . . . we left behind."

The next day we piled into three cars and drove across the Hudson to Manhattan for a boat ride around the island. It was a warm, close day and it felt good to be on the open deck with the breeze sweeping across the river. I sat with Doc DeWeese and Charles Whitfield for a while. The Doc had settled down some, though he was still not sure of his place among us. Louie spent most of the cruise at the snack bar and was needled mercilessly with every munch. Some of the others leaned along the rail, heads together, deep in the particulars of the past.

Later we wandered through the South Street Seaport along the East River. It was bustling with tourists and we did not stay long. We drove north, up to the Plaza Hotel to run the gauntlet of posh emporiums on Fifth Avenue. Squeaky and Georgia scooted across Fifty-ninth Street to the south wall of Central Park, where artists had set up their easels and stalls. The Oklahomans were enchanted with the city.

That night we again took dinner beneath the oaks; this time, large pans of lasagna. Afterward Louie, drowsy from the meal, tried to settle himself in our Pawley Island hammock. It was an impossible maneuver for him and his gyrations drew an audience. "I'll tell you what," said Belknap, perfectly deadpan, "you get in there, boy, and we're gonna need a crane to get you out."

After dark a few of the men gathered on the front porch. I was in the kitchen cleaning up and could hear them talking. They were telling war stories and they were laughing loud and long. It had been years since I'd heard such a hearty chorus.

I billeted half the men at my in-laws a few towns away. The family was gone for the summer and we stocked their refrigerator with provisions for breakfast. The two Docs, Mike Caron, and Charles Whitfield later told me that each night, after they returned from a long day of reunion with the rest of us, there was still so much to talk about, the borders sat around the kitchen table till dawn.

Sunday we went to a swim club for steaks and corn on the cob. It rained as soon as we arrived and the club emptied. But thirty minutes later, the storm passed, the sky cleared, and we had the grounds and swimming pool to ourselves.

Doc DeWeese wandered down one of the paths to the pool's edge. "You remember the swimming hole at Ca Lu and how we used to dive from the rocks into the Quang Tri River?" he said. "It was so peaceful there."

No one wanted to end it, but that evening Charles Whitfield caught a flight home to Savannah. He was the first to leave, and he wept in the parking lot of the club as he said his good-byes.

The next day, Monday, Doc Hefright climbed into the cab of his pickup truck and set out for Lick Ridge. "I can't tell you what this has done for me," he said. Then he drove off, leaving Belknap smiling.

Craig and Jean flew home to Texas Tuesday morning. A few hours later, Squeaky and Georgia, with Doc DeWeese hitching a ride in their pickup, left for Washington, D.C., where they planned to see the sights. At week's end they headed west.

Let me tell you about camping in Virginia. We set up camp atop Loft Mountain and deer roamed through the camp, seemingly unaware of people. It is amazing how deer can adapt. . . . Also in the same campground were BEWARE OF BEARS signs. We didn't see any bears in the park but Georgia spotted a black bear alongside the road. Being an ex-Marine, I am not scared of bears, at least not pictures of bears. . . . Anxious to return to the heat of Oklahoma. . . . The reunion was great.

Doc DeWeese also dropped me a note, but there was not much in it. He came close to the circle that weekend, but never really took the place reserved for him. Although he did not say so, I think he later regretted the distance. At all events, he did no damage. In the months that followed, he came to see that there was never any danger of censure. None of his comrades cared how he spent his nights. His office was secure.

Beth and I decided to drive north to her family's summer place on Guffin Bay. Beth said she was glad to leave; with the men gone, the house seemed so empty.

Around Labor Day Mike Caron called from Connecticut. "If it had meant my job, I was comin' to that reunion," he said. "Heck, I never experienced anything like it. To have that strong a tie was unbelievable, to feel all that camaraderie, the love."

I know now why men who have been to war yearn to reunite. Not to tell stories or look at old pictures. Not to laugh or weep on one another's knee. Comrades gather because they long to be with men who once acted their best, men who suffered and sacrificed, who were stripped raw, right down to their humanity.

I did not pick these men. They were delivered by fate and the U.S. Marine Corps. But I know them in a way I know no other men. I have never since given anyone such trust. They were willing to guard something more precious than my life. They would have carried my reputation, the memory of me. It was part of the bargain we all made, the reason we were so willing to die for one another.

I cannot say where we are headed. Ours are not perfect friendships; those are the province of legend and myth. A few of my comrades drift far from me now, sending back only occasional word. I know that one day even these could fall to silence. Some of the men will stay close, a couple, perhaps, always at hand.

As long as I have memory, I will think of them all, every day. I am sure that when I leave this world, my last thoughts will be of my family—and my comrades, such good men.

EPILOGUE

THE WAY FORWARD

CRAIG BELKNAP kept close. In the years following the reunion, we saw each other often. At one point he even spoke of moving east. I would have been pleased to have had my great friend so near, but that was not to be. Texas was native soil and he simply could not leave it. In the fall of 1988, after a bitter dispute with his board of directors, he resigned his post as the executive director of a drug and alcohol treatment center and established himself as an independent consultant. His hip pain got worse, his limp more pronounced, but he still would brook no talk of surgery. "I'm just not ready to get back on the table again," he said. At last it was clear he never would.

SQUEAKY and GEORGIA WILLIAMSON set about improving their ten acres of virgin land in Bengal, Oklahoma, a tiny hamlet hard by the Arkansas border. They cleared brush, planted grass, put in a gravel drive, and parked their fourteen-by-sixty-foot house trailer on a concrete slab. Squeaky tried to dig for water, but came up dry and had to hook up to the county pipes. He's been healthy of late, no longer afraid of losing the eye. He and Georgia still live on his disability pension, working occasionally as barn painters, or baling hay for Georgia's parents. They do not travel much anymore. Small-town life is adventure enough.

It's turkey season and I've been out in the mountains searching for that old gobbler. You get up before dawn and from the top of the mountain you hoot like an owl. Turkeys hate owls and will usually gobble when they hear one. If the owl call does not work you try a crow call. Turkeys hate crows. If for some damned reason the turkeys will not respond to the crow you get out your turkey-box and gobble away. Turkeys hate turkeys.

DAVE TROY stayed in the insurance business, most recently in New Jersey as an executive with a new firm. He and Frank Ciappio meet regularly for lunch or dinner. Sometimes I join them. Dave is still full of stories, our comic chronicler of war, Golf Company's epic poet.

FRANK CIAPPIO twice switched jobs, finally starting his own small brokerage near his home in Sparta, New Jersey. He said he "lost his shirt" when the stock market crashed in October 1987, but reckoned in time that he would recoup his losses. He talked of moving to Colorado, his Golden Land, but never put his house on the market. Frank just likes to grumble.

DOC HEFRIGHT was still trying to heal himself, keeping close to his house high on Lick Ridge. Belknap tracked him closely. For a while they talked once a month on the telephone. Sometimes, when Doc was out leading his Boy Scout troop, Craig would chat with Judy, Doc's wife, to get the news. In time it got better. Doc finally won his disability claim against the state prison system and was awarded what amounted to retirement pay. He took some of this money and went to a local trade school where he studied electricity, but he never used his new skill. I got the sense that he was not yet ready to work, that he still had not conquered the great anger that had kept him on the ridge. I last saw the big bear in April at a gathering of the men in Washington. He looked fine, no sign of depression. At one point we had a moment alone together. "How's it going?" I asked. He smiled. "I'm okay . . . in here," he said, and put his large hand over his heart.

CHARLES WHITFIELD gave up driving a battery truck and returned to teaching, this time high-school mathematics at a state adult education center in Savannah. "I tell you, I've been lucky," he said. "Everything just seems to keep falling into place. It's been like that ever since the war."

CORA and JACK HAGAN still live in Savannah, not far from Charles. I rarely hear from them now. From time to time I send Cora a letter with news of the other men. Each Christmas we exchange cards. "Thank you for staying in touch with us," she wrote two years ago. I have tried to respect the distance. A presence from the past sometimes comes on like cold weather; it only deepens old aches. As of this writing, Maj. John Robert Hagan, USMC, has been missing in action for twenty years.

MIKE CARON was laid off from his job as the manager of a tire store in West Haven, Connecticut. After a stint selling automatic garage doors, he became a partner in a local weightlifting and fitness center. His end of the business is sales. He has more independence than profit at this point, but he is content.

DAVID NELSON BUCKNER and Anne Victoria Riffey were married on March 7, 1987, at the Navy Chapel in Washington, D.C. It was a bright, clear day, especially warm and cheerful for early spring. Marigolds were in bloom at the base of the chapel. Anne, in white with pearls, carried a bouquet of lilies. The Skipper was in his dress-blues. The ceremony was intimate but unaffected, the perfect metaphor for the moment. They repeated their vows; the Lord's Prayer was said; then came the "Wedding March," followed by Beethoven's "Ode to Joy." Outside, under a portico, six of David's brother officers and men from his command formed an arch of swords, and the colonel, with his new bride on his arm, walked smartly under it. At a reception later, he offered a toast: to family, he said, then, looking at the men in uniform, "to old friends and bold friends, too."

DOC DEWEESE ended seven years of service to the quadriplegic lawyer from Seattle. In the summer of 1987, through the good offices of his friend, Jim Burke, Doc was hired as a "mental health associate," or counselor in a PTSD program, at the American Lake Veterans Administration Medical Center, a neuropsychiatric hospital with three hundred beds near Tacoma, Washington. "I'm here. I'm happy, I'm busy doing *my* work," Doc wrote of his work with his brother veterans. "The issues often 'hit very close to home.' But I'm able to remain objective enough to be effective." In truth, the Doc had trouble at first. "He's [got to learn he is] not the medic anymore, he's a therapist now," said Burke, a counselor for many years. "At war, everybody loved the Doc. Now they are going to hate him because he's going to have to hurt them to get them better. The hardest thing he has is dealing with Marines. He opens himself up and often they turn on him." That summer Doc's friend Gene and his former roommate, Tom, died of complications arising from Acquired Immune Deficiency Syndrome. Doc was a pallbearer at Tom's funeral. Despite the urging of his friends, Doc refused to undergo a blood test to determine if he was carrying the disease. He did not, he said, want the weight of knowing. To date, he has shown no symptoms. He lives by himself in an apartment in Tacoma, looking for balance. "I move on," he wrote, "hoping to survive AIDS the way I survived the war."

LOUIE TARTARO won election to another term as chairman of the union at his bus garage on Long Island. Out of some 340 members, only a handful of "dissidents," as Louie dismissed them, voted against him. "Hey, Norman. How's it goin', Norman. I love ya, kid." We saw him last at our spring 1988 gathering in Washington. He was wearing a matching gold watch and ring and driving a sleek black Jaguar sedan, every inch the big shot.

"NO! . . . NO! . . . NO! . . . Norman . . . help me . . . I'm hit. . . ." I still hear Jim Payne's cry. I know now I always will. But it no longer haunts me.

One day in the spring of 1988, I received a call from a woman named Sheryn Scherer. She said she had read an essay of mine in a book of photographs. I had mentioned Jim in that piece, and as soon as she spotted his name, she tracked me down. She was his cousin, she said. "we were as close as brother and sister. How well did *you* know him?"

It was a weekend morning. I had been scooting about the house finishing some chores. The call caught me flat-footed.

I told her the story of Bridge 28: how Jim had taken my place before the battle, how he was killed going to the aid of the wounded, how he had seemed to follow me across the years. I spoke slowly, measuring the phrases, but I gave her all the details, repeated his last words.

She was silent for a long time. "Oh, Mike," she said at last, "we didn't know any of this."

A few days later I sent Sheryn some photographs of Jim at war. Not long after that she replied with a six-page letter.

She said she was married to a former Navy captain and lived in San Diego. Her father and Jim's father, Andrew James Payne Sr., were brothers-in-law. In the 1950s they'd moved their families west from Washington, D.C., to Glendale, California, where, with the aid of a relative, they secured jobs as technicians in the movie industry. A grandmother and a great-aunt followed and soon the small clan was together.

"The hardest part of all is relating my memories of Jim," she went on:

We were two kids who passed from childhood to adolescence side by side. I remember playing hide and

*seek, jumping off the garage roof, throwing darts at
the rabbits in his wallpaper, going to the movies, playing
both chess and baseball so he could practice, trying to
get him to dance with me so I could practice, letting
him drive with me [she was eighteen months older]. . . .
I have a little step stool he made and sold as a Junior
Achievement project. "This Little Stool Is just Dandy/
For Reaching Things That Are Not Handy." Those
words wore off long ago, but I think of them every time
I step on that stool. . . .*

*One of my fondest memories of Jim happened one
day after school when our mothers were going somewhere. While riding in the back seat Jim was telling me
some story that sounded very fishy. In an effort to
convince me, he insisted I talk to Joey Donner who
could confirm every detail. "Just who is Joey Donner
and why should I believe him?" I asked. "A boy in my
class," he replied, absolutely amazed that I didn't
know him. In an effort to save face I asked him if he
would know who I meant if I told him to go talk to
Patty Chandler. "Of course," he said, "she lives on
Harvard St. and has a brother named Eddy. I played
him in the carom tournament at the park." I tried this
three more times, giving up in utter frustration when I
couldn't find anyone Jim didn't know. We were only
about 8 or 9 at the time. His ability to make good
friends stood him in good stead throughout his life.*

Jim's death settled hard on the small family that had mi-
grated to sunny Glendale. Eight months after Jim was killed
at Bridge 28, his grandmother died of complications result-
ing from a stroke. Five months after that, on the evening
after Mother's Day, Jane Payne, Jim's mother, died of
cancer. Then, right after the new year, Aunt Etzie, the
great-aunt, died of a heart attack before reaching the
hospital.

In two years' time, the Paynes buried four of their kin.
"The ensuing years were terrible," Sheryn reported. "I

could not accept Jim's untimely death. . . . Apathy, withdrawal, all followed." In the end, she said, she simply accepted the losses as fate. "Sometimes, things just happen."

Jim's father still refuses to talk about his son's death and the family has not tried to draw him out, "not yet, anyway," she continued.

Then, toward the end of the letter, she described the last time she saw her red-haired cousin.

> *I remember his funeral. [There was] the largest crowd I ever saw at an event that wasn't a parade or a public celebration. The procession of cars was so long it blocked two freeway exits while in progress and required 10 motorcycle escorts. There were so many cars at the cemetery they had to double park. And when I looked up on that dreary, rainy day, all I saw was a sea of tear-drenched faces: pretty girls and young men, middle-aged adults and old people, all mourning his death.*

At mid-morning on the 14th of May 1987, I had another son. We named him Ben. A few hours after his birth, I called Belknap and asked him to be the boy's godfather.

The christening took place on a cool Saturday in September at home in Montclair. We rented folding chairs and tables, laid on a large catered spread.

The guests began to arrive before noon. By the time the priest had slipped on his white vestments and was in place beneath the stairs at the head of the living room, the house was packed.

An impromptu altar was fashioned from a card table covered with a plain white cloth. A molded glass punch bowl served as our baptismal font; candles burned softly in silver candelabras; marigolds of red and white spilled from a miniature carafe.

I stood to the right of the table in a doorway leading to the kitchen. Ben was sleeping heavily on my shoulder.

From under the arch, I could look out on the assembly of intimates and kin now waiting silently in their seats.

Beth was wrapped in the moment. She had badly wanted another baby; I had not. We held so hard for so long to our opposite ends, we almost pulled the marriage apart. At last, I surrendered ground on which I should never have stood: the safe place, the status quo. Josh sat nearby, a finger hooked inside the top button of his shirt, pulling at his collar. He had just turned eight, a sweet boy, fair and dark-haired like his mother. In the front row was my father, distracted for the moment. He planned to offer a prayer for his grandson and was studying what he wanted to say. Often, now, when we are together—the baby, the boy, the white-haired paterfamilias, and me—people stare, for we look so much alike. A few rows back sat Frank Ciappio and Dave Troy, mixed in—felicitously, it seemed to me—with those I call family.

At length, Father Dowd turned and nodded. I stepped from beneath the arch and handed Craig the baby.

In that moment, aspersed with holy water and anointed with oil, Ben tied anew the bond between Belknap and me. My son became our anchor; now, no matter which way the current flowed, there would be no drift. The baby brought us forward, out from under the shadow of a small bridge, and replaced the past as the agent of our friendship.

And yet, standing in a crowded room watching Craig cradle the baby in his arms, I suddenly realized that there was more to the moment than even I had intended, for what was truly taking place beneath the staircase went well beyond the offering of a holy sacrament or the consecration of a private pact.

In the middle of the ritual, I was overcome with a sense—a sudden understanding, really—a sense of winning. It was a curious feeling to have at such a tranquil moment, with the good Father reading softly from his missal. It caught me unaware, but it was unshakable nonetheless, so strong and so clear. On that Saturday in September, far from the field of battle, long past their moment of strife, I knew that the men of Golf Company had done more than just survive the fighting or come through the long aftermath. When I looked across the baptismal font to where Belknap was standing with Ben, I could not stop myself from thinking that in the tally of the years, we had truly come out ahead. Here, at last, was victory worth having—my son in the arms of my comrade.

ACKNOWLEDGMENTS AND
END NOTES

I am grateful to my longtime teacher, Jean Merritt Armstrong, for her help in shaping the book. We met right after the war when I was at college. She has been my editor, literary conscience, and friend ever since. Her words will always itch at my ears.

Three gifted writers, good men, too—David Maraniss, Daniel Laskin, Sam Freedman—also spent many hours with the manuscript. Their suggestions were invaluable in the preparation of the final draft. I was fortunate that such skilled hands and honest minds could be brought to bear on this work.

Thanks also to Elise Yousoufian, Bob Stock, Jeff Schmalz, Dennis Stern, Lynn Blodgett, and Paul Gray for various kindnesses; to Gail Hochman and Barbara Grossman for five years of forbearance.

I owe a particular debt to Peter Dawson, a comrade at Parris Island in 1967. The assistant principal of a local high school, he lives now with his wife, Monica, and daughter, Mackenzie, on the shores of Crystal Lake in Gray, Maine.

When I first began to search for the men of Golf Company, I drove to Maine to talk with Pete. Although we served in different units in the war, by a bit of luck we flew home together and, across the years, kept in touch. After I had finished the research, I went back to Crystal Lake to consult with Pete again. He always seemed the most level-headed of men and I wanted to bring that kind of clear thinking to my subject, one still charged with fire. Pete helped quell the flames and clear the air. For that and the enduring friendship of such a fine man, I am grateful.

The title is meant both to evoke a modern idiom and echo an ancient idea. For the latter, I refer the reader to Aristotle's *Nichomachean Ethics*, Books 8 and 9, and Cicero's "Laelius: On Friendship."

Overall, I was greatly influenced by J. Glenn Gray's remarkable essay about combat in World War II, *The Warriors*. As a soldier, he knew well love and loss, the possibility of individual virtue, violence and the corruption of the soul, the problem of redemption through suffering, strength, spirit, and the meaning of self-sacrifice.

Some readers will hear here echoes of T. S. Eliot's "Four Quartets." I have drawn on some of his themes. A few of the chapter titles were either taken from or strongly suggested by lines in those poems, but, as fragments, do not bear quotation marks.

Of the scores of books used to prepare for this effort, the following were the most worn: *Men Against Fire*, by S.L.A. Marshall; *Men Under Stress*, by Roy R. Grinker and John P. Spiegel; *When Johnny Comes Marching Home*, by Dixon Wecter; *The Veteran Comes Back*, by Willard Waller; *Man's Search for Meaning, An Introduction to Logotherapy*, by Viktor E. Frankl (particularly Part I); *Home from the War*, by Robert J. Lifton (a useful foil); *Goodbye to All That*, by Robert Graves; *The Face of Battle*, by John Keegan; *The American Soldier, Combat and Its Aftermath*, by Stouffer et al.; and *Men at War*, edited and with an introduction by Ernest Hemingway.

A note on the text. The word *gook*, like other racial

derogations, seemed to soil the page, but it survived several dozen edits because no other word, in context, was right. An enemy was a gook, a gook was an enemy, nothing more. Also I have eliminated the distraction of most misspellings in the letters, diaries, and documents quoted herein. Where it was necessary for clarity, I have added punctuation.

Finally, I salute my most devoted reader, the woman whose name appears at the beginning of this book and for whom it was written.

Montclair, New Jersey
March 1989

Index

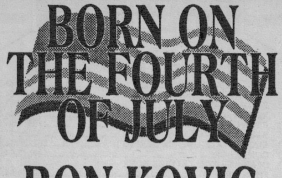

BORN ON THE FOURTH OF JULY

RON KOVIC

A true story of innocence lost and courage found.

He was a natural athlete, a shy teenager, an All American working-class kid. He shipped out to Vietnam with the Marines. Ron Kovic didn't come marching home. He was wounded, paralyzed permanently from the chest down.

This is Ron Kovic's story - a searing, graphic, deeply moving account of a young man whose real war began in the devastating aftermath of Vietnam.